Global Citizenship Education

ALSO AVAILABLE FROM BLOOMSBURY

Comparative and International Education, David Phillips and Michele Schweisfurth

Education and International Development, edited by Tristan McCowan and Elaine Unterhalter

Global Citizenship Education and the Crises of Multiculturalism, Massimiliano Tarozzi and Carlos Alberto Torres

Globalization and International Education, Robin Shields

Peace Education, edited by Monisha Bajaj and Maria Hantzopoulos

Global Citizenship Education

A Critical Introduction to Key Concepts and Debates

EDDA SANT, IAN DAVIES, KAREN PASHBY AND LYNETTE SHULTZ

Bloomsbury Academic
An imprint of Bloomsbury Publishing Plc

BLOOMSBURY ACADEMIC
LONDON • NEW YORK • OXFORD • NEW DELHI • SYDNEY

Bloomsbury Academic
An imprint of Bloomsbury Publishing Plc

50 Bedford Square
London
WC1B 3DP
UK

1385 Broadway
New York
NY 10018
USA

www.bloomsbury.com

**BLOOMSBURY and the Diana logo are trademarks
of Bloomsbury Publishing Plc**

First published 2018

© Edda Sant, Ian Davies, Karen Pashby and Lynette Shultz, 2018

Edda Sant, Ian Davies, Karen Pashby and Lynette Shultz have asserted their right under the Copyright, Designs and Patents Act, 1988, to be identified as Authors of this work.

All rights reserved. No part of this publication may be reproduced or transmitted in any form or by any means, electronic or mechanical, including photocopying, recording, or any information storage or retrieval system, without prior permission in writing from the publishers.

No responsibility for loss caused to any individual or organization acting on or refraining from action as a result of the material in this publication can be accepted by Bloomsbury or the authors.

British Library Cataloguing-in-Publication Data
A catalogue record for this book is available from the British Library.

ISBN: HB: 978-1-4725-9243-9
PB: 978-1-4725-9242-2
ePDF: 978-1-4725-9245-3
ePub: 978-1-4725-9244-6

Library of Congress Cataloging-in-Publication Data
A catalog record for this book is available from the Library of Congress.

Cover image © ulimi | GettyImages

Typeset by Newgen KnowledgeWorks Pvt. Ltd., Chennai, Great Britain

To find out more about our authors and books visit www.bloomsbury.com. Here you will find extracts, author interviews, details of forthcoming events and the option to sign up for our newsletters.

Contents

List of Tables   vii
About the Authors   viii
Acknowledgements   x

Introduction   1

PART ONE Key Questions, Concepts and Dimensions

1 Why Global Citizenship?   13
2 Why Global Citizenship Education?   21
3 Global Rights and Duties   31
4 Imagining Global Communities through a Decolonial Ethic of Global Citizenship   39
5 Global Identities   45
6 Local and Global Citizenship   55
7 National and Global Citizenship   63
8 Planetary and Global Citizenship   71

PART TWO Key Educational Frameworks

9 Citizenship Education   81
10 Social Justice   91
11 Development Education   101
12 Character Education   115
13 Global Education   125
14 Peace Education   135

15 Diversity Education   143

16 Education for Sustainable Development   153

PART THREE Key Issues in Research and Practice in Teaching and Learning about and for Global Citizenship

17 Research   167

18 Curriculum   177

19 Community Action   187

20 Teaching and Learning Methods in Global Citizenship Education   197

21 Evaluation   207

Bibliography   215
Index   231

Tables

5.1 Suggested questions for the collaborative research 53
9.1 Arguments for and against enfranchising 16-year-olds 88
10.1 Different approaches to distributive justice 94
13.1 Discourses on global education and their ideal global education curriculum 127

About the Authors

Edda Sant worked in different secondary schools in Spain as a Social Sciences and Citizenship Education teacher. Following this, she worked four years in the Universitat Autònoma de Barcelona, Spain, after obtaining a fellowship from the Spanish Department of Education (Beca FPU) to conduct her PhD on teaching and learning political participation. In 2014, she joined Manchester Metropolitan University, UK, where she is a senior lecturer in Education Studies. Her research focuses on citizenship, democratic, political and history education, areas in which she has published in European and American journals and books.

Ian Davies was a teacher in state schools in England for ten years. He completed his PhD in 1992 with a thesis on political education. He is currently professor in the Department of Education, University of York, UK, where he is the director of the Graduate School of Education, director of the Centre for Research on Education and Social Justice and deputy head of department. He has worked for the Council of Europe as an expert on education for democratic citizenship, is a past Fellow of the Japan Society for the Promotion of Science and is a visiting professor at the University of Education, Hong Kong. He has published widely.

Karen Pashby joined Manchester Metropolitan University's Department of Childhood, Youth and Education Studies in 2016. She lectures and does research in the Global, Citizenship and Education stream. Previously, she held postdoctoral fellowships at the University of Oulu, Finland, and the Centre for Global Citizenship Education and Research at University of Alberta, Canada. She completed her PhD at the University of Toronto where she coordinated the Global Citizenship & Sustainable Development cohort in teacher education. An experienced secondary school teacher in Canada and Brazil, her research – grounded in critical and post/de-colonial theory – considers the complexities of global citizenship education in multicultural contexts and the implications of the rush to internationalize higher education.

Lynette Shultz is professor and co-director of the Centre for Global Citizenship Education and Research at the University of Alberta, Canada. She has studied global citizenship for the past fifteen years and has published several books and articles on the topic. She has also published widely on global social justice and internationalization of education. She is currently on the executive committee of the World Council of Comparative Education Societies and the Comparative and International Education Society of Canada.

Acknowledgements

We are very grateful to Dr Eleanor Brown for providing valuable advice at various points of the writing process.

Introduction

In this introduction we explain the purpose of the book, provide definitions of key terms, explain the structure of what we have written and make suggestions for how the book could be used.

We have written this book with a passionate sense of commitment. Global citizenship and education provide us with enormous challenges and opportunities, encapsulating matters of the highest priority. It is not an exaggeration to say that locked within these fields are the ideas and issues that must be understood and enacted if we are to make a better world. Our hugely ambitious approach in this book is to illuminate and discuss some of the fundamental perspectives and approaches to the topic through multiple lenses that capture the complexity of histories, issues and interconnections that currently play out in the lives people in the world and demand an education that supports learning how to be in this world.

The authors of this book are based in different parts of the world. We feel our expertise is limited to certain regions of the world (Europe, Canada, the United States and to some extent Latin America and Australia and some of the countries of East Asia). Our reading has been deliberately expansive and we have attempted to include Africa, the Middle East, Russia, India, Pakistan and Bangladesh in our thinking and writing. But, of course, our knowledge, understandings and experiences are not comprehensive and the countries and regions that we have just mentioned certainly do not constitute the whole globe. The ambitions we refer to above need, obviously, to be carried through realistically, with a considerable degree of caution and humility.

In this introduction we aim to do several things. We will:

- outline the purpose of the book;
- discuss definitions or characterizations of key terms so that we ensure – as far as is reasonably possible – that the dynamic fields of global citizenship and education are explored coherently and meaningfully;

- describe the structure of the book indicating how our chapters align with the definitions we are using and the aims we have for the book;
- indicate how we feel the book could be used.

The purpose of the book

In this book we are aiming to make a contribution to discussions and practice relevant to global citizenship and education. We are not – as noted above – claiming that we will cover everything. The world is a big place and debates about what is important are not of recent origin. The ancient Roman playwright, Terence, suggested that there are as many opinions as there are people (*quot homines, tot sententiae*), and we would not find much disagreement with that basic idea (even if we would disagree with the sexist way in which he expressed it). This is not to suggest that in this book we wish simply to draw attention to the very broad range of what others have said. We have our own views, and while we wish to operate inclusively, we begin from a position in which we value pluralist, inclusive perspectives. While we do not suggest an 'anything goes' approach, we recognize that all ideas come from a particular context that is historically, socially and politically located, and any work claiming to understand 'the global' must acknowledge that what is understood as universal is often what is dominant and not necessarily shared by others in a world impacted differently by people's sense of their own locations, positions and relations with others. And, we do see that when working with the concepts of global social justice and global citizenship, some ideas and practices are indeed better, fairer and more likely to result in equity and justice than others. The challenge in global citizenship education is to sort through what ideas matter and to explore who should – and who actually – gets to decide. In order to achieve a better world, in, and through education, we need to ensure that a commitment to different forms of social justice (as we will identify later in the book) are honoured in both substance and process, allowing for a multitude of voices to be heard and for outstanding professional and other forms of practice to be celebrated, enhanced and brought to the attention of others. As such, we aim in this book to provide:

- Discussions of key foundational ideas and principles, drawing on ideas, experiences and histories beyond 'the west' to contribute to a perspective of global citizenship and global citizenship education that is both decolonizing and pluriversal;
- Discussions of how those ideas and issues are considered and included in key contexts (research, policy and pedagogical practice in international contexts);

- Globally informed reading lists and educational exercises that help students, teachers and others understand key ideas and develop the necessary openness to discuss multiple perspectives and worldviews.

Definitions or characterizations of key terms

The central threads running through this book are global citizenship and education. We are resisting the possibility of giving definitions endlessly of all terms relevant to these central threads, and so we restrict ourselves here to outlining globalization, citizenship and education while being alert to many other key areas including community, diversity, cosmopolitanism, planetary perspectives, post-colonialism and others.

We try as often as possible to bring 'globalization', 'citizenship' and 'education' together in order to discuss global citizenship education. We also recognize (but do not explore to the same extent) that it is possible – and often entirely appropriate and necessary – to describe and discuss 'globalized citizenship', 'citizenship education' and 'global education'. Each of the three words with which we are using as our focus – 'global', 'citizenship' and 'education' – is open to dynamic interpretation (across time, place and in relation to purpose). We have separate chapters on these areas. But unless we say something generally about what these things mean then we run the risk of continuing some of the confusion and complexity that is part of debates about global citizenship and education. We want to discuss clearly and propose appropriately, and so, with some tentativeness, we suggest that:

- **Globalization** is essentially concerned with the increasing interdependence of people around the world.

This simple and possibly simplistic statement is made complex by a range of significant issues. 'Global' may have geographical meaning but simply including references to people and places in different parts of the world is not sufficient for our purposes. 'Global' is not simply descriptive. If we were to use the word 'international' we would be emphasizing the significance of connections between nation states. The 'inter' in international may be a link as opposed to an interweaving; a connection rather than a more profound coming together. If 'international' is limited and perhaps limiting then 'global' may mean – without suggesting that this is an exclusive or discrete characterization – that the understandings of and commitment to nation states have been more significantly transformed.

In order to understand economic, political, social and environmental issues that affect each of us (individually and collectively) on the planet, we require ideas and language to discuss the relations and impacts of these issues. Thinking 'globally' helps us read the world through a *multiscalar* perspective, providing important knowledge about people, systems and structures that work locally, nationally, internationally and transnationally. Issues about government (or, at least governance) and about identity and perhaps by immediate association by particular values and perspectives are relevant (including those that are affective such as toleration and respect as well as – or, perhaps more than – the cognitive). It may allow for a focus on particular trends or contexts through which the interdependence that has been referred to above may be achieved. Economics, technology (especially those forms that facilitate communication) and population and environment are probably some of the most important social and political contexts to consider in any consideration of the meaning of 'global'.

In order to reflect properly on globalization, it is necessary to ask searching questions about it. We feel it is unhelpful for sensational claims to be made. Globalization in its current form is new mainly due to its intensity. This is, however, not to deny that there have been previous versions. Mongolia, China, Britain, Russia, Spain, the Arabic countries, the United States and others have had (or have) global ambitions or capacities. The significance of these empires indicates that colonialism was (and is) a very significant globalization project. And the continuing power of the nation state – despite or because of the rise of transnational forces and institutions – should be recognized in any consideration of what globalization means.

The intentions behind the activities of nation states and other transnational actors are of relevance to how we characterize globalization. The extent to which – even today – all are involved in globalization is open to question. While everyone may be impacted by global economic, political or environmental relations, there is great disparity in how these impacts are distributed. Some argue that current global economics have created a global economic elite and a global economic poor or lower class. In this system the poor in, for example, Johannesburg and London may have a more similar experience of globalization than the wealthy in these two global cities.

There are parts of the world that have had various labels (with varying degrees of acceptability) attached to them. Simplistic (and at times negatively stereotypical) terms such as the 'third world', 'low income countries', the 'global south' may fail to recognize the complexities associated with considerations of the nature of globalization. Whether or not globalization is culturally as well as economically a force for good that allows for and promotes diversity and inclusivity is highly contested. There are times when words such as 'global' and 'international' are meant to stand as some sort of quality mark: an indication, in other words, of excellence that will be of interest to others wherever they might be in the world. University-based researchers in some parts of the world, for example, are used to having their work graded as 'international' if it deemed to be of high quality. But it is possible, of course, that globalization indicates that an iniquitous and assimilatory force is being unleashed: if so, we should, of course, be wary of fostering forms of education that support its further development. The sort of interdependence we see as being part of the globalization we want is one that is aligned with justice, diversity and inclusivity. Such seemingly obvious 'good things' require much further thought and will be discussed in this book.

- **Citizenship** is a matter of one's formal legal and political status and a sense of belonging. It also entails the right and responsibility to make rights claims regarding those issues that impact one's well-being.

Immediately one can see from the above statement that citizenship is essentially bound up with particular elements. A citizen is an individual person but not all individuals are citizens. The legal status that is so beneficial in terms of allowing for the possibility of rights to be realized does not indicate that the most necessary rights have actually been included in what is deemed appropriate for those citizens. Further, the formal assignation of rights and duties to a limited number of people makes apparent its exclusionary nature. Similarly, there are challenging issues in relation to a sense of belonging. Citizenship may exclude as much – perhaps more than – it includes.

The collective nature of citizenship may emerge (in what might be regarded as traditional European, US or 'Western' perspectives) from issues about public and private matters as an agglomeration of individuals as opposed to applying to groups. So, for example, people may not be regarded by themselves or others as citizens in light of their sex or gender but (in alignment with perspectives about human rights) due to their individuality. Singularity through citizenship is collectively expressed with other individuals. But the UN Declaration of the Rights of Indigenous People which is significant in all parts of the world and very explicitly in Latin America, Africa, Canada and elsewhere challenges these traditional perspectives.

The actions that are taken or encouraged give an indication of the meaning of citizenship. This connects with traditions of citizenship in which the liberal (or rights based) exists alongside – and, at times, within – an emphasis on duties or responsibilities associated with civic republicanism. Action is often a key idea of citizenship but is difficult to define. A simple example is enough to illustrate this complexity: is it my right as a mother/father to bring up my children, or is it a duty? Surely it is both, but the action and the perspective on that action (as well as the source of authority connected with the characterization of the action) are all important in considering the meaning of citizenship. To use another example of an issue from which we may develop our reactions to global citizenship: is it my right to fly despite the impact on many others due to negative effects of carbon emission; do I have a duty to change my actions for the collective good? And, of course, the absence of action – whether in the form of passive resistance or something else – is perhaps as indicative of participation as something which is generated more directly in an explicit form of engagement. Is it the case that sometimes not doing something, doing something? Placing too much emphasis on action, however, may serve not only to help point out where things need to change fundamentally, but may also inadvertently privilege those who are better positioned than others to take the time and use resources to enact change. The very young, the very old and those with different abilities or disabilities or those who lack social or other forms of capital (including refugees, those suffering from poverty, racism, sexism and other iniquities) will not do be judged fairly in their capacity as citizens well if certain forms of engagement are valued more than others.

The place where citizenship might take place is important not only, as suggested above, in geographical terms relating to single or multiple local, national and global citizenships but also regarding what constitutes the public and private contexts in which actions and thoughts occur. Reliance on institutional and constitutional engagement may be an expression of civics but not necessarily of citizenship. We wish to see citizenship aligned with our preferences regarding globalization, i.e. not narrowly bound by individualistic, nationally oriented and duty bound perspectives but instead as a recognition and drive for a justice-oriented, inclusive, collective, responsible focus.

- **Education** is the means by which we learn.

Throughout the book we will for practical reasons devote most of our attention to formal, often compulsory, teaching, learning and assessing in schools. But no book on global citizenship and education can afford to ignore the greatly varied sites of learning across the world and we endeavour to explore as best we can the non-formal and informal sites and processes of learning. We explore very different purposes and perspectives about learning. We feel that education is always *for* something. We do not develop our argument so generally as to highlight in great detail the philosophical, political and economic aspects of education that highlight the imposition through education of liberal culture, supposed economic efficiency and attempts at political democracy. But we do use these fundamental matters to outline our ideas and to draw attention to issues and ways forward. Our concern for purpose will entail describing and reflecting on the ways in which education is framed. Citizenship education may stand at times as an umbrella phrase for many different approaches in which efforts are made to help learners understand and take part in current contemporary society and to develop a more socially just world. The major forces relevant to globalization and the key aspects of citizenship (a formal legal status and identity) provide a platform from which we may identify areas that are developed educationally. These broad framing devices lead us to consider matters such as development, peace, sustainable development and others. In addition, getting closer to immediate and direct work with learners, there is a need to reflect on broad issues regarding curriculum construction, pedagogical development (including assessment) and evaluation.

The structure of the book

Our aims for this book as well as the definitions and characterizations given above influenced our writing structure. We contextualize the notion of global citizenship education within key concepts, perspectives and educational frameworks. We discuss different ways in which global citizenship can be taught, learned about and assessed in formal and informal contexts of education. We analyse these different examples by considering the different approaches to global citizenship education. Predominant scholarly debates about global citizenship education have tended to frame matters principally in relation to Western perspectives. We will attempt to meet the need to approach global citizenship and global citizenship education with appropriate expansiveness. And, very importantly, we want to write in an accessible style. We aim to provide a much needed educational resource for MA students and final year undergraduates, their tutors and others. We highlight key ideas and issues and provide a practical way for students to work by themselves and with the help of peers and their tutors to develop their understandings and skills.

The above means that we have decided to, following this introduction, to divide the book into three main sections: key questions, concepts and dimensions; key educational frameworks; and, key issues in research and practice in teaching and learning about and for global citizenship. Section 1 contains eight chapters in which we explore the fundamental ideas and issues about globalization, citizenship and education. This Section is divided into three parts. In Part 1 we deal with two key questions: 'why global citizenship?' (we review neo-liberal, social-humanitarian and de-colonial discourses about global citizenship and global social justice) and 'why global citizenship education?' (we explore its fundamental nature in relation to different notions of education, globalization and citizenship). The second part of Section 1 is made up of three chapters in which the following key concepts are explored: global rights and duties; global communities and global identities. In these chapters we move beyond justifying the attention that we are devoting to global citizenship and education and instead focus more directly on the ideas that are essential in realizing global citizenship. In Chapter 3, global rights and duties, we explore ideas regarding the civic republican and liberal traditions of citizenship in Western societies, alternative understandings of citizenship and belonging from non-Western societies, and we include a discussion of the links between global rights and human rights and post-colonial considerations. Global communities (Chapter 4) contain a discussion about the nature and expression of communitarianism and pluriversalism in local, national and global contexts. It considers global communities through a de-colonizing lens. Chapter 5 (global identities and global subjects) includes discussion of conscientiousness and imagination so that we may consider the ways in which people may or may not see themselves as global citizens. The final part of Section 1 contains three chapters that deal with key spatial dimensions allowing us to articulate the contexts through which global citizenship and education are developed. We have framed these chapters in ways that link with place, so we consider local, national and planetary issues.

Section 2 contains eight chapters in which we discuss the educational frameworks that are relevant to global citizenship education. We will explore, in turn, citizenship, social justice, development, character, global, peace, diversity and sustainable development education. This set of different approaches to global citizenship and education is an indication of the complex fundamental philosophical issues and also at times the political splintering of what could broadly be described as social studies. There are strong similarities across these different frameworks but also extremely strong differences. Questions of individual or collective responses, cognitive or affective considerations and the extent of the reliance on academic disciplines or social objectives are all apparent. This complex situation has long been apparent with arguments about whether these differences reflect a healthy dynamism that is appropriate for fast moving democratic debates or, simply, intellectual incoherence and a failure to build a platform that, in harsh political terms, will lead only to the further lowering of the status of approaches to education that strive to achieve understanding and action. The struggle to define and agree on an approach that articulates the heart of global citizenship education will probably – and rightly -never be finally resolved. By outlining the different educational frameworks we hope to clarify understanding and build a dynamic consensus, avoiding the negative potential associated with too close a reliance on a series of 'adjectival educations' (such as 'peace education', 'development education', 'citizenship education' and so on) with proponents negatively pitted against each other.

The final Section of the book focuses on issues in research and practice in teaching and learning. There are five chapters. We examine research in Chapter 17 discussing what has been done and what needs to be done. We then, in Chapter 18 explore how different approaches to global citizenship frame different curriculum constructions. In Chapters 19 and 20 we focus on the detailed actions that are taken by teachers and learners. The first of those two chapters deals with community action with some attention to whole school initiatives and also projects involving those outside the school (e.g. using social media; service learning; political activism; the digital divide etc.). The second of those two chapters deals with teaching and learning methods through 'mainstream' subjects and discretely. The final chapter explores evaluation. This gives us an opportunity to discuss how we can determine whether educational initiatives have been successful and how we may develop recommendations for future improvements.

Using this book

Global citizenship and education are of concern to everyone. We feel, however, that probably most of our readers will be final year undergraduates and masters students in a wide range of locations. Many, but not all, will be based in education departments but we also expect students in sociology, social policy, politics and other fields are attracted to this book. There are a growing number of undergraduate courses that explore global citizenship and education. Higher education institutions are developing full degrees in International Education or Global Studies. We would hope that the instructors/educators who work on those programmes would find this book useful as an aid to their teaching and perhaps as some support as their own insights grow.

We do not have a narrow 'party line' on how global citizenship and education should be characterized. This, we hope, is shown very clearly by the wide range of perspectives that we have included. We repeat, however, that education is not neutral, and we wish to confirm our commitment to inclusive, democratic means that lead to understanding and actions congruent with social justice. Within those confines – which we cannot imagine our readers disagreeing with – we strongly wish to encourage critique of what we have written. We do not wish to encourage, simply for the sake of it, the voicing of opinions. We do want to promote knowledgeable, reflective critique that is evidence through and leads to enhanced inclusive engagement.

In order to attempt to achieve these aims, our chapters are divided into different parts. Each, relatively short, chapter contains an outline of key ideas and issues; a short (4/5 titles) annotated list of key resources through which, in most cases, students would be inspired to then read the original; a practical exercise through which understanding and action is encouraged; and a further reading list (not annotated and relying on easily accessible resources). The practical exercises are either desk-based or involve engagement, individually or with others face to face, virtually and at times with people from more than one country. Throughout there is explicit coverage of examples, case studies and issues drawn from across the world. This will include examples from a wide range of education institutions (primary, secondary and higher, governmental and non-governmental international institutions and corporations and political and social movements).

One book will certainly not cover all the issues in global citizenship and education. But this one is, we hope, a start and we hope that readers of our book are inspired to develop their critical understanding and commitment to making the world a better place.

PART ONE

Key Questions, Concepts and Dimensions

In this section of the book, there are eight chapters that explore fundamental matters. These eight chapters are loosely in three groups. The first group contains two chapters in which we ask 'why global citizenship' and then 'why global citizenship education'. The second group comprises three chapters in which the building blocks of global citizenship education are discussed: rights and duties; global communities and identities. Finally, there are three chapters in which there are discussions from a conceptual/geographical focus: local, national, and planetary. By the end of this section, you will have a clear understanding of the fundamental matters that characterize global citizenship education.

1

Why Global Citizenship?

This chapter explores the multiple ideas that are attached to the term 'global citizenship' and discusses why this is considered a term for our time. Global citizenship pulls us to think in a multiscalar way, from the personal and local to what we think of as a global, transnational or planetary view. Our lives tend to be organized, to a large extent, around local and national-level systems and events, particularly in the areas of social and political engagement. In recent years, as economic activity became more organized through a formal global financial system, it became clearer how people around the world were connected through this capitalist system. As environmental issues became more severe, people around the world became familiar with making links between local and global views in order to understand both the issues and solutions to these intensified environmental threats. It is at this point where the idea of global citizenship emerged and at its foundation are understandings and experiences of globalization. In his 2007 book *The Creation of the World or Globalization*, Jean-Luc Nancy compares two processes, globalization and mondialization, at play in our world that are often bound in the one word of 'globalization' but each holding a different possibility for human destiny (p. 1). Globalization, he argues, involves the capture and production of uniformity through global economic and technological logics and, ultimately, leads to an uninhabitable world, a world where there is a disintegration of the 'convergence of knowledge, ethics, and social well-being' (p. 34). Mondialization, on the other hand, describes processes of engagement with humans and non-humans in what we might think of as the creation of the world. In this way, all relations are thought to be important as a piece of the creation of a world where everyone is considered a part. Nancy argues that the space for this to happen is inherently one of justice (pp. 1–28). We see these things happening in projects that protect refugees, support indigenous communities to maintain their lives on their land, or to when people and governments come together to develop strong policies to protect the environment. Nancy concludes that 'between the creation of the world OR globalization, one must choose, since one implies the exclusion of the other' (p. 29). This description of the complexity of globalized systems and relations helps us to understand how global citizenship, working in and through either or both of these processes, continues to be a contested but durable idea. Will global citizenship be part of creating a world for all or will it serve a more destructive project of mono-economic, mono-cultural and mono-political engagement that serves only a small elite and destroys what is vibrant about human life on the planet?

Global citizenship began to appear in NGO and school curriculum materials in the mid-1990s, mainly in the UK and North America. Who were these super-citizens? Initially, the idea was used to describe people working on both sides – Nancy's mondialization and globalization. In most cases, global citizens were understood as people able understand the emerging relations of globalization and an increasingly globalized financial system. Activists who built anti-globalization social movements linked across national and sector borders to claim their rights from a growing number of international organizations, corporations, and a small but wealthy elite who saw all borders as an impediment to their liberty and access to improved lifestyles. These activists were described as 'global citizens', working in new global policy arenas and linking globally to enact local, national, and global policy changes. It wasn't long until the corporations, international organizations, and their mobile staffs were also being described as global citizens. From these early times, the idea of global citizenship has been a contested and undefined concept and while such a problem might suggest it lost its meaning and use, there is a durability in the term that requires our attention.

Neoliberal ideas of global citizenship

How can we understand the globalization that Nancy has described? Many scholars describe the global policy regime through ideas of neoliberalism. For example, David Harvey (2005) describes how neoliberalism acts as a powerful hegemonic discourse making ideas such as individual freedom and autonomy being guaranteed by a free market rather than the state, common sense. Neoliberalism differs from previous liberal economic theories in that it demands that all political and social systems be re-designed to support the principles of a global free market. Citizens started to be understood as self-interested individuals rather than members of nation states or communities, and governments shifted their primary focus to creating and protecting markets rather than concern for something understood as 'society' or those things in society that were of common concern. Often this shift of roles was evident in the removal of policies that protected the social, labour, health and safety, and environmental rights, or that limited government supports to local or national businesses in order to allow global businesses access to 'global markets'. The neoliberal idea of a global economic system working in these cases was that all individuals, regardless of their circumstances, should compete in the global market. Of course, the global system was not a level-playing field and a few very powerful transnational corporations began to take over local markets throughout the world. The overall impact of neoliberalism has been to increase social inequality and allow a single global market system to be supported in local and national policies, even when this system seems contrary to the best interests of local communities (Harvey, 2005; 2008). Global corporations, within this economically liberalized environment, have used globalization's intensified technological and mobility capacities to expand their interests around the world. In the early 2000s, C. K. Prahalad and A. Hammond were very influential in both the corporate and development assistance institutions. In their 2002 article in the Harvard Business Review, they argue for corporations to expand their reach:

> Everyone knows that the world's poor are distressingly plentiful. Fully 65% of the world's population earns less than $2000 per year [Note: this % is much higher in 2016] . . . But despite the vastness of the market it remains largely untapped by multinational companies. (p. 49)

They conclude:

> Ethical concerns aside, we've shown that the potential for expanding the bottom of the market is just too big to ignore. (p. 57)

Global citizenship soon followed as a way to defend this expansion against anticolonial and anti-globalization resistance. This position, part aspiration and part organizational branding strategy, is expressed here in a definition of corporate global citizenship (2008):

> International business leaders must fully commit to sustainable development and address paramount global challenges, including climate change, the provision of public health care, energy conservation, and the management of resources, particularly water. Because these global issues increasingly impact business, not to engage with them can hurt the bottom line. Because global citizenship is in a corporation's enlightened self-interest, it is sustainable. Addressing global issues can be good both for the corporation and for society at a time of increasing globalization and diminishing state influence. (para 3)

> Global corporate citizenship is a logical extension of corporations' search for a consistent and sustainable framework for global engagement – and one that adds value for both the companies and the global space in which they engage. It is a form of corporate engagement that can reinforce the positive role of business in society and enhance profitability in the long term. Indeed, global corporate citizenship integrates both the rights and the responsibilities that corporations have as global citizens. (para 32)
>
> Global Corporate Citizenship: Working with Governments and Civil Society. Foreign Affairs. Jan/Feb 2008 https://www.foreignaffairs.com/articles/2008-01-01/global-corporate-citizenship Accessed July 15, 2016

As Nancy (2007) highlighted, globalization (and the global corporate citizen described above) sits alongside other understandings of how actions create the world, a world of ongoing interspecies and interpersonal/ intergroup relations. As we look back to these years, we can see how the dominant global actors have chosen by looking at the data reported in the Global Wealth Report 2015 by Swiss bank Credit Suisse (October, 2015):

- In 2015, just sixty-two individuals had the same wealth as 3.6 billion people – the bottom half of humanity. This figure is down from 388 individuals as recently as 2010.

- The wealth of the richest sixty-two people has risen by 45 per cent in the five years since 2010 – that's an increase of more than half a trillion dollars ($542bn), to $1.76 trillion.

- Meanwhile, the wealth of the bottom half fell by just over a trillion dollars in the same period – a drop of 38 per cent.

- Since the turn of the century, the poorest half of the world's population has received just 1 per cent of the total increase in global wealth, while half of that increase has gone to the top 1 per cent.

- The average annual income of the poorest 10 per cent of people in the world has risen by less than $3 each year in almost a quarter of a century. Their daily income has risen by less than a single cent every year.

Under neoliberal rationales (Harvey, 2005; 2008) economic models should shape and reform all aspects of how people live to create the greatest increase in wealth. The data here shows that that has been the case for about 1 per cent of people, but with more and more people, and certainly all non-human life on the planet, seeing their livelihoods diminish (see Dorling, 2014; Piketty, 2015). The good global corporate citizen appears to be more about brand than equality. The alternative proposed by development organizations, meant to ameliorate the inequalities of the global economic system, has also failed to improve the life chances of the majority of the world population who remain poor and decitizenized, particularly when considered under the umbrella of a 'global citizenship'.

Humanist responses to global issues

The corporate global citizen idea stands in contrast with definitions coming from more humanist perspectives at the same time (cf. Abdi, 2008; Singer, 2002). Clearly people suffered under the intensely globalized system and the impulse from many sectors was to intervene and these interventions were often gathered under the idea of global citizenship as a way to educate people about the global systems that often masked the way the system worked in favour of large corporations, wealthy individuals, and the most powerful countries. This Oxfam definition informed many of the global citizenship projects in the UK, Canada, the United States and Australia in the late 1990s and 2000s:
We see a Global Citizen as someone who:

- is aware of the wider world and has a sense of their own role as a world citizen;
- respects and values diversity;
- has an understanding of how the world works economically, politically, socially, culturally, technologically and environmentally;
- is passionately committed to social justice;
- participates in and contributes to the community at a range of levels from local to global;
- works with others to make the world a more sustainable place;
- takes responsibility for their actions.

Oxfam 1997/2015 (file:///User/Downloads/ml-global-citizenship-guide-schools-091115-en.pdf) Accessed 15 July 2016.

The definition itself points out some of the problems that globalization created not only economically but also socially and culturally. Media and advertising promoted a global modern culture (which was mostly the 'culture of consumption' understood as American culture). There was pressure around the world to consume the 'lifestyle' of food, clothing, entertainment, art, music, and literature offered by the global market. Of course, the question that needed to be asked was: Whose local was the global in this system? It was not a system that came out of 'nowhere' and it was certainly not benefiting people in most parts of the world. Humanist education projects approached this context by promoting global citizenship as both charity and social justice (Andreotti, 2006). These approaches argued for better distribution within the system to alleviate some of the poverty and despair but few addressed the deep troubles that underpinned the world system as a whole (Shultz, 2007).

An anticolonial response to globalization and global citizenship

In the past decade, many people have started to include a decolonial analysis to global citizenship (cf. Andreotti & de Souza, 2013; Abdi, Shultz & Pillay, 2015). While much of the early global citizenship discussion took place within a limited geographical area of the UK, the United States, Canada, Australia and some European countries, there were many ideas circulating among people living in previously colonized areas of the world that challenged the notion that these areas were somehow failed versions of Western nations, in need of 'development' and a modern education that would allow them to participate in the global economy. It seemed clear that such efforts perpetuated violent colonial relations that diminished the life chances of people living outside the 'Western' centre of world economic and political power where people claimed their ideas and systems were universal and global (see Abdi, 2008; de Sousa Santos, 2014; Escobar, 1995; Kapoor, 2008; Rodney, 1981; Simpson, 2008). As people schooled in Western ideas of universalism encountered these ideas, they began to shift how they understood global citizenship (see Jefferess, 2008). Global citizenship was viewed through the lens of colonialism and was again positioned in a contested position, holding both the possibility of being used to continue forms of colonizing interference in the lives and social relations of people living differently that those people in the 'west', and also as a decolonial resistance and a way to identify and disrupt global processes that perpetuated colonial legacies of violence and diminished citizenship.

We are left now with a need for a concept that will help us understand and engage with the citizenship relations that play out beyond the nation state but also one that does not easily slip into the norms of traditional colonial relations. Can global citizenship be such a concept?

Annotated bibliography

Abdi, A. A. & Shultz, L. (Eds.) (2008). *Educating for Human Rights and Global Citizenship*. Albany, NY: SUNY Press.

This set of short essays provides insights on global citizenship from multiple perspectives. Authors, writing from ten countries and indigenous nations, discuss citizenship and global systems, the problem of misrecognition of indigenous rights and citizenships within global human rights and citizenship efforts, and the problems of racism, sexism, and poverty as barriers to citizenship at all levels. Together they provide insight into the need for a global perspective on citizenship.

Jefferess, D. (2008). Global citizenship and the cultural politics of benevolence. *Critical Literacies*, 2(1), 27–36.

This article critiques humanist ideas of global citizenship education that emerge from ideas of cosmopolitanism and a transnational identity that positions some people as 'helpers' for a deficient 'Other'. Jefferess provides an important analysis of actions that neglect to consider how the winners and losers in the global system are connected together, the winners' benefits depending on the burdens of the world system being shouldered by the rest of the world, the millions who are kept without access. Jefferess poses important questions that anyone working in global citizenship education must engage.

Odora Hoppers, C. (2009). From bandit colonialism to the modern triage society: towards a moral and cognitive reconstruction of knowledge and citizenship. *International Journal of African Renaissance Studies*, 4(2), 168–80.

This article describes the demand that the rest of the world comply with Western cultural norms and standards and how it impacts the lives of the majority of people on the planet. Odora Hoppers argues that if there is ever to be a way for those living in lands that had been colonized to contribute to the wellbeing of the world, there needs to be a transformation, a decolonization, of global relations starting with the foundations of knowledge and science.

Activity

1. In his 2008 essay, 'Are we all global citizens or only some of us?' Nigel Dower provides an important discussion of who is considered to be a

global citizen. Many international non-governmental organizations provide materials for educators to use for global citizenship education. Although these materials seldom provide a definition, each activity is based on a narrative of who a global citizens is. Even a cursory check of examples (for a reference of examples of activities, see http://www.globalhive.ca) suggests a narrow vision of who is or can be considered a global citizen. Drawing on your own experience with global citizenship activities, describe the 'global citizen' imagined in the activity. (For a reference of examples of activities, see http://www.globalhive.ca). Does this imaginary include everyone (i.e. is it universal?).

Dower, N. (2008). Are some of us global citizens or are only some of us global citizens? In Abdi, A. & Shultz, L. (Eds). *Educating for human rights and global citizenship.* New York: SUNY.

2
Why Global Citizenship Education?

Historians of education usually explain how mass education was created with the purpose of educating citizens of nation-states. Schools were in charge of transmitting a set of values and knowledges that would encourage social cohesion and a national sense of belonging. We still have examples of this all around the world. In Nigeria, students follow a textbook on civic education called 'We are Nigerians', in China, the government created a guideline on patriotic education, in Britain, teachers are expected to promote 'British Values'. And yet, a simple search in any internet search engine illustrates that citizenship education is no longer exclusively national but also 'global'. 'Global Citizenship Education' is part of international policies (e.g. UNESCO, 2015) and it is included as part of some national curriculums (e.g. Ecuador, Republic of Korea, and Scotland). We feel that, without leaving behind the education of the national citizenry, global citizenship education is probably one of the educational priorities in the twenty-first century. However, what do we mean when we talk about global citizenship education?

Global citizenship education (GCE) is a complex concept, which in our understanding, cannot be fully defined with complete agreement across all groups and individuals. GCE contains in itself different underlying ideologies about the meaning of citizenship, globalization and the role of education in a global society. In the introduction, we have discussed how 'global citizenship' brings together the contested meanings of 'globalization' and 'citizenship', plus complex new questions. The combination of 'globalization', 'citizenship' and 'education', generates an even more complex field. Each time we talk or write about GCE, we are be taking a particular approach about globalization, citizenship and education that derives into a particular approach to GCE. Since there are different views on globalization, citizenship and education, the views on GCE are, probably even more diverse. That makes it impossible, in our view, to provide a single definition of GCE. We feel that any teaching and learning activity whose aim is the education of the global citizenry should be considered in relation to different meanings of global citizenship and different purposes of education. We have discussed in the previous chapter the relations between global and citizenship. In this chapter we want to discuss how global citizenship might be understood in relation to different purposes of education.

Global citizenship and the purposes of education

Philosophers of education have largely discussed what education is for, Biesta (2009) identifies three main purposes of any education activity: subjectification, socialization and qualification:

- The qualification purpose of education is associated with the acquisition of knowledge, skills and understandings that will lead to 'do something', mainly in relation to the world of work.
- The socialization purpose of education can be defined as the ways in which, 'through education, we become members of and part of particular social, cultural and political orders' (Biesta, 2009, p. 40).
- The subjectification purpose of education implies fostering students' independence and autonomy from the political, economic, social and economic orders they live in.

In the following, we discuss each of these purposes in relation to global citizenship education, considering the arguments for and against each of these views.

Global citizenship education as qualification

Global citizenship education can be related to the qualification purpose of education. If we look at global citizenship education through the lens of this purpose, we can understand that global citizenship education can be reduced to some learning outcomes, related to the acquisition of a certain set of knowledge, skills and understandings that some have called 'global' or 'intercultural competences'. The international organization UNESCO (2015), for instance, defines the global competences of a global citizen in terms of (1) knowledge and understanding of specific global issues and trends; (2) cognitive skills such as critical thinking and problem-solving; (3) non-cognitive skills such as empathy and openness and (4) behavioural capacities such as social engagement. Global citizenship is therefore understood as an outcome towards which education contributes. As an extreme case, global citizenship education would lead to some sort of qualification, as the 'global citizen award' or the 'global mention' that some universities (e.g. University of Kent) are already offering to their students if they demonstrate the acquisition of these knowledge, skills and dispositions.

Three main arguments are used to justify global citizenship education as qualification:

- Global citizenship can be associated with the economic purpose of education. Students might need to compete for jobs in an increasingly globalized world in which attributes such as global perspectives in knowledge, flexibility or linguistic skills, are increasingly compatible with employability. Some jobs today and probably more jobs in the future will require employees who can work and communicate with partners and customers from all around the world. In this respect, having certain global knowledge and skills can be an advantage for these workers.

- Global citizenship education can be associated with human capital theory that we will discuss further in Chapter 11 and 13. When a country positions itself in the global market, having a large number of citizens holding global competences might be considered a resource and can be appealing for international corporations. For example, having a higher proportion of citizens who speak English as a second language might be a reason for establishing a business in a country rather than in another.

- Some educational institutions, such as universities and also schools, often want to attract students from other countries. Offering courses, specialists or global educational approaches can be a way for these institutions to place themselves in the global market. We can understand that, in particular, for international students a global approach to any degree programme (e.g. education, health, and geography,) might be more appealing that a national approach to the same degree. In this respect, government and institutions promote practices of global citizenship education, not to attract corporations but to attract students to their educational systems.

This approach to global citizenship education has highly been criticized. Biesta and Lawy (2006) discuss how, if we understand citizenship as an outcome that education promotes, we are failing in two un-ethical assumptions. First, we understand, before 'being educated', students were not 'global citizens'. Second, we consider that some people (e.g. curriculum developers, and teachers) have more rights to define what 'global citizenship' means than others creating something like 'first-class' and 'second-class' global citizens. 'Citizenship as an outcome' can lead to process of inclusion/exclusion, pre-determining who is/who is not and who might become/who might not a global citizen.

Global citizenship education in its qualification dimension can also be criticized for being essentially a neoliberal and competitive form of global citizenship. Indeed, the three different justifications we have highlighted above emphasize the competition between individuals or countries in the global market. If global citizenship education is about competition, we wonder whether the humanistic ideal of 'global citizenry' is transformed into some sort of consumer citizenry. In addition, concerns can also been raised in relation to the unfair nature of this competition. Those who decide the meaning of global citizenship and the content of these global competences are always going to be in an advanced position to win this competition. For instance, if those who speak English as a first language establish English as the international language of communication, English speakers are always going to be in advantage and will be more likely to 'win the competition'.

Global citizenship education as socialization

Global citizenship education can also be understood in terms of socialization. Global citizenship education, in this approach, is mainly understood in terms of the promotion of certain values and identities that will allow us to become 'better' citizens of the world. More precisely, under this approach, UNESCO (2014) understands global citizenship education mainly in relation to:

- Human rights. We can understand a global citizen as the individual who is committed to human rights. In this respect, global citizenship education would be similar to the notion of human rights education, including teaching and learning awareness; and the defence of these rights. Some post-colonialist theorists (e.g. Mignolo, 2009) criticize the notion of Human Rights that they perceive as an attempt to impose some Western values into non-Western societies. In this respect, Global citizenship education can be understood as a way to impose the Western version of what a 'Global citizen' should be to non-Western countries in order to maintain the Western hegemony. We will develop these ideas further in Chapter 8.

- Peace education. Peace education not only relates to international peace and understanding but also to actions against violent extremism. Global citizenship education might be linked to peace education in terms of promoting pacifist values and a more cohesive global citizenry. Some post-colonialist theorists have also raised concerns about certain understandings of peace education. Does the defence of pacifist values implies, they ask, a compliant acceptance of situations of discrimination, inequality and exploitation? In Chapter 14, on Peace education, we will discuss these issues in more depth.

- Education for sustainable development (ESD). For some, global citizenship is intrinsically linked to environmental issues, particularly to the promotion of some sort of planetary identity, the encouragement of sustainability values and behaviours; and the commitment for the protection of the environment. However, there is a question of whether some ESD initiatives fails in internal contradictions. First, individuals, rather than economic powerful groups, are made responsible of the environmental problems when the responsibility is, at least, shared. Second, individuals are often encouraged to promote sustainable development at the same time that consumption is boosted. We will discuss education for sustainable development in Chapter 16.

The three ways in which we understand global citizenship education as socialization are, as we have seen, controversial. There is also a more general question when we discuss global citizenship education in its socialization function: who decides what a good 'global citizen' is? There are no global democratic institutions that can take this decision and if some countries take the lead in deciding, aren't these countries imposing their views, and values, on the others?

Global citizenship education as subjectification

Global citizenship education can also be discussed is relation to the subjectification function of education. Under this approach, Vanessa Andreotti stated that global citizenship is not about '"unveiling" the "truth" for the learners, but about providing the space for them to reflect' (2006, p. 49). In other words, in contrast with the two previous forms of global citizenship education, the subjectification form promotes a global citizenship from below. The problem here is: how do we do this?

We feel that in the literature associated with what Biesta (2009) defines as subjectification there are, at least, three different understandings. Each of these schools of thought is, in our understanding, connected to different views and practices of global citizenship education:

- The progressive education school tends to understand subjectification in terms of encouraging students' natural freedom (Standish, 2003). Education, for this school, should be about giving students the spaces to develop their own areas of interests, and values. In relation to global citizenship, this approach would assume that all the students are already global citizens and educational settings should only provide them with the space and resources to develop further their ideas. For some, this approach fails in building a theory on the naïve assumption that all students' values and beliefs would contribute to a better society. But what happens if, for instance, a student wants to develop a notion of global citizenry based on oppression and inequality? Should the teacher, the schools, and the educational system encourage any views on global citizenship?

- The liberal school of education tends to understand subjectification in terms of encouraging certain knowledge and processes that foster students' autonomy from the system they live in (Standish, 2003). In the basis of this theory lays the assumption that if the students are provided with something like the appropriate knowledge and skills they will become critical and autonomous. The question here is, if global citizenship education is linked with 'appropriate knowledge and skills', what makes this approach different to the qualification approach we have previously discussed?

- The critical education school tends to understand subjectification in terms of counter-practice. Counter-practice implies education on non-dominant knowledges and values. In the case of global citizenship education, this would be, for instance, to develop a critique of human rights based on post-colonialist approaches. It could also result in criticizing the notion of global citizenship education in itself as an attempt to impose Western culture in other societies. But the question is, how do we know critical educators are right in their analysis? And, in addition, if critical educators are the ones who define who is and who is not a global citizen are we not failing again in line with the criticisms associated with global citizenship education as socialization?

Conclusions

In the introduction to this book, we mentioned that we felt it was impossible to provide easy definitions for the terms we are discussing. We hope that after these first two chapters you are able to better understand our position.

However, we want to finish this first section emphasizing three aspects that we consider essential to discuss about global citizenship education. First, the notion of global citizenship education cannot be examined without considering the assumptions we make about globalization, citizenship and education and about global citizenship. Second, there is nothing like a correct approach to global citizenship that can be taught and learnt. There are multiple and contradictory views about the need and the form of global citizenship education. Third, we do not believe that global citizenship education can be reduced to a specific set of educational practices. We feel that nobody can offer a manual about how teachers could better teach global citizenship. Because as we have said there is nothing like a 'universal global citizenship' and therefore there is not a single 'proper way' of educating for global citizenship. We think, however, that perhaps there are more reflective ways of educating the global citizenry. It is one of our tasks in this book to help you to examine and challenge different views to encourage this reflection.

Annotated bibliography

Andreotti, V. (2006). Soft versus critical global citizenship education. *Policy & Practice*, 3, 40–51.

The Brazilian post-colonialist educator, Vanessa Andreotti discusses in this paper two main approaches to global citizenship education. In the first part of the paper, Andreotti draws upon the work of Andrew Dobson and Gayatri Spivak to contextualize theoretically the notion of global citizenship education. We recommend engaging with some more introductory readings to post-colonialist theory to ensure an appropriate understanding of this first part. In the second part, entitled, 'Soft versus critical citizenship education and the notion of critical literacy', the author presents a more comprehensive comparison between what she describes as 'soft global citizenship education' and 'critical global citizenship education'. Andreotti's views on global citizenship education can help you to better understand what global citizenship education as counter-practice means.

Davies, L. (2006). Global citizenship: abstraction or framework for action? *Educational Review*, 58(1), 5–25.

In this paper, Lynn Davies attempts to cross the bridge between global citizenship theory and educational practice. She briefly contextualizes the notion of global citizenship and she examines and compares actual curricula and programmes of study of global citizenship. Although having a clear British focus, the paper illustrates how different understandings of global citizenship inform different educational practices. It also demonstrates how global citizenship education policies and practices might be examined to identify underlying ideologies.

Torres, C. A. (2015). Global citizenship and global universities. The age of global interdependence and cosmopolitanism. *European Journal of Education*, 50(3), 262–79.

This article illustrates some of the critiques of global citizenship education understood as qualification and as socialization. By looking at the particular case of higher education, Carlos Alberto Torres discusses different views on global citizenship education and on the purposes of higher education and how these views are having an impact on higher education policies and practices worldwide. By highlighting different discourses, strategies and dilemmas, the text represents a good introduction to the topic of global citizenship education in the context of higher education

UNESCO (2015). *Global citizenship education. Topics and learning objectives.* Paris: UNESCO. Retrieved from http://unesdoc.unesco.org/images/0023/002329/232993e.pdf

UNESCO develops the basis of their global citizenship education approach on this report published on 2015. The report is the result of the meeting of the Experts Advisory Group (EAG) on Global Citizenship Education (GCED) (Paris, June 2014) and it is implicitly associated with the Education For All agenda (see Chapter 11). The document can be examined to understand UNESCO's approach to global citizenship education. With the purpose of being a comprehensive and practical guide, global citizenship education is presented in this document in its qualification function. UNESCO presents a single definition of global citizenship followed by a set of outcomes, knowledge and skills that can contribute towards this form of global citizenship. The report is rich in providing worldwide examples of how UNESCO's understanding of global citizenship can be taught and learnt.

Activities

1. In this exercise, we suggest that you analyse different views on global citizenship education. We would like you to examine your views together with the views of other higher education students. It is our aim here to encourage you to reflect about your own understanding of global citizenship education. We recommend that you to follow the instructions below in the order in which they appear but you should feel free to use this activity in the way that best suits you.

a) Write a definition of global citizenship education that summarizes the way you understand this concept.
  b) Consider the following views of some pre-service teachers about the ways they would contribute to the 'global citizenship education' project through their practices.
     - 'I would have a debate in which students will discuss their views on global citizenship and we could finally a agree a definition together'
     - 'I would promote values such as empathy and understanding that are necessary for a global citizenship and for a better global society'
     - 'I would teach my students the skills to examine sources from around the world and to recognize similarities and differences'
  c) Identify the approaches to global citizenship education implicit in these views in relation to: (a) the different purposes of education; (b) the different reasons for and against global citizenship. Examine your own definition in a similar way.
2. Now we encourage you to examine the way in which global citizenship education is framed by different institutions. First, we would like you to find public and private institutions that explicitly aim to educate the global citizenry. UNESCO (http://en.unesco.org/gced) and OXFAM (http://www.oxfam.org.uk/education/global-citizenship) can be examples of these but you can find other examples such as national governments, universities or schools. Second, we would like you to examine the ways in which the concept of 'global citizenship' is constructed in these institutional policies. Consider whether global citizenship is constructed in relation to neoliberal, humanistic or anticolonial principles (Chapter 1). Finally, you should analyse what are the educational purposes underlying these institutional policies and how they can be discussed in relation to the framework we presented in this chapter.

3

Global Rights and Duties

There is a vast literature on rights and duties. There are significant challenges in interpreting the many official and unofficial declarations and the huge number of academic, professional and popular publications. There is actually little international law that would help us encapsulate global rights and duties, although there are laws made in one place that apply elsewhere – at times this may be due to transnational citizenships (e.g. those that apply in the European Union). There are, in a globalizing world, increasing attempts to clarify who is entitled to – and responsible for – what.

We do not have a simple consensus about the meaning of rights. There are fiercely contested debates about many issues including, for example, whether the discourse of rights is theoretically and in practice largely a Western notion. We will not be able to secure a reasonable grasp of the complexities associated with rights unless throughout fundamental questions of who 'offers' rights; who holds those rights; and, who is in charge of ensuring that these rights are not merely *de iure* (in theory) but also de facto (in reality).

Many see the most obvious starting point in relation to global rights and duties to be those high-profile statements that are issued by international bodies such as the United Nations. This does not mean that all these things are universally accepted (and it does not mean that these international bodies are democratic). The Universal Declaration of Human Rights was proclaimed in 1948 in the aftermath of the devastating destruction of World War II. It highlights those fundamental human rights that are to be universally protected (http://www.un.org/en/universal-declaration-human-rights/). This was followed by several other declarations (e.g. International Covenant on Civil and Political Rights) and it has clear links to statements in particular parts of the world. The Charter of Fundamental Rights of the EU, for example, brings together in a single document the fundamental rights protected in the EU. The Charter contains rights and freedoms under six titles: Dignity, Freedoms, Equality, Solidarity, Citizens' Rights and Justice. Proclaimed in 2000, the Charter has become legally binding on the EU following the Treaty of Lisbon, in December 2009. The Charter applies when EU countries adopt or apply a national law implementing an EU directive or when their authorities apply an EU regulation directly (http://ec.europa.eu/justice/fundamental-rights/charter/index_en.htm). There have also been developments that are directly related to children and connected to these overarching statements. For example, the United Nations Convention on the Rights of the Child (http://www.unicef.org.uk/Documents/Publicationpdfs/UNCRC_PRESS200910web.pdf).

The statements referred to above might best be described as international rather than global. In other words, they carry the ambitions of people who are largely based in Western countries and who are idealistically and at times politically concerned with the world order (in varying degrees of commitment to democratic accountability). Some have declared their uncertainty about some aspects of these declarations. For example, groups such as Amnesty International have questioned whether the declarations are comprehensive, suggesting that other things might be added, including, for example, a right not to kill. Some countries have not signed the Universal Declaration (indicating a problem with the universality of its acceptance and application). Initial signatories (58 countries) to the Universal Declaration did not include South Africa who wished to preserve its apartheid system. Some countries have their own approach to the achievement of human rights. In China, for example, the four Cardinal Principles (introduced by Deng Xiaoping in 1979) of upholding the socialist path, the people's democratic dictatorship, the leadership of the Communist Party of China and the thought of Mao Zedong and Marx and Lenin is set alongside the Fundamental Rights and Duties of Citizens in China (http://www.helplinelaw.com/law/china/constitution/constitution03.php). In Islamic countries key principles may be based on the *Qur'an* and Hadith and codified in the form of Sharia Law variously interpreted involving five pillars of Islam for worship and community interaction.

How then may we make sense of not only what is said but also how those things should be interpreted? A fundamental starting point is consideration of the overarching perspectives of universalism and relativism. The latter suggests that cultural difference allows for the possibility of particular principles and actions. Universalism does not mean that things will require a simple application of a pre-arranged formula to problems. The Universal Declaration is not a complete philosophical model and it does not provide a guide to concrete action in specific cases. The Universal Declaration, however, offers an opportunity to discuss different understandings of justice. It may help address certain weaknesses of a relativist approach. If, for example, we wish to avoid the possibility of a dictator declaring that an oppressive practice is suitable in a particular area given supposedly cultural justification then a universal declaration could be extremely useful (and there is more discussion on this point in Chapter 10 on social justice). But these issues about rights and duties will remain contested. Ahmed (2012) has suggested that only an unhelpfully limited form of diversity is currently accepted by those within the liberal tradition in which the roles of private individuals are prioritized within an Enlightenment-inspired approach to rationality:

> The difficulty for liberals is that individual autonomy rests on truths they consider to be 'self-evident' and universal. Whilst liberalism argues that reason must challenge dogma, many non-western peoples challenge non-negotiable liberal truths as dogmatic and oppressive. (p. 728)

Related to these fundamental concerns are issues about the meaning of global citizenship and to where it applies. In part this is a matter of geographical reach. Some will suggest that rights and duties may only be framed in relation to areas which are legislatively relevant. In other words, the power to act would reside with a state or a transnational body with legal powers. This however raises three other matters: first, to what extent is a distinction to be made in who has what rights and duties between 'person' and 'citizen'; second, what counts as an appropriate perspective on the legitimate space within which these rights and duties would apply; and third, what is the nature and the purpose of the rights and duties that are accepted or imposed?

The distinctions between 'person' or human being and 'citizen' connect with the formal political and legal status of citizenship. Currently, little international law exists, and there are very high ambitions referred to above about declarations of universalism. Further, there are seismic shifts in populations in economic and political migrations. As such, identifying who has the rights of a citizen is extremely complex and challenging. There are issues about how one gains citizenship rights and duties. The two legal traditions of *jus solis* and *jus sanguinis* (the former allowing for citizenship through place of birth; the latter based on heredity) give rise to very different considerations. While in Singapore, for example, a person's ethnic group is included on an identity card, details of cultural background are not collected in a census in France. The rights and duties of ethnic groups in one place matter greatly but not at all elsewhere. Something like 'human rights' or 'global rights' in contrast with national rights are currently impossible to define officially – there are no universally accepted bodies that may decide who is and who is not a global citizen.

The question of perspectives on legitimate space entail consideration of whether rights and duties are seen in terms of seeing oneself as a member of the human race, someone who is broadly responsible for the condition of the planet, someone subject to moral law or, most concretely, and aligned with the conception of citizen referred to above, someone who presses for a world government (Heater 1997). This has implications for the ways in which rights and duties are enacted. The vertical relationship between a state and a citizen may be as significant as the horizontal relation between people and citizens. In short, what do we take from and contribute to not just the state, but what do we commit to and owe each other? And, as above, who decides that this is to be accepted?

There are many issues that are relevant to the nature and purpose of the rights and duties that we have. Group as well as individual rights and duties need to be considered. To what extent, for example, is it legitimate to talk of women's rights as opposed to the particular right of an individual person to decent treatment during childbirth? Are certain rights available only to groups of a certain age (such as a pension) or is the right only to fair treatment and cannot be expressed specifically? To what extent is it appropriate to specify a right in relation to consequences (as opposed to a right to take action whatever the outcomes)? Is it reasonable to consider a reciprocal relationship between rights and duties? The absence of such reciprocity may be deemed unfair (e.g. 'you're not entitled to unemployment benefit until you have worked for a specific period of time'). But this may be problematic if vulnerable members of society (the very old, very young and those who are unwell) come to be seen as second-class citizens and as such people who are not deserving of rights. The question of rights to have a particular thing and not to be subject to certain conditions also tells us a great deal about rights and duties. This is often cast in the form of debates about freedom: what I am free to do; what I am free from? This is relevant to what we see as the full range of our commitments. Do animals have rights? Do we have duties to the environment? Does a tree have rights? And, finally, what areas of action do we see as being significant? Are there any distinctions to be made between political, moral, economic and other rights and duties? Crucially, models of citizenship (e.g. Westheimer & Kahne 2004; Oxley & Morris 2013) provide different ways in which people may approach their citizenship. Whereas one person might see her legally enshrined rights and duties as the means by which one is personally responsible, another may see those same rights and duties as allowing for social justice orientation. And, perhaps most fundamentally of all, there is a need to consider the relationship between rights and duties in the form of liberal and civic republican traditions of citizenship. Whereas the latter is essentially about responsibilities enacted in public, the former emphasizes rights of a private citizen. Heater (1999) includes a very good discussion of the nature of and issues about these traditions. It is interesting to note when new developments occur in our consideration of rights and duties. When Marshall (1963, pp. 67–127) discussed the development of citizenship in relation to civil, political and social rights the connections he made with global citizenship were very limited. These and other matters are explored further in this book, especially in the chapter on citizenship education (Chapter 9).

Annotated bibliography

Joppke, C. (2008). Transformation of citizenship: status, rights, identity. In E. F. Isin, P. Nyers & B. S. Turner (eds). *Citizenship between past and future* (pp. 36–47). Abingdon: Routledge.

In this chapter Joppke seeks to develop an overarching conception of citizenship. He argues that this is a necessary task as it is possible that different conceptions of citizenship lead academics and professionals simply to talk past each other. Following the work of others he declares that citizenship may be thought of in terms of status, rights and identities and that while these things combine into an overarching characterization, it is possible and necessary to explore each part of the whole. In relation to rights he suggests that there has been a shift in emphasis 'from redistributive social rights to procedural civil rights, particularly minority rights' (p. 40). This means that there have been two legal developments: 'the extension of citizenship rights to non-citizens and the creation or strengthening of minority rights' (p. 41). This focus on minority rights allows him to comment on the nature of anti-discrimination and multicultural recognition: 'in a nutshell, anti-discrimination is universalistic; recognition is particularistic' (p. 42). These debates about rights clearly (as Joppke intends) connect with other aspects of citizenship.

Kiwan, D. (2005). Human rights and citizenship: an unjustifiable conflation? *Journal of Philosophy of Education*, 39, 37–50.

Kiwan argues that human rights and citizenship are not the same thing. Whereas human rights are universal, citizenship is framed more particularly. She develops this argument by exploring citizenship in terms of five categories – moral, legal, identity-based, participatory and cosmopolitan – and concluding that attempts to bring citizenship and human rights together are intellectually incoherent and may actually obstruct citizen engagement. This is a very important contribution to the debate about rights and duties as there have been fiercely conducted debates about the national limits placed on citizenship and the tension between 'citizen' and 'person'. The debate over the meaning of a country – broadly whether we are dealing with a geographical entity, an ethnic identity or a political state – is thrown into sharp relief.

Soysal, Y. (1994). *Limits of Citizenship. Migrants and Postnational Membership in Europe*. Chicago, IL: University of Chicago Press.

This book is regarded by many as a modern classic or at least a key reference point in discussions about rights. Soysal focuses on the rights of immigrants, and by discussing global forces and specific national responses (especially in France,

Germany, the Netherlands, Sweden, Switzerland and the United Kingdom) suggests that non-citizens are increasingly recognized as having rights. She suggests that different countries adopt specific means of recognizing groups, individuals and national government action (corporatist, liberal, statist) to allow for the extension of rights to 'guest workers' and others. This post-national citizenship is a positive and significantly challenging contribution to discussions about formally established citizenship in the context of charters and conventions that emphasize universal human rights and in the concrete reality of mass movements of people as political, economic or other refugees and immigrants.

UNICEF rights respecting schools. http://www.unicef.org.uk/rights-respecting-schools/about-the-award/child-rights-in-schools/

UNICEF is extremely active in supporting schools and other bodies that work with young people. It is possible for schools to apply for an award that recognizes positive work. The award is awarded on the basis of evidence provided in four areas: leadership of the school; knowledge and understanding of children's rights; ethos and relationships; and the empowerment of children and young people. There are three levels of award: recognition of commitment, level 1 and level 2. A clear description of what is involved is given on the web site mentioned above:

> A Unicef UK Rights Respecting School is a community where children's rights are learned, taught, practised, respected, protected and promoted. Children and young people and the school community learn about children's rights by putting them into practice every day. The Award is not just about what children do but also importantly what adults do – in Rights Respecting Schools, children's rights are promoted and realised and adults and children work towards this together'. There is an expectation that children will learn about rights, be able to access key information, participate and work within an environment that is rights-friendly.

United Nations (2004). *Teaching Human Rights*. New York and Geneva: UN.

This teaching and learning resource is easily available on the web (see http://www.un.org/wcm/webdav/site/visitors/shared/documents/pdfs/Pub_United%20Nations_ABC_human%20rights.pdf) It is divided into three main sections: an introduction in which key ideas and issues are described and explained; a chapter containing activities for pre-school and lower primary school students; and a chapter with activities for upper primary, lower and senior secondary school. Not all teachers like all activities but there is a wealth of interesting and valuable material for use in classrooms and other less formal settings and this resource is a very good example.

Activities

1. The poem 'Dooley is a traitor' by James Michie is easily available and provides plenty of interesting material to debate rights and duties about going to war. Other poems not originally in English such as 'Human Rights' [Derechos Humanos] by Ernesto Galeano? (https://www.facebook.com/CartogramAmericana/posts/1552515945010373) Pablo and Neruda's 'The enemies' [Los enemigos] (http://dude-pablo.tripod.com/id6.html) also provide very stimulating starting points for discussions about rights and duties. Michie's Dooley asks why he should fight against an enemy who has not done anything to him. Issues about duties to the state and personal responsibility are immediately apparent. Galeano raises issues about human rights in very immediate contexts that allow us to reflect on lived experience as well as the big questions about law and philosophy. Neruda's poem is essentially a call to punish the enemies, raising questions about the right to take – if this is the right word – revenge.
2. The Universal Declaration of Human Rights could be presented and discussed. Exercises could be done on classifying and prioritizing rights and duties. What sorts of rights and duties have been included (political, social, economic, cultural and others)? Students could be asked to think about their relative importance. Beyond this general framework it might be interesting to ask students to transform the rights which are generally phrased into particular expressions. So, for example, what is meant by right to education? Is it for all, for a specified number of years and in named subjects, taught and assessed in particular ways? And if those specifications cannot be given, are we still reasonable in our determination to call it a right?
3. Students could be asked to consider the relationship between 'freedom from' and 'freedom to'. There is an excellent activity created by Ted Huddleston (2004) in which a group of vigilantes insist that they have had enough of young people causing trouble, and in the light of police inactivity, will ensure that the local area is secure and that people are well behaved. A poster is displayed which asserts that anyone causing trouble will be dealt with. Issues about the legitimate source from which rights emerge are obviously relevant here as well as things referred to above about 'freedom from' and 'freedom to'.
4. Read the play 'Enemy of the People' by Henrik Ibsen and read the novel 'The Quiet American' by Graham Greene. (Or, you can read summaries of them online or watch the films that have been made of them.) This play and novel are among the many that present the reader with complex issues about what counts as people's rights and duties, what we can do

to make the world a better place (and what may go wrong in the process). Think about how you would decide if the main characters are promoting global justice. Think about the distinctions between consequentialist and categorical justice (the former emphasizes the results of one's actions; the latter emphasizes the need to do the right thing).

4

Imagining Global Communities through a Decolonial Ethic of Global Citizenship

The idea of global communities is relatively new and certainly contested. We need to use caution in employing the idea without first understanding more about what is being imagined in such communities. Often 'global community' is conceptually employed as a way of gathering people together across borders to recognize commonality and shared purpose. Critiques of the idea come from post-colonial, decolonial, and anti-poverty theorists and activists. This chapter examines the possibilities and critiques of a global community from the perspective of global citizenship as an ethical way of claiming membership in such a community. Participation as a global citizen is often viewed through an overly-romantic notion that appeals to only a small elite who have the financial, social, and political capacity to be globally mobile. For most people on the planet, global mobility is impossible if they live in a country with a devalued currency, oppressive social norms, or even a passport that isn't recognized as legitimate in crossing borders. If you live in the United States, Canada, the UK, Australia, New Zealand or much of Europe, you are more likely to have access to currency that is 'mobile', a passport that opens doors rather than closes them, and an international relations system that has prepared you to expect to 'know' the world without borders and to move without impediment. This is certainly not a universally shared experience of the world.

Willie Ermine (2007) articulates the importance of attending to the encounters of different worldviews and cultures in any project of knowledge or legal engagement across borders of many kinds but particularly in relations where there is historically or currently relations of domination. He suggests that processes of reconciling ethical, moral, and legal principles necessary in these encounters will require a depth and intensity of cross – cultural cooperation that has few examples in modern history (ibid). Ermine describes how the universalism imagined in Western philosophy and enacted in centuries of political and economic domination around the world tends to separate most worldviews from that of Western thinking, with the idea that Western thinking and ways of living are inherently superior.

> One of the festering irritants for Indigenous peoples, in the encounter with the West, is the brick wall of deeply embedded belief and practices of Western universality. Centre to the issue of universality is the dissemination of a singular world consciousness, a monoculture with a claim to one model of humanity and one model of society. This is the claim to a God's eye view on humanity and that this perspective is appropriately located in the West . . . This monocultural existence suggests one public sphere and one conception of justice that triumphs over all others. (p. 198)

The colonialism inherent in the mobility of Western ideas and people is described as dismembering by Ngũgĩ Wa Thiong'o. Here the people subjected to colonialism lost their land, their social and political systems, and also their languages and knowledge. 'Wherever they went, in their voyages of land, sea, and mind, Europeans planted their own memories on whatever they contacted' (Thiong'o, 2009, p. 4). Not only was the economic system based on imperialism but also colonial education systems forced on the world began to teach whole regions of the world that they did not have anything worth knowing. In this, people in Africa, indigenous lands of North and South America, and Asia learned to forget knowledge that did not fit into the European canon and specifically that there was not any legitimate way to organize their lives or communities outside of the capitalist- imperialist economic and political system that underpinned much of Western knowledge (Amin, 2011; Rodney, 1972; Thiong'o, 2009). The colonial/ colonized mind was trained to imagine, not a global community, but a unified European empire (albeit with tensions among Europeans about land and power within this empire). Enrique Dussel (2013a) describes the continuity of the colonial project and the need for a decolonial ethic to guide us to a global knowledge trust that in fact, de-centres Western thought and makes room for other knowledge:

> Colonial praxis has from the beginning relied upon a philosophical justification as its foundation, and this is the point of departure for modern European philosophy with its universality claim, which unfortunately is accepted by most of the members of the South. This justification also had an anthropological character (expressed in the assumption of the superiority of European human beings over those of the South, as reflected in the

interpretation of that superiority by Gines de Seulveda in his re-reading of Aristotle in the 16th Century, or by Kant in the 18th century, based upon his conception of the origin of inequalities in the climates of the Earth and its regions) – one aspect of which was historical (where Europe was, for example, the 'centre and end of universal history' for Hegel) and another which was ethical (in terms of the inclusion within European culture of the peoples of the Americas, Africa, or Asia, upon whom was imposed its vision of an ethics which is non-conventional, individualist, founded upon rational argumentation, universal, and not merely particular such as those characteristic of the cultures of the South) which served to demonstrate the legitimacy of colonialism. (p. 9–10).

It is important that we disrupt this idea of what the 'global' constitutes – universal and European – if we are to imagine anything that might be able to include the worldviews, knowledges, and experiences of the many different people on the planet. This is a decolonizing process, long overdue by most accounts.

Ubuntu: a southern African world view

One example of a worldview that differs at an ontological and epistemological level, it that of 'Ubuntu' in southern Africa. Mbiti (1969) describes the deep relationality of this view: 'I am because we are, since we are therefore I am' (p. 215). It stands in contrast to the position of most Western philosophies: '[w]estern philosophy accepts as its starting point the notion of unconstrained and uncontextualized 'I' – that is, an 'I' defined in relation to the self and its inner being, rather than in relation to others. The African mode, however, seems more communal and emphasizes an 'I' that is always connected to and in relationship with others' (Mudimbe, 1988, 1). Assie-Lumumba (2017) describes this as a wider ontology that is at the foundation of African knowledge throughout the continent. In the general African ethos, 'to *be* is necessarily to be in relation' to others, and the 'center is a human being who is free and at the same time highly dependent upon others, on the memory of the past, and on emphasizing the balance between nature and culture' (Assie-Lumumba, 2017, p. 14). The individualism that is considered natural and universal in Western thought is not possible to 'think' from this relational worldview. This is just one example of differing worldviews. It does highlight the peril in claiming a 'global community' as we can't be sure of what worldview informs such a community and if what is imagined are good global relations based on inclusion of difference or of a kind of universalism that sees difference as a way to distinguish a person or group on a hierarchy of humans on a trajectory of Western enlightenment (Andreotti, Stein, Ahenakew & Hunt, 2015).

Ethical space of encounter

Ermine (2007) provides us with an important framework, one of 'ethical space', from which we can begin to sort through our global relations with the intention of creating more just and durable international relations. While Western philosophy provides a rich background of ethical inquiry, as we have discussed in this book, the limits of the relevance of Western universalism in this philosophical background is questioned when the ideas have been applied outside of Western cultures and geo-political institutions. Ermine addresses this disagreement in his use of 'ethical space'.

> Shifting our perspectives to recognize that the Indigenous-West encounter is about thought worlds may also remind us that frameworks or paradigms are required to reconcile these solitudes . . . The notion of an agreement to interact must always be preceded by the affirmation of human diversity created by philosophical and cultural difference. Since there is no God's eye view to be claimed by any society of people, the idea of the ethical space, produced by contrasting perspectives of the world, entertains the notion of a meeting place, or initial thinking about a neutral zone between entities or cultures. (p. 201)

In order to enter into this ethical space, one must understand that different worldviews exist and contribute to human knowledge in ways that will be unknown and outside our own worldview. In this, all knowledge is understood as incomplete. From this position, we can understand the importance of people who live and see the world differently to be able to contribute to what might be called a 'global knowledge commons'. Walter Mignolo (2000; 2011) uses the idea of 'pluriverse' to disrupt our idea of universalism. He argues that it is necessary in the current globalized world to be able to communicate in a pluriversal sphere if we are to address the many global issues that impact all life.

> I would like to use pluriverse in the sphere of decolonial projects coming from the global political society (deracializing and depatriarchalizing projects, food sovereignty, economic organization of reciprocity and definancialization of money, decolonization of knowledge and of being, decolonization of religion to liberate spirituality, decolonization of aesthetics to liberate aesthesis, etc.) and multi-polarity in the sphere of politico-economic dewesternization, lead states projects. (Mignolo, n.d. Accessed at waltermignolo.com/on-pluriversality)

These critical global projects highlight the urgency of the education task ahead of us.

How then should we approach global citizenship as an ethical way to imagine global communities? The global issues that face us on the planet present an urgent and extensive reimagining of how humans should and can live a sustained life on the planet. Tlostanova & Mignolo (2014) describe the need to shift the geo- and body politics of knowledge if we are to learn to listen to the knowledge and experiences of people on the periphery of the global systems that now work in the world. This will take first, an unlearning on the part of people throughout the world. Global citizenship education can contribute to this unlearning through the creation of ethical spaces for unlearning coloniality. Following Ermine's suggestion, people can develop agreements for interaction across these differences that do not require that non-dominant people or groups give up their worldview in order to fit the dominant Western perspective. This can happen in classrooms, and on research projects; on international agencies and wherever people meet as not just members of a small, shared community but as members of a global community. In this way, participants must acknowledge their own location and contribution and those of others. Global citizenship can contribute to a decolonial future when it engages the multiscalar (global to local) understanding of citizenship rights and responsibilities based on pluriversality. In this, a global citizen is not a person with a view from 'nowhere' or 'everywhere' but a person who understand his or her own location in the world and acknowledges that this location provides only one of many views of the world and how it does and should work. A global citizen would then be able to understand global systems and their local manifestations as related to many readings of the world and to create ethical space for diverse perspectives and ways of living in the world. Global issues require a reimagining of how we live on the planet. It is not possible to predict what new possibilities this will create but we can understand that the projects that we collectively need to undertake to make the world more just and more liveable for human and non-human life requires such a great global transformation of thinking and relating.

Annotated bibliography

Abdi, A. A. (2013). Decolonizing educational and social development platforms in Africa. *African and Asian Studies*, 12, 64–82.

In this article, Abdi brings together the key anti-colonial and decolonial arguments as they relate to the experiences of people in Africa. He highlights the role of education and it potential for reproducing colonial relations and systems or, with some reconfiguring education actors and goals, assist in setting African people and their communities off into toward a future that includes the wisdom and worldviews that provided a foundation for well-being for thousands of years. This is not a call for a romanticized past but an acknowledgement of the generous social epistemological view of the world that can address the legacies of colonialism that cast this worldview as deficient against the liberalism and individualism of the European colonial project.

Schooling the World (video) http://schoolingtheworld.org/

This video is a documentary covering the role of education in colonization in different parts of the world and particularly the intentional focus on the world's land-based cultures. It begins with a provocative question: if you wanted to change a culture in a generation, how would you do it? With interviews with Vandana Shiva, Wade Davis, Helena Norberg-Hodge, this question is viewed from different worldviews and experiences of colonial education and its more recent form, development education.

Simpson, L. B. (2014). Land as pedagogy: Nishnaabeg intelligence and rebellious transformation. *Decolonization: Indigeneity, Education and Society*, 3(3) 1–25.

In this article, Leanne Betasamosake Simpson describes how the resurgence of Indigenous political, social, and intellectual life is supported by land-based education where indigenous people are immersed in the lands, languages, and spiritualities that supported life for millennia. She describes the need for education that disrupts education to create capitalist consumers to one where people are education as cultural producers.

Activity

Ramón Grosfoguel (2013, p. 74) poses these questions: 'How is it possible that the canon of thought in all the disciplines of the Social Sciences and Humanities in the *Westernized university* [italics in original] is based on the knowledge produced by a few men from five countries: Italy, France, England, Germany and the United States? How is it possible that men from these five countries achieved such an epistemic privilege to the point that their knowledge today is considered superior over the knowledge of the rest of the world? Why is it that what we know today as social, historical, philosophical, or Critical Theory is based on the socio-historical experience and world views of men from these five countries?'

Analyse your experience with social and educational theories based on these questions. Where do these theories come from? What knowledge comes from outside Western Europe or United States?

How might global citizenship shift this problem?

5

Global Identities

Do you think of yourself as a 'global citizen'? Your answer to this question may connect to whether or not you hold a global identity. In 2014, two of the authors of this book together with another colleague conducted a comparative research project in two European countries in which we examined how fourteen-years-old identified themselves (Sant, Davies & Santisteban, 2016). Overwhelmingly students identified themselves as citizens of their countries, nations, villages and schools. Of the 583 students who answered a questionnaire, only six students identified themselves as 'citizens of the world'. As we wrote then:

> Despite the obvious significant increase in everyday expressions of a global society seen in the use by young people of social and other media potentially involving interactions with peers and others from around the world and general increased international flows of people and goods, there was little explicit indication of global identity or citizenship. (Sant et al., 2016, p. 21)

Although we don't assume here that the findings in that research can be generalized to everywhere else, we understand that this research illustrates how global citizenship education cannot (and should not) avoid discussions on global identity. It is our intention in this chapter to do so.

Citizenship, identity and education

Citizenship is often discussed as a legal status, as an identity or as both (Kymlicka & Norman, 1997). For instance, a citizen of Guatemala can be considered someone who is recognized legally as citizen by the Guatemalan state; someone who identifies herself as Guatemalan; or someone who, being recognized as Guatemalan by the state, also feels the Guatemalan identity. The scholarship on citizenship notes that a sense of belonging with the community is essential in the constitution of the citizenry. Those who identify themselves with their communities are probably more likely to participate and to show solidarity with the other members of the community. In other words, having a sense of belonging contributes to the social cohesion of the community. In contrast, if the members do not identify themselves with the community, the community can disappear. In the national context, for instance, if citizens identify themselves with the country and with the other citizens within this, they often make a stronger contribution, for instance, in terms of their participation, and willingness to pay taxes. If citizens, on the contrary, do not identify themselves with the country, the country might disappear, perhaps through separatism movements that create alternative countries.

If we look at Western philosophy, one of the main questions raised in relation to identity is how identities are constituted. For some, identities are essentially produced by the social. According to Althusser (1972), the individuals are 'recruited' (in Althusser's term 'interpellated') by state institutions such as schools or police forces. In Althusser's account, the individual does not participate in the constitution of these identities but instead, they are imposed to each of us. For instance, Althusser critics how schools 'impose' national and 'a-political' identities to working-class children. Another French philosopher, Michel Foucault (1982) partially disagrees with Althusser. Identities, in Foucault's understanding, are a consequences of dominant discourses associated with social practices and institutions that are incorporated by individuals through what Foucault defines as 'technologies of the self'. Following Foucault's theory, the feminist Judith Butler (1997) and the sociologist Stuart Hall (2000) contribute that individuals do have some agency in this process. They discuss how individuals, while participating in social practices that promote identities, are be able to challenge the nature of these identities in a process she describes as performativity. In an illustrative text, Hall argues:

> On the one hand, the discourses and practices which attempt to 'interpellate', speak to us or hail us into place as the social subjects of particular discourses, and on the other hand, the processes which produce subjectivities, which construct us as subjects which can be 'spoken'. (2000, p. 19)

Butler discusses how in the case of gender, individuals participate in discourses of gender, by reproducing and repeating (performing) certain practices. Through this performance ideas of gender become set and reproduced; however, new ideas on gender can also be introduced (e.g. queer movement) that might challenge the original notion of gender. Whereas Butler does not believe the individual rationally decides this performance but that the societal norms and discourses do, Goffman (1959) understands individuals are able to manage their identities, performing the identity that will better suit their objectives.

Trying to determine exactly how individual and social identities are formed has thus been a topic of much debate and research. The creation and reinforcement of an identity and sense of belonging, with the nation and as a citizen is no simple. The importance of identifying as belonging to one's nation is often perceived as one of the reasons why mass schooling has been introduced worldwide. Beyond national identities, we are also aware of school national curricula promoting regional, European, religious and school identities. In most of these cases, particular subject areas such as language, history, geography and citizenship contribute towards this purpose. For functionalist theorists such as Durkheim and Parson, the reinforcement of a national identity could contribute to social cohesion and peaceful coexistence. For conflict theorists, such as the French philosopher Louis Althusser, the creation of a national identity through schooling encompasses the imposition of a dominant ideology and the attempt to dilute other political consciousness, essentially working-class. For post-colonialist theorists, Western schools 'were used to help social structures to fit in with European concepts of work and interpersonal relations' (Carnoy quoted in Coloma, 2013, p. 649). In this respect, the dissemination of the national identity represented not only the imposition of that particular nation identity and an undermining of local identities, but the attempt to reconfigure what can be understood as an identity in itself as to be a citizen was to be a member of a colonial state.

(Global) identity: the (global) self and the (global) social

From Althusser who understands identities as essentially created by the social, to Goffman who discusses identities as something the individual critically decides to perform, there is a wide range of theories that attempt to discuss the links between the self and the social. In what follows we discuss seven different approaches to 'identity' as presented by Benwell and Stokoe (2006). We add a final approach considering the limitations of Western philosophy as discussed by post-colonialist authors. We examine the possibilities and challenges of each approach for the constitution of a global identity and its links with education.

(Global) identity as enlightened self. Associated with the liberal philosophical tradition (mainly with the philosophers Descartes and Locke), the enlightened or civic approach to identity understands that individuals are able

to decide whether or not they identify with the community. In this respect, one would expect that each of us, after a careful and reflexive consideration of our knowledge and previous experiences, would choose to belong or not to belong to the global community. If we understand identities in this way, global citizenship education in its subjectification approach (see Chapter 2) could encourage students to reflect about their previous knowledge and experiences with the global. Critics of this approach, however, challenge the view that individuals have the agency to make such a decision. For instance, someone holding a Syrian passport can take a reflexive decision and decide that she or he wants to have an Austrian identity. However, unless this person is recognized by the Austrian authorities as a citizen holding the rights to stay in Austria, she will not have the rights of an Austrian citizen, and she will not be able to participate fully in the Austrian community.

(Global) identity as romantic self. The romantic approach understands identity as something innate. One does not decide to belong to a community but she is born into it. Identity here is essentially associated with culture (including customs, language, and religion). In this approach, the sociologist Anthony Smith (2005) understands that identities can only be constituted through shared experiences, including shared memories of specific events and personages, a sense of continuity between succeeding generations and a sense of common destiny. In this respect, the role of education would be the commemoration and transmission of these shared memories, through, for instance, learning the history of the nation. In Smith's view, given the plurality of human beings' experiences and the lack of common memories, the constitution of a global identity must be premature at least for some time. In Norris' (2005) examination, in contrast, globalization is creating the conditions for people to share these memories and constitute a cosmopolitan identity. She points to, for instance, people sharing experiences of migration, creating international networks or sharing memories in the digital space. From a postcolonial perspective, there have been shared, while diverse, experiences of colonial oppression experienced by various populations for centuries.

(Global) identity as psychoanalytic self. The psychoanalytic approach to identity is mainly based on some interpretations of the work of Sigmund Freud and Jacques Lacan and the later development of other philosophers such as Zizek and Kristeva. Lacan understands that identities (better described as identifications) are constituted through the interaction of three different registers: the imaginary, the symbolic and the real. The imaginary register encompasses the ways one 'imagines' oneself and the social to be. The symbolic, instead, refers to something like a pre-existing social space (e.g. practices, and institutions) that encourage individuals to be and behave in certain ways. The real register is associated with the 'space in which the Imaginary and Symbolic are enacted' (Brown & England, 2005, p. 453). The real is always uncertain,

impossible to encapsulate and predict even after a careful consideration of the imaginary and the symbolic. In this understanding, the identification with the global could be the result of the interaction between individuals having particular global imaginaries and global institutions (e.g. United Nations) and practices.

(Global) identity as the social self. Based on the work of the social psychologists Tajfel and Turner, social identity theory discusses how individuals identify with groups through a combination of knowledge and emotional attachment to the community. Social identity theory assumes that identities need to be created in relation to an ingroup and outgroup. In other words, only by excluding those who do not belong to the ingroup (the others), our community and our sense of belonging with it is constituted. In certain ways, social identity theory challenges the possibility of a global identity. Although we might gain some knowledge about the global community, it is difficult to think how an emotional attachment associated to the ingroup and the outgroup would look like in the global context. If, the members of the global community are to be all human beings, the question of who could be the 'excluded' remains. If, instead, the global community is only inclusive to certain human beings, questions about who has the right to decide the criteria for inclusion can be posed.

(Global) identity as the narrative self. The narrative approach to identities is based on the work of different philosophers such as Ricour and Lyotard and different linguists such as Propp. Essentially, narrative theorists argue that we constitute our identities through narratives, stories that we explain to ourselves. We make sense of the social and our participation in this social space through these identities. For instance, one can explain how she 'became' a global citizen through an adventure narrative, highlighting different travels around the world, and the different she people met. Someone else, instead, could explain how he 'became' a global citizen through a dramatic narrative, highlighting a story of emigration, and loneliness. The way in which both identify with the idea of global citizenship could be completely different.

(Global) identity as postmodern self. Some postmodernist theorists (e.g. Bauman and Beck) understand that the late twentieth century and the twenty-first century are characterized by fragmentation, relativism and uncertainty. Identities are not an exception. The postmodern self is considered to have multiple identities, which might be simultaneous or characterized by their fluidity. A cosmopolitan identity, in this respect, can be constituted without having to renounce to other identities (e.g. national, or local). Indeed, in the research we presented in the beginning of this chapter, one of the students identifies herself as 'Catalan, Spanish, European and world citizen'. Postmodern identities, in addition, are also considered to be 'hybrid' with individuals mixing different parts of themselves into a new identity (e.g. third culture kids).

(Global) identity as the political self. The postmarxist theorists Chantal Mouffe and Ernesto Laclau discuss how identities are essentially flexible and political. Identities, in their account, are political because they are antagonistic, this is how they are constructed in opposition to others. For instance, in the context of the movements of de-colonization on Africa, individuals from different ethnic groups joined to struggle against the colonizing powers. By doing so, these individuals constituted a differential identity built on opposition (against) the colonizer. However, in Laclau and Mouffe's account, these identities are flexible. Therefore, after the process of decolonization, this common identity disappeared and alternatives identities (perhaps opposing one to the others) occupied this place. In terms of global citizenship, Mouffe and Laclau's theory would probably challenge the view that a universal form of global citizenship is possible. Instead, they would understand education for global citizenship in its subjectification function and they would understand the peaceful struggle to define global citizenship as a political act.

(Global) identity as the Western self? Some post colonialist authors argue that the same notion of identity is often examined only considering Western assumptions of what constitutes an identity (Connell, 2007). In theory and practice, these Western assumptions are often universalized and this represents a challenge for more inclusive approaches to global identities. In this respect, post colonialist authors are particularly concerned with the possibilities of examining non-Western identities and global identities assuming the principles of Western theories. Before engaging in a discussion on global identities, they argue, we would need to engage in a process of decolonization of the same notion of identity, and this would continue as a key element of on-going discussions of global citizenship. As we have mentioned in Chapter 4, Western knowledge is framed by certain ontological and epistemological assumptions that present as universal but are actually very much bound by specific ideas about individuals their role in the world that are not universally shared.

Conclusions

The relation between identities, citizenship and education is extremely complex and especially so in the case of global identities. Global citizenship, at least in the moment of writing this book, can be associated with a broad idea of holding a global identity, and this can be taken-up in different ways, but whether or not it can be associated to a global status is matter for discussion. Although the United Nations through the Universal declaration of Human Rights, provides, theoretically, all human beings with a set of rights, there is no guarantee that these rights are practically granted. What we challenge here is 'who' is the social entity that can contribute to the creation and reinforcement of identities.

The romantic and the psychoanalytic approaches highlight the relevance of social imaginaries in the constitution of identities. If, as Stein and Andreotti (2015) suggest the dominant global imaginary is linked to the myth of Western supremacy, one might wonder whether only those who imagine themselves as 'Western' are able to identify themselves with a global identity. In this respect, if this dominant global imaginary prevails, there is a question of whether there are opportunities for those who do not identify themselves as Western to identify themselves as 'global'.

There is also a question of how global identities are constituted if, as social identity theory and Laclau and Mouffe assume, they are constituted in opposition to other identities. In this respect, we wonder whether human beings might have different experiences in relation to the global. Norris (2005) highlights that contemporary beings share experiences of migration, and international networks. Human beings, perhaps, tend to have 'hybrid' identities in the line of ideas discussed in the postmodern self. There is a question, however, of whether human beings experience these events in the same way. For instance, Baumann (1999) critiques the notion of 'cosmopolitan identity' for bringing together those who feel free to travel around the world and enjoy the opportunities offered by globalization, and those who do not have any other option rather than emigrate. In this respect, we could not talk about 'global identity' but 'global identities' that could be constructed against each other.

In the field of education, the discussion between functionalist and conflict theorists is still relevant. For the functionalist theorists, the education on a global identity would contribute to peace and global cohesion. This approach can be partially linked with the socialization function of global citizenship education. For the conflict theorists, instead, there is a risk of promoting a dominant ideology and the preservation of power relationships by promoting one version of a global identity through education. The nature of educating about having a global identity will involve considering different perspectives on the nature of identities. In this understanding, associated with critical forms of global citizenship, only through a subjectification approach to global citizenship, this risk can be assumed.

Annotated bibliography

Bauman, Z. (1998). Tourists and vagabonds. In Z. Bauman (Ed.). *Globalization: the human consequences* (pp. 77–102). Cambridge: Polity.

'Tourists and vagabonds' is one of the chapters in Zygmunt Bauman's book *Globalization: the human consequences*. In the chapter, the sociologist Bauman discusses the different impact of globalization on human beings. In his understanding, whereas for some, the tourists, globalization offers a wide range of possibilities including travels and discovery, for others, the vagabonds, globalization forces them to move to try to escape their local realities. We feel that Bauman's chapter is helpful for a better understanding of some of the critiques to the enlightened and romantic approaches to identities.

Benwell, B. & Stokoe, E. (2006). *Discourse and Identity*. Edinburgh: Edinburgh University Press.

In this book, Benwell and Stokoe present a comprehensive introduction to the concept of identity particularly aimed at postgraduate students. The book is divided into two main sections. In the first section, the authors cover different approaches to identities. We find particularly helpful the detailed first chapter on theories on discourse and identity. In the second section, the authors cover particular identities that are interesting from a global point of view: commodified, spatial and virtual identities. The book is well written and accessible considering the topic covered. This accessibility, however, does not have a negative impact on the areas covered. The book covers the main issues related to identities that might be relevant for global citizenship education.

Connell, R. (2007). The northern theory of globalization. *Sociological Theory*, 25(4), 368–85.

This article exposes some of the challenges academics might face when social constructs such as 'identities' are only examined through the lens of Western theory. Connell discusses how ideas on globalization -such as the discussion on global identities we undertook in this chapter – often exclude non-Northern viewpoints. In contrast, she argues that, if we want a genuinely global analysis of global issues, sociological theory in itself needs to be reconsidered.

Nilan, P. & Feixa, C. (Eds.) (2006). *Global youth?: hybrid identities, plural worlds*. London: Routledge.

This book gathers different research papers examining how young people identify themselves all around the world. Following a comprehensive introduction in which the postmodernist view of hybrid identities is discussed, each chapter summarize the research conducted worldwide. More precisely, case studies are reported from Iran, Indonesia, Japan, Sénégal, Australia, Spain, France, Britain, Canada, Mexico and Colombia. We found this book an excellent resource for looking at how young people constitute their identities in the twenty-first century.

Smyth, A. D. (2005) Towards a global culture? In D. Held & A. McGrew (Eds). *The Global Transformations Reader* (pp. 278–86). Cambridge: Polity Press.

GLOBAL IDENTITIES

The ethno-symbolist sociologist A. D. Smyth discusses in this chapter the notion of global culture and global identities. The author provides an accessible account of how global identity can be discussed from an ethnic-romantic approach. In brief, Smyth argues that there is nothing like a shared past by the whole humanity that can inform the basis of a common global identity. In this respect, we find particularly relevant the section entitled 'Ethno-history and posterity'.

Activity

1. In this activity, we would like you to conduct some collaborative research to examine whether or not your friends, family or acquaintances identify themselves as global citizens and the reasons behind this identification or lack of identification. You can conduct this small-scale research face to face or virtually. In table 5.1, we suggest some questions that you can consider using in this inquiry. Once you have conducted your research, apply the theoretical framework we have presented in this chapter to analyse the answers of your participants.

TABLE 5.1 Suggested questions for the collaborative research

Aim	Suggested questions	Questions for the analysis
To examine whether or not your friends, family or acquaintances identify themselves as global citizens	1. Do you identify yourself as belonging to particular groups / communities? 2. What are these groups / communities? 3. Do you think of yourself as a global citizen?	1. Do they identify as global citizens without you asking? 2. Do they identify as global citizens when explicitly asked?
To analyse the reasons behind this identification or lack of identification	4. Why do you think of yourself / do you not think of yourself as a global citizen? 5. Why do you think other people think of themselves as global citizens? 6. Why do you think other people do not think of themselves as global citizens?	3. Do they link global citizenship to any of the discussed approaches to identity? 4. How do they explain the relation between the self and the social?

6

Local and Global Citizenship

The national curriculum of Chile for Primary Education in the subject area of History, Geography and Social Sciences covers sixteen units on History. This includes five units on Greek and Roman civilization, the Medieval period on Europe and Modern Times on Europe. The curriculum, therefore, includes five units on non-local history that some might understand as global history. The curriculum also covers one unit on Chilean Native Americans, two units on Maya, Azteca and Inca civilization and one unit entitled 'Discovery and conquest of America'. The syllabus specifically recognizes that the purpose of mixing American and European history is to ensure that students understand the confluence of different civilizations in the present Chilean society. Similar examples can be found in other Latin American (and non-Latin American) countries.

In our understanding, this curriculum illustrates the complex local-global dynamics that we will examine in this chapter. Some local forms of history (essentially Greek, Roman and European) have become global in Chile and in other parts of the world. In other words, certain local history has been assumed to be world history. Simultaneously, Chilean history – and several other histories – is understood as a confluence of civilizations where different communities are integrated to create a new local history. Similar issues are often experienced in the curriculums of language, geography, citizenship, science, and the arts worldwide.

In this chapter, we introduce some of the approaches to the local-global dynamics and its links with global citizenship and global citizenship education.

The local and the other 'locals'

The concept of locality is highly ambiguous. Although references to the local are often associated with cities, villages and towns, there are at least ten different forms in which the term local is used (Urry, 1995). For instance, 'local' is sometimes used to refer to lower areas of administration, to refer to municipalities or to distinguish people from those who are non-local or outsiders. 'Localness' is often understood as a synonym of proximity or closeness. But for something to be 'local', proximal and close, something else has to be distant. The 'local' in this respect is socially constructed in relation to something else (Appadurai, 1996). For instance, imagine someone who grows up in small village in Poland. The local, there, can be constructed as the village in relation to the distant city of Krakow. Imagine this person goes to live in Spain. She might start missing some 'local' Polish meals such as the pierogi. Let us now imagine she later moves to Qatar. She might also miss 'local' Christian traditions such as celebrating Christmas. In the example in the Chilean curriculum, some will understand the Chilean pre-Colombian 'local history' to include only the Chilean Native American history (e.g. the history of the Mapuches) while others will understand that this also includes the Maya civilization (as Native Americans) which lived 1,000s of km/miles away.

The 'local' is usually understood as being spatially bounded and 'at risk' (Appadurai, 1996). As such, boundaries, borders and borderlands have often been perceived as zones of danger. However, most scholars agree that 'local' as something that is 'pure' does not exist. Rather, different 'locals' have always been connected through flows of ideas, traditions, resources and people. The acceleration of the globalization process has fostered these flows. If the 'local' had always been (at least) partially influencer and influenced, the level and the number of influences has now grown exponentially.

In education, processes of policy transfer are usually described as the most visible example of influence between two locals. Policy transfer implies the identification of 'good educational practices' happening somewhere else and the adoption of these other practices into local context. The concept of policy transfer, however, implies a wide spectrum of practices from extreme forms of imposition to a subtler spread of ideas (Phillips & Schweisfurth, 2014). In one extreme, for instance, nineteenth century empires such as the British or the French imposed into their colonies Western-type schools. In another extreme, in 2009, students from Shanghai, Singapore and Hong Kong excelled in PISA evaluation for maths. Since then, a number of countries have attempted to learn from the 'Asian style' of teaching maths. But processes of policy transfer are extremely complex. The importation of external policies requires a consideration of the complexities of the 'local' contexts including local economy, demography, culture, etc. For instance, the 'Asian style' of teaching maths -based, among others in the whole-class interactive teaching- is difficult to separate from communitarian values that are held in some 'Asian' locals. It is hard to imagine that this 'style' can be integrated to other 'local' contexts holding competing values.

In this first section, we have briefly analysed the relations between 'locals'. But processes of influence – including processes of policy transfer – do not always imply a direct influence between two 'locals' but rather the mediation of 'global' agencies (e.g. World Bank). We will discuss below these second type of influences by examining the relations between the 'locals' and the 'global'.

The local and the global, interpretations and analysis

In schools' learning and teaching materials, the concept of 'local' is often constructed in opposition to the concept of 'global'. The local is frequently perceived to be particular, immediate and concrete, whereas the global is constructed as universal, distant and abstract. But the relations between global and local are actually extremely complex and require further consideration. In what follows, we examine some of the philosophical and sociological interpretations and analysis of these relations.

Interpretations: does the 'global' exist?

The relation between the global and the local mirrors deep philosophical questions about the particular and the universal. The main question here is, is anything 'universal' or 'global' that is shared by all 'particulars' or 'locals'?

World culture theorists take a universalist stand and understand that there are some 'global' principles and forms of knowledge that apply to all 'locals'. As we discussed in the Chapter 2, human rights, sustainability and democratic principles are often described as these 'global principles'. Similarly, world culture theorists believe that certain forms of knowledge are valuable in all possible locals. Maths and science -in the way most of us learn in schools- is often considered to be the essence of this 'universal' knowledge. World culture theorists understand that, if Western type schools are being universalized, this is because they are the 'best' possible form of education in all local contexts. As such, it is possible to have a 'global criteria of quality' against which all education systems can be assessed. The very notion of international achievement test is based on this assumption. 'To do well in education means the same thing in every social context, and, by extension, that education fulfils the same role in every society' (Shields, 2013, p. 78).

Post-colonialist authors, in contrast, take a particularist stand. They understand that there are no universal principles and forms of knowledge that apply to all local contexts. Instead, some local forms of knowledge (mainly Western) are imposed upon everybody else through processes of economic, political and cultural imperialism. In this understanding, if schools have become the dominant form of education worldwide, it is not because they are the 'best' form of education in all local contexts but rather, because some local forms of education (Western type) have implicitly or explicitly been imposed on all other local contexts. For the post-colonialists, there are no global criteria of quality. Each local system might have its own criteria. The type of knowledge that is valuable in the Indian Himalayas, for instance, is not the same type of knowledge valuable in the city of Berlin. Education fulfils different roles in different local societies.

Analysis: are all the 'locals' integrating into a single 'global'?

In contemporary societies, the links between the global and the local are also considered when scholars analyse the process of globalization. The question here is whether globalization is contributing to the homogenization of all 'locals' into a single global?

Some scholars understand that the acceleration of the globalization process is homogenizing all 'locals' in cultural, linguistic, economic, political and educational terms. Culturally, certain meals, shows, music, and celebrations, have been integrated into a wide range of places beyond where they were created. In linguistic terms, it is calculated that almost 10 per cent of the world population speaks English as a foreign language. Economically, capitalism has increasingly become the dominant economic system globally. Certain corporations (e.g. Coca-Cola, Suzuki and McDonald's) make their business in factories in many countries; and other industries have been de-localized usually to lower-salary countries. Politically, the central ideas of nation-states have become dominant worldwide including those countries that traditionally had alternative forms of governance. In education, certain social institutions including educational institutions such as schools, nurseries, universities have become global.

Homogenization is perceived in contradictory terms. For the world culture theorists, homogenization is a way to ensure that all locals have access to the 'best' of the world culture. For instance, the homogenization of the school curricula will bring the best possible curricula to all local contexts. For some post-colonialist authors, instead, the spread of Western culture is destroying non-Western local forms of knowledge. Schools contribute to the spread of Western culture and values and to the destruction of local cultures. In a study on the Baiga community in India, for instance, Sarangapani (2003) argues that whereas the local knowledge of the Baiga community is contextualized and oral, modern (Western) forms of schooling are based on abstraction, descontextualization and literacy. The differences are so fundamental that, 'Baiga knowledge tradition', she argues, 'cannot survive in the modern school institutional structure' (p. 208).

Other scholars understand that globalization implies both processes of homogenization and processes of differentiation. The philosopher Walter Mignolo (2000), for instance, provides a sophisticated account of the local-global relations. According to Mignolo, certain local forms of knowledge (mainly Western) – that he defines as local histories – have become universalized – global designs. In the Chilean example we used, European history (including, for instance, the Roman Empire) is taken to represent the global. But these global designs are not necessarily appropriated by all locals in the same way, they are modified and adapted to local contexts. The example we used in the beginning of this chapter can be used to illustrate Mignolo's understanding. The arrival of Cristobal Columbus to America in 1492 is often described in worldwide history textbooks as the 'discovery of America'. This is, a local history (European understanding of the event) becoming a global design (global understanding of the event). But the way in which this 'discovery of America' is received might be different in different local contexts. Whereas in Spain the term 'discovery' can be used to examine the implications for the 'discovery' for the modern Spaniards, in Chile, teachers can use the notion of 'discovery' to challenge the ways in which Spanish conquerors perceived America.

The sociologist Roland Roberston (1995) also understands that globalization brings both homogenization and differentiation. According to Roberston, the process of globalization has brought a number of global social imaginaries. The way in which each local is adapted and integrated this social imaginary, nevertheless, is highly different. Global ideas, business, services, and institutions adapt to the particular reality of each locality. For instance, although McDonald's is settled in 119 countries, its menu is different in each local context. In Catalonia (Spain), McDonald's breakfast menu includes bread with tomato, one of the traditional Catalan meals. In India, the breakfast menu includes Veg McMuffin. In Costa Rica, the breakfast menu includes McPinto based on the local speciality Gallo Pinto. In education, although schools have become universally institutionalized, the school is not exactly the same in all local contexts. For instance, some areas privilege single-gendered schools whereas in other these schools are forbidden. In some countries, private and public schools coexist whereas in others, only public schools are recognized.

Global citizenship: the local and the global

Discussions about local-global dynamics might be very helpful to consider how the concept of global citizenship is constructed. For the universalists, global citizenship in itself might encompass the 'best' of all local societies.

Education for global citizenship is here understood as socializing young generations in these shared principles and forms of knowledge. For the particularists, in contrast, global citizenship is a more problematic concept. Global citizenship is here understood as a 'local' form of citizenship defining itself as 'global'. Education for global citizenship can be perceived as an attempt to homogenize all locals into the same principles, values and forms of knowledge (see, for instance, Mannion, Biesta, Prisley & Ross, 2011). Educating a global citizenry, in this respect, can put 'at risk' the existence of the 'local' citizenry.

Within post-colonialism, some authors prefer to talk about 'global citizenships' rather than 'global citizenship' (Marshall, 2011). Here, there is an acknowledgment that different 'local' understandings of global citizenship are possible and sometimes they might be in conflict. Talking about 'global citizenships' rather than 'global citizenship' also responds to Mignolo and Roberston's analyses of globalization. Perhaps global organizations such as UNESCO promote a particular understanding of global citizenship (process of homogenizations) but perhaps there are also opportunities in local contexts to interpreted and adapted this particular understanding (process of differentiation).

Annotated bibliography

Delgado, L. E., Romero, R. J., & Mignolo, W. (2000). Local histories and global designs: an interview with Walter Mignolo. *Discourse*, 22(3), 7–33.

This article reproduces an interview with W. Mignolo, one of the main theorists of the local-global dynamics. The interview is a good introduction to Mignolo's work mainly to the notions of global designs and local histories. For the purpose of this book, we find particularly interesting the educational examples Mignolo describes. He focuses on discussing how through the dynamics global-local, education can contribute and to reinforce or challenge power relations and inequality processes.

Fielder, M. (2007). Postcolonial learning spaces for global citizenship. *Critical Literacy: Theories and Practices*, 1(2), 50–7.

Global citizenship education can be understood as a third space where ideas on global citizenship are negotiated. In this article, Matthias Fielder analyses post-colonialist frameworks. He particularly focuses on the work of Homi K. Bhabha and his concepts of hybridity and third space to discuss educational practices. Fielder focuses on the role of literacy in order to investigate students' identities and how these identities might be constantly negotiated and rewritten.

Juhász-Mininberg, E. (2012). Local-global. In R. M. Irwin & M. Szurmuk (Eds). *Dictionary of Latin American cultural studies* (pp. 211–16). Gainesville: University Press of Florida.

In this chapter, the author Emeshe Juhász-Mininberg synthesizes some of the key discussions on local-global dynamics. The chapter is a comprehensive introduction for those who are interested in these dynamics and in identifying relevant literature in this topic. We find particularly interesting the examples provided in which the local-global is examined in the case of Latin America considering the work of Latin American scholars.

Kwan-choi Tse, T. (2007). Whose citizenship education? Hong Kong from a spatial and cultural politics perspective, *Discourse: Studies in the Cultural Politics of Education*, 28(2), 159–77.

This article examines the global-national-local dynamics in the particular case of Hong Kong citizenship education. The author, Thomas Kwan-choi Tse, analyses these dynamics as encountered in the official discourses and NGO's alternatives on citizenship education. The article illustrates how whereas the local-global dynamic produces, in some occasions, hybrid discourses on citizenship, on others there is a clash of discourses between different institutions of power (the local authority, the state, and the IGOs).

Mignolo, W. (2009) Who speaks for the 'human' in human rights?. *Hispanic Issues on Line*, 5, 7–24.

In this article, Walter Mignolo examines the construction of Human Rights in relation to his notions of global designs and local histories. The article provides a detailed and comprehensive account of how Western understandings of 'human' and 'rights' became the contemporary global human rights. Drawing upon an historical and world-wide contextualization, Mignolo critiques how the political and economic power of Western countries has allowed them to universalize local views on humanity. The article ends by providing a set of examples that illustrate how alternative local interpretations can inform the basis for a de-colonizing education.

Activities

The first activity of this chapter is probably more relevant if you are enrolled in an educational or social science course. The second activity is particularly addressed to those of you who are enrolled in a teacher training course or similar.

1. In this chapter, we would like you to watch the film *Babel* by the Mexican director, Alejandro González Iñárritu. The film focuses on four interrelated different settings in four countries, in Japan, Mexico-United States and Morocco. We would like you to examine the film considering the following questions for discussion:

    a) Think about the United States and Mexican story:
    - In what ways might the United States and Mexico influence each other?
    - To what extent do you feel this influence is 'voluntary' or 'imposed'? Why?
    - Would you say the relation between the United States and Mexico is a relation between two 'locals' or a relation between a 'local' and a 'global'? Why?
    - In what ways might Amelia's (the nanny) understandings of 'local' be different from Debbie and Mike's (the children) understandings?

    b) Think about the Japanese story:
    - To what extent are the ways in which the Japanese group of youth behave in the film different from or similar to the ways in which groups of young people behave in your local community?
    - How may globalization (including processes of homogenization and differentiation) explain these similarities and differences?

    c) Think about the Moroccan story:
    - What are the Moroccan ('local') understandings of the shooting?
    - What are the US ('local') understandings of the shooting?
    - In your experience, what 'local' understandings would be more likely to become global?
    - How could you explain the 'shootings' considering Mignolo's theory?

    d) How could this film be used for the education of the global citizenry as (a) qualification (b) socialization and (c) subjectification? (see Chapter 2 'why global citizenship education?')

2. We would encourage you to compare a set of citizenship, history, geography or social studies school textbooks/teaching materials. You can examine your own or you can look at some online research studies such as (http://www.mariocarretero.com/ingles/img/carretero_jacott_lopez_manjon.pdf) or (http://www.blackhistory4schools.com/articles/empire%20in%20ww2.pdf). We would encourage you to consider:
    - to what extent do the textbooks illustrate a global design in the line of what is described by Mignolo?
    - to what extent the textbooks are 'glocalized' in the line of what is described by Roberston?
    - to what extent do these textbooks contribute to 'homogenization' or 'differentiation' forces?

7

National and Global Citizenship

Almost everyone lives in a country but what is a nation and what constitutes a nation-state? What sort of connections exists between a nation and global citizenship?

Perhaps a starting point is simply to identify the location of a nation – but, as we shall see, even that is not straightforward. The geographical boundaries that are established around countries seem at first glance to allow for a fairly straightforward approach to be adopted. It would not be hard to point to the United Kingdom on a map (even if I did have to ensure that it was appropriately detailed and that I did not accidentally exclude particular areas, especially perhaps all the islands off the mainland). But then what about areas that are distant from the UK, for example, the Scilly Isles, the Channel Isles, Gibraltar, the Falklands, the Bahamas? The same identification challenges could apply to many countries including for example the thousands of islands that make up Indonesia, the overseas territories of France and the many places that are officially classed in some atlases (but not others) as belonging to one country (e.g. there are different views in different parts of the world about the national status of Taiwan). In what ways do these places belong to the country, state or nation? It's possible that many people do not know and as such the concepts of nation and state are in practice somewhat fluid. Whereas it is possible to be very clear in a state about who has citizenship those who see themselves belonging to nationhood cannot always have recourse in the same way to legal documents.

The uncertainty referred to above has led to many pointing to nations, in Benedict Anderson's memorable phrase, as 'imagined communities'. We know that the overuse of this phrase (which was first coined as part of his discussion of identity in colonial America) has led him to refer to 'a pair of words from which the vampires of banality have by now sucked almost all the blood'

(Anderson, 2006, p. 207). But 'imagined communities' is a good phrase and it does have meaning. Smith (1991, p. 14) defines the nation as:

> A named human population sharing an historic territory, common myths and historical memories, a mass, public culture, a common economy and common legal rights and duties.

Hobsbawn and Ranger (1983) have shown clearly how identities are invented in the development of a nation. Colley (1992) in her modern classic about the history of Britain refers to the *forging* of the nation as it was hammered out on the anvil of war but she also alludes to the *forgery* that has taken place. There is nothing natural about a nation. Most countries are of very recent origin (e.g. 1870 Germany; 1949 China; the UK was established in 1922 – and this may soon be revised in light of the likely break up following the 2016 EU referendum). Nation states come and go.

The nation state is still powerful but the boundaries of time and space (illustrated by the above references to the history and geographies of state citizenship) that limit our discussions and practices are increasingly subject to critique. Discussions about nations involve territory and that overlaps with issues covered in other parts of this book, for example in our chapters on rights and duties and identities. This new geometry of citizenship may help us see changes in citizenship as:

> being experienced only in terms of coherency, unity, and homogeneity and occupying instead new times and spaces linked to ideas of encounter, fragmentation, heterogeneity and process. (Ní Mhurchú, 2014, p. 126)

If this imaginative perspective is the essence of a nation then we need to be very careful to consider the ways in which we reflect on the connections between the nation and global citizenship. We need to know what is considered as essential in a nation. It is important not to suggest that this imagination might be seen entirely negatively. Barton, for example, has suggested that:

> If citizens are to work together as members of a democratic society, they must share a sense of identity, and that identity must be parallel to the political system within which citizen action takes place – and in today's world, nations enjoy a privileged position in that regard. (Barton, 2005, p. 4)

John Stuart Mill suggested that:

> A portion of mankind may be said to constitute a nationality if they are united amongst themselves by common sympathies which do not exist

between them and any others – which make them cooperate with each other more willingly than with other people, desire to be under the same government, and desire that it should be government by themselves or a portion of themselves, exclusively.

in *Representative Government* (1861), under the heading of 'Nationality'

However, the ideas given by Barton may be expressed in rather more provocative terms. Brendan Nelson, Australian education minister asserted:

If you want to be in Australia, if you want to raise your children in Australia, we fully expect those children to be taught to accept Australian values and beliefs . . . We want them to understand our history and our culture, the extent to which we believe in mateship and giving another person a hand up and a fair go. And basically, if people don't want to be Australians and they don't want to live by Australian values and understand them, well basically, they can clear off. (http://www.theage.com.au/news/war-on-terror/accept-australian-values-or-get-out/2005/08/24/1124562921555.html)

Even when these sentiments about a nation are expressed with a desire to bring people together there can also be a sense that some members of a national group are expected to be loyal. The question then arises as to what are people expected to be loyal to? There is a sense in the quotation shown below of a shock at the disloyalty of fellow citizens as opposed to shock that anyone could do this to anyone (whatever their nationality). Gordon Brown, following a terrorist attack in London, said as a high-profile government minister,

we have to face uncomfortable facts that while the British response to July 7th was remarkable, they were British citizens, British born apparently integrated into our communities who were prepared to maim and kill fellow British citizens irrespective of their own religion . . . We have to be clearer now about how the diverse cultures which inevitably contain differences can find the essential common purpose also without which no society can flourish. (http://news.bbc.co.uk/1/hi/uk_politics/4611682.stm)

What might we expect from fellow citizens? Are some citizens in different places across the globe possibly part of the same nation? A distinction is made by Peter Seixas (2014) and others between celebratory and critical patriotism. The former may at times come closer to nationalistic fervour in which the particularities of one place are asserted unproblematically as being almost entirely positive. In extreme examples there may be points made about ethnic groups that may be perceived as racist. Critical patriotism on the other hand may allow for a positive regard and even love of one's country but also deliberately encourage a reflective and critical (but not negative) approach to what has been achieved. The boundaries between these two rather crudely sketched positions are often fluid. Laclau (2005) suggests that the nation and nationalism mean nothing in themselves but much depends on the discourses associated with them. Would it be fair, for example, to criticize politicians (in this case Michael Gove in 2011 when Secretary of State for Education in England and Wales and David Cameron UK Prime Minister), who referred to the history of his country as 'one of the most inspiring I know' and chose 'Our Island Story' as his favourite children's book as being overly committed to positions unacceptable to someone of liberal sensibilities or would it simply be perfectly reasonable attachment to one's own country?

What are the constituent elements of nationality? Rules about the formal political and legal status may be contested but they can be identified. What about other matters that may help someone feel that they belong to a nation? Is the way in which a person identifies themselves to do with things like language, religion, culture and values? And is there a connection of sorts between questions of status and matters principally about identity? A formal, legally established status leads to requirements to undertake duties; and, it is a guarantee of rights. But this guarantee is available only in name unless certain practical conditions are in place. Those practical matters often relate to the expressions that are about identity. Some countries, for example, insist that a certain level of language ability is achieved as part of a citizenship test. This has a strong functional element. The language most widely used in a country allows people to access basic services and benefits, as well as being vital in attempts to achieve employment (raising questions about possible distinctions and overlaps between civic and ethnic nations – a language allows one to achieve what could be referred to as civic citizenship whereas another or the same language may be relevant to a sense of ethnic or cultural citizenship). In a less immediately obvious way, but also very significant and recognized as such in the make-up of citizenship tests in various countries, are knowledge and understandings of the values that are deemed to apply in national contexts. At times this will include religion (many countries have an established church and not to be a member of it is seen as an indication of an outsider's identity and may be used as a justification for the withholding of rights available to those who have no such membership). A key point however is that difficulties may occur when adherence to these values is not fully aligned with individuals' and groups' sense of who they are. The dividing line between single and multiple identities are not straightforward. Issues of national diversity in relation to global citizenship are extremely important.

There are several ways in which issues about nation and state are revealed. In some countries there are officially recognized arrangements regarding national variation. In China, within the context of one – strongly emphasized – nation state, Hong Kong and Macau are Special Autonomous Regions. The policy of 'one country, two systems' is in place and currently being tested. Many countries (e.g. Spain) have officially recognized autonomous regions which are described as 'historical nationalities'. Within Europe (see Ross, 2015) and in many other parts of the world (including, e.g. immigration in Japan) post-colonial and other forms of migration as well as other factors has led to the existence of many what could be called below state national groups. Within the United States many are daily finding ways to give meaning to the phrase *e pluribus unum*. The multiple loyalties envisaged by Heater (1999) and the distinctions between country, state and nation are a recognition of the dynamism and messiness of national and global citizenships. And we need to consider whether national and global citizenship are harmoniously arranged in a framework of multiple citizenships or whether they are in conflict.

The fundamental values that a country commits to are based on at least two different possible formulations. Either they are an indication of what exclusively applies to one country. In other words, they sum up what a country – in and of itself – signifies. In this sense US values would be distinct, perhaps almost entirely, from any other countries' values. On the other hand, it could be argued that these are the values that the people currently living in a particular place feel that they wish to declare. In that sense those values may be the same as those adhered to by others. And there is a possibility that these values could be more dynamic, more prone to change than something which purports to be a fixed indication of the essence of a nation.

The tensions that emerge in educational contexts from these different perspectives are very closely connected to ideas about the boundaries between nation (and state) and global matters. The essential dividing point is about whether critical or celebratory perspectives are adopted. This can be very obviously seen in curriculum and textbook controversies. Evans (2015), for example, shows the tensions that can be caused by the intention on the part of a government – in this case in South Korea – to write about the past in a way agreed by a national government. The tension in Hong Kong over the production of a set of guidelines for national education led to street protests.

The examples given above are specific flashpoints that emerge around the tensions between nation-states and global citizenship. It is necessary to look a little more deeply at the attempts that are made in an effort to resolve things. Generally, there are three approaches. Firstly, as implied above there is the nation state approach. Values are asserted as being inherently and exclusively linked to a country and asserted against all opposition. Secondly, and this is an approach that has been argued by some (see Sears, Davies & Reid, 2011) as applying to very many places in the world, is a generic focus on values and skills. The nation-state is not recognized very strongly. This position may be developed so it seems almost as if place does not exist and the citizenship education that is provided may only be to develop very general skills such as analysis. Thirdly, there may be an approach which explores knowledge and issues about national groups within nation states. This can occur, especially in the areas of development education, various social justice programmes and especially in the field of anti-racist and multicultural education. There may be challenges here about the extent to which meaningful connections are made between ethnic groups and nations but it is an approach which is argued for very strongly by some (e.g. Ross, 2015).

What may we conclude from the above? It is not possible simply to declare the best way forward. But what is needed is a properly professional form of citizenship education that will allow for these difficult matters to be considered: the three flashpoints referred to above are the means by which issues about the connections between national and global citizenship may be identified, considered and enacted. Not to do so would be either to ignore contestation (and so in effect allow the dominant ideology to prevail as 'common sense') or to assert one form of connection between the nation and the globe which, again, would allow for an unacceptably hegemonic approach to global citizenship education

Annotated bibliography

Chong, E. K. M., Davies, I., Epstein, T., Peck, C., Peterson, A., Ross, A., Moreira dos Santos Schmidt, M. A., Sears, A. & Sonu, D. (2015). *Education, Globalization and the Nation State*. Basingstoke: Palgrave Macmillan.

This book provides an overview of the issues that face individual countries in the context of a globalizing world. There is an introduction and a first chapter which reviews key matters followed by case study chapters on Australia, Brazil, Canada, China, the UK and the United States. There is also a chapter which discusses the transnational European Union. Each of the case study country chapters have a common structure which looks at the historical background of that nation, the educational context and the specific issues and initiatives in which education takes place about and for the nation.

Grimley, N. (2016). Identity 2016: 'Global Citizenship' Rising, Poll Suggests. Retrieved from http://www.bbc.co.uk/news/world-36139904.

This is an internet-based source that gives a fascinating insight into the identities offered by people from many different countries. The range of differences between countries is striking. But there is also a clear indication that increasing numbers of people see themselves as global citizens. The interest in relation to the material covered in this chapter is the interaction between individual countries. Why might some be more likely than others to see themselves as global citizens? Is this a matter of history, of economic interest, of perceived cultural affinity or something else?

Reid, A., Gill, J., & Sears, A. (2010). *Globalization, the Nation-State and the Citizen: Dilemmas and Directions for Civics and Citizenship Education.* Abingdon: Routledge.

This book provides an overview of the development of civics and citizenship education policy across a range of nation states. Citizenship is discussed dynamically with consideration of different meanings of that term. The book is divided into three sections: an introduction is followed by twelve chapters that address issues in individual countries (Australia, Canada, Brazil, Singapore and so on) and the book ends with four reflective chapters which pull together some of the main threads of the debates. There is consideration of cosmopolitanism, post-statism, and post-globalization as well as other matters.

Activities

1. Read and discuss the article 'why there's no such thing as global citizenship' (see http://www.theatlantic.com/national/archive/2012/08/why-theres-no-such-thing-as-global-citizenship/261128/ This article was published in the Atlantic magazine. It explains what is meant by global citizenship. Or, rather it states in a strongly opinionated manner what some people feel is global citizenship and then it tells us that those people are wrong. It suggests that world consciousness; transnational governance; and globally active economic entrepreneurship are supposed to be global citizenship but that this is not enough or simply inappropriate. The article ends on this rather strident note: 'Want to be a citizen of the world? Help America be all it can be. There's nothing more cosmopolitan than a true American patriot.' Analyse this article. You might agree with and, if so, explain why. You might have questions about the content – write those questions down on a piece of paper. You might have comments about the style of the piece – why has the author decided to write in this way?

2. Take some citizenship tests. Review the material provided by a few countries. Take the practice tests and then discuss the appropriateness of the statements that have been included. Did you pass the test – why, why not? How could you improve the test? Would you include items on politics, society today, international affairs, cultural values and other things? Would you require a language test? Why? Most important of all – when taking a national citizenship test what do you need to know, understand and be able to do about global citizenship? What is the current situation

and what should happen? Some examples of these tests may be seen at https://my.uscis.gov/prep/test/civics; https://www.border.gov.au/Trav/Citi/pathways-processes/Citizenship-test; http://www.cic.gc.ca/english/citizenship/cit-test.asp;

3. List five advantages and five disadvantages of free movement of people across national borders. In a few limited contexts (parts of the European Union is an example) this freedom of movement is allowed. Many value it strongly as an indication of harmony and tolerance and democracy. But some people oppose it vigorously. Some argue that it is damaging economically and culturally. And some suggest that if it occurs only in limited transnational contexts (such as within Europe) there is actually a buttress against global citizenship rather than a route to it. What do you think?

4. Read the original or comments about Ernest Gellner's classic book Nations and Nationalism (Gellner, E. [1983. 2nd edition 2009]. *Nations and Nationalism*. Ithaca, New York: Cornell University Press.). Gellner produced several key publications but it is probably in this book that his ideas are stated most clearly and in full. His work is subject to much critique but he has been influential in his suggestions that nationalism is a key feature of a modern society. That society is dependent on a formal education system, a coherent system of government, political control, similarity of language and culture and a sense of identification. It would be interesting to discuss these ideas with others perhaps focusing on the limits to nationalism. Using some of the comments given above in this chapter consider where positive patriotism ends and unpleasant political ideology begins.

8

Planetary and Global Citizenship

Planetary citizenship is an important way to understand global citizenship. In addition to the impact of economic and technical globalization on how people imagine themselves engaged on multiple levels from the local to the global, many ideas are shifting in relation to 'the planet'. For example, most countries in the world are involved in setting climate change goals that would see great changes to the amount of carbon released into the atmosphere. Other people are involved in removing plastic from the ocean as it has become clear that at least eight million tonnes of plastic are dumped into the ocean each year (https://www.weforum.org/agenda/2016/01/how-much-plastic-is-there-in-the-ocean/.).We see people connecting around the world to repair damage to the earth caused by excessive development that involved clear cutting of forests, damming rivers, and depleting soil. If the air, the water, and the land are at risk, so too are humans! These global environmental issues with their social and economic connections have helped people think about how the planet's wellbeing is linked to human wellbeing. As the evidence of the dire condition of many of the planet's basic systems becomes visible, efforts are being made to change human thinking and actions to ameliorate the damage and suffering for humans and non-humans as well as their shared planet. Global citizenship can be helpful in rethinking the scales, actors, and acts of citizenship needed to create such changes (see Shultz, Pashby & Godwaldt, 2016).

A key area that stands to change how we understand citizenship is *Earth Jurisprudence*. Modern liberals valorize human rights as being key to organizing a civil society, identifying individual rights as being inherent to all humans, and demanding that states as well as private actors establish laws, governance structures, and relations based on rights being universal, indivisible, and inalienable (see http://www.ohchr.org). In this, the planet, as our refuge, exists without recognition, an object for human benefit if not consumption. However, as scientists and environmental activists tell us, we have entered into a time where the integrity of human life and the planet itself are in question because of the vast changes humans have made to the land, air, and water. This era is referred to as the anthropocene (see Crutzen and Schwagerl, 2011; Schwägerl, 2014; Stephan, Crutzen & McNeill, 2007). Anthropocene is meant to describe a geological epoch defined by the scale of human impact. As Crutzen and Schwagerl (2011) state; 'For millennia, humans have behaved as rebels against a superpower we call 'Nature' (para 2) and the result has been a tremendous impact on all relations within the natural world. Western science says we have acquired the status of a geological force and now act 'outside of Nature'. It is important to investigate this claim because one of the projects of Western modernity has been to dominate nature based on the concept of the superiority of humans (Battiste, 2000; Mignolo, 2000; Davis, 2009). What does it mean to consider that humans might be able to live 'outside of nature'? Is this Western modernity's universal claim to power and the completion of the project of modernity where humans and the natural world are seen as strategically indifferent? Clearly, we live in a precarious time where planetary systems are in danger of collapse and there seems an uncritical arrogance in the notion that humans could exist outside of this collapse. Scientists at the 'Stockholm Resilience Centre' (see http://www.stockholmresilience.org) have identified 'nine planetary boundaries' (ibid) that, if breached, will result in unprecedented collapse of current systems that support life (ibid). Their research has tracked changes since 1950, and the findings indicate we are near crisis in at least four: biosphere diversity/ genetic diversity, biochemical flows, land-system change, and climate change. Other scholars describe our time as one of 'The Sixth Great Extinction' (see Wagler, 2012). The Secretariat of the Convention on Biological Diversity (2010) estimates that humanity could extinguish one out of every three species on Earth within the next one to two hundred years.

Donna Haraway (2016) argues, we must make the link between these collapses and global capitalism, understanding how our global system of capitalism has worked to amplify the depletion of resources by refusing any limits, and in fact, has made the extraction and destruction of the land, water and air so rapid that we are extremely vulnerable to planetary collapse. Jason Moore (2013) and Donna Haraway (2016) suggest an epochal name for our time should be *The Capitalocene* rather than Anthropocene because, while humans have lived on the planet for millennia, it is only our system of modern capitalism that has brought about the destructive human impact on the planet. Haraway (2016) and Moore (2013) contribute an analysis of relations of class, state, and capital to understandings of the massive geophysical changes we see (and experience) on the planet. We need to find ways to survive on our damaged planet that shift us away from the deadly relations that threaten the collapse of the planetary life sustaining systems. Haraway describes how we might live and relate differently as a way to not only end the destruction, but to live more fully human lives based on good relations with humans and non-humans. 'A common livable world must be composed, bit by bit, or not at all' (p. 40). Here she proposes that we are moving into a time, the Chthulucene, where we are forced to take 'response-ability (p. 2) for the damaged earth. The key here is that this suggests an urgent need to halt the destruction as we learn to live on our damaged planet. Haraway states that in doing so, we will 'require each other [human and non-human] in unexpected collaborations and combinations' . . . we will make 'oddkin' (ibid) through sympoeisis or 'making with', ways of being in the world that have been neglected or diminished through systems of colonialism, capitalism, patriarchy, which are, as Walter Mignolo describes, the darkness of modernity (2011), the shadow side of the modern agenda of progress. This kind of decolonial analysis is emerging as more and more people question the universalism of Western thought and look to relational worldviews that make sense of the world by understanding humans as part of, but not dominant, in a system of human and non-human relations.

Peter Burdon (2012) and Ben Mylius (2013) both suggest that we are making a very important epistemic change that is beginning to be reflected in a new legal (and philosophical) area of 'Earth Jurisprudence'. (See the United Nations Concept Note and Final Report for the UN General Assembly's April 2015 Dialogue on Harmony with Nature (incorporating discussion of the importance of nature's rights http://www.un.org/en/ga/search/view_doc.asp?symbol=A/RES/70/208).

Referencing Foucault's (2002) discussion of the 'erasure of humans', Mylius shifts our understanding from apocalyptic extinction to a deeper understanding of our capacity (and now urgent need) to think and live without humans being 'the centre of all things' (Mylius, 2013, p. 104). Earth jurisprudence – the rights of the planet and nature – leads us to eco-centrism where there is 'no apex at which humans, or any entity, can be placed' (p. 106). Burdon (2012) describes the importance of recognizing this shift in our key institutions including law, education, and economics. Bruno Latour (2004) provides a philosophical platform for the shift in scientific orientation for us to in turn, shift our belief that humans and nature are separate (and that Man is inherently superior).

We are clearly at an important point in history, and continuing to organize life on the planet in the same way as we have since European colonization, is not going to solve the problems we face. Here, the idea of global citizenship can be helpful.

Global citizenship in the anthropocene/capitalocene/chthulucene

Both the United National Declaration on the Rights of Indigenous People (http://www.un.org/esa/socdev/unpfii/documents/DRIPS_en.pdf) and the 2010 Proposed Universal Declaration of the Rights of Mother Earth (https://pwccc.wordpress.com/2010/04/24/proposal-universal-declaration-of-the-rights-of-mother-earth/) suggest ways that we might begin institutionalizing changes for planetary citizenship. These have informed the discussion of Harmony with Nature (United Nations, 2016) that

> Decide[d] to initiate, in 2016, a virtual dialogue on Harmony with Nature among, inter alia, experts on Earth jurisprudence worldwide, including those who have been active in the interactive dialogues of the General Assembly, in order to inspire citizens and societies to reconsider how they interact with the natural world in order to implement the Sustainable Development Goals in harmony with nature, noting that some countries recognize the rights of nature in the context of the promotion of sustainable development, and requests that the experts submit a summary to the General Assembly at its seventy-first session and that the virtual dialogue be hosted on the website on Harmony with Nature. (p. 3/4)

According to the United Nations, without significantly shifting how we understand ourselves in relation to nature, we will not only be unable to implement the vision of sustained life on the planet that is expressed in the Sustainable Development Goals 2030 (https://sustainabledevelopment.un.org/post2015/transformingourworld), but life on the planet will itself be in jeopardy. Richard Kahn (2010) draws on Herbert Marcuse to develop his approach to ecopedagogies that could provide a transformational platform for a time of global crisis. Marcuse theorized the link between advanced capitalism and environmental breakdown (1992) and he contributed to understanding a 'post-anthropocentric form of cultural work in which nature and the nonhuman are profoundly humanized, meaning that they are revealed as subjects in their own right' (Kahn, 2010, p. 24). This develops the idea of planetary citizenship as belonging to all living and non-living entities on the planet. Current efforts to link education to sustainability (see Chapter 16) would be strengthened if the foundational ideas included a multispecies ecojustice based on the rights of humans, non-humans, and the planet itself.

Global citizenship has the possibility to locate our engagement in a planetary focus, shifting patterns of citizenship that are tied to nationalism or a localism that seeks to exist without relations to either the natural world, or with humans who do not share the same geographical, cultural, class or racialized histories. The epistemological (ways of knowing about the world) and ontological (ways of 'being' in the world) shift that is required for such a transforming, and according to many, a decolonizing global citizenship, are very demanding but necessary given the urgency of the planetary conditions. There are hints that change is coming. As Arandati Roy stated at the World Social Forum in Brazil in 2003, 'Another world is not only possible, she is on her way. On a quiet day, I can hear her breathing'.

Annotated bibliography

Haraway, D. (2016). *Staying with the Trouble: Making Kin in the Chthulucene.* Durham: Duke University Press.

Donna Haraway is a 'multispecies feminist theorist' and presents a compelling argument for the necessity of deep change in how we relate to other people and other species on our planet. This relational shift is challenges the individualism of liberalism that has dominated Western thinking for many centuries. Instead, with human and non-human life intertwined in relations, we find ourselves living as 'kin' on our suffering planet.

Kahn, R. (2010). *Critical Pedagogy, Ecoliteracy, & Planetary Crisis: The Ecopedagogy Movement.* New York: Peter Lang.

In the area of education, ecopedagogy is located as a response to dire environmental problems and the severe human conflict that often rises in places of environmental degradation. Drawing on the work of Paulo Freire and other critical theorists, critical educationists use ecopedagogy for transformational education that can shift social and political relations of power. Kahn argues that the global call for sustainable development isn't up to the task of transforming human's domination of nature to the point of extinction but instead we need education with a focus on place based relationships.

Mignolo, W. (2011). *The Darker Side of Western Modernity: Global Futures, Decolonial Options.* Durham/London: Duke University Press.

For the past two decades, Walter Mignolo's work has provided important critique of Western modernity and highlighted the violence and destruction that follows projects that see some humans as superior to others, and all humans as superior to other life on the planet. He argues for creating space for non-Western knowledge that has sustained human life for millennia. This project of decolonization is an urgent one if we are to address the inequality, environmental destruction, and social upheaval we are experiencing on a global scale at this point in history.

Misiaszek, G. (2016). Ecopedagogy as an element of citizenship education: the dialectic of global/local spheres of citizenship. *International Review of Education*, 62(1), 587–607.

In this article, Misiaszek studies ecopedagogues in Argentina, Brazil and the Appalachian region of the United States. He studied how these pedagogies linked to global citizenship. His findings indicate that when local knowledges and national citizenships are decentred in citizenship studies, the full impact of globalization is not addressed. However, through an ecopedagogical approach within the differing spheres of citizenship: local, national, global and planetary, education can play a part in transforming the thinking and actions toward a more critical consciousness of planetary responsibility.

Mylius, B. (2013). Towards the unthinkable: earth jurisprudence and an ecocentric episteme. *Australian Journal of Legal Philosophy*, 38, 102–38.

In this article, Mylius argues that a change in thinking (episteme) is necessary if we are to avert major planetary crises due to the impact of humans acting without understanding their own interconnection with life on the planet. Mylius points out the shift from anthropocentric to an ecocentric episteme needs to be institutionalized through laws and policies.

Warren, K. (Ed.) (1997). *Ecofeminism: Women, Culture, Nature*. Bloomington: Indiana University Press.

This set of essays takes on an eco-reading of the world from the perspective that is not only feminist but also anti-racist, decolonial, and interdisciplinary. This view of ecofeminist scholarship presents the rich array of ideas that compel humans in many parts of the planet, to read the world differently and to live their lives and build cultural practices that recognize humans as part of nature. The authors explore how eco-feminism is taken up as a political position and as a growing social movement.

Activities

1. Watch these two videos from the organization Bioneers:
   https://www.youtube.com/watch?v=couHXnRdIc4 (Kenny Ausubel: Plants Are Sentient Beings)
   https://www.youtube.com/watch?v=5OiOpSiWq9Q (Xiuhtezcatl Martinez: What Are We Fighting For?)
2. Discuss the shifting understanding of human in the world that these speakers are discussing. What is an epistemological shift that is part of planetary citizenship? What is an ontological shift that is part of planetary citizenship? What are the citizenship rights and responsibilities indicated by these changes?
3. Create an ecocentric policy for your community or university based on this epistemological stance (see Mylius, 2013).

PART TWO

Key Educational Frameworks

There are eight chapters in this section reflecting some of the perspectives that are brought to global citizenship education. Social studies education is at times represented as subject to a range of framing devices. Occasionally this has been described as the adjectival educations – in other words a describing word sums up the particular approach that is being promoted. We have included here a range of frameworks that relate to global citizenship education: citizenship; social justice; development; character; global; peace; diversity and sustainable development. We accept that there may be other framing devices that we have not included; we highlight the contested nature of the frameworks that we do include; we discuss the varying strength of their relationship with global citizenship education; and, we also indicate within chapters vitally important ideas and perspectives that are not given a separate chapter title. By the end of this section you will have considered a wide range of ideas and issues in which global citizenship education may be characterized and begun to think about the ways in which implementation is attempted.

9

Citizenship Education

In this chapter it is necessary both to explain what citizenship education is and to outline the ways in which it connects with – and, at times, does not connect with – global citizenship. What sort of framework could and should be developed in order to ensure that citizenship is global?

Citizenship is, of course, of ancient historical origin. The societies of Greece and Rome and then, in the modern era, the revolutions of England, France, Latin America and the United States created and allowed for the expression of ideas and systems of governance that were aligned around rights and duties. But it is not just in relation to rights and duties and not just in the 'West' that citizenship has been significant. The deep rootedness of Confucianism influences many aspects of education in East Asia. Across the world ideas about (and practices of) religious groups have had a significant impact on citizenship. The role of the Catholic Church for example in Spain and South and Central America is (or has been) immediately noticeable. Many countries that until recently would not have engaged with citizenship are now doing so (e.g. recent developments in Saudi Arabia are very interesting).

Given the wide geographical spread for the implementation of citizenship education and the very varied ways in which it has been characterised we need to try to be a little more specific about this educational framework. The significant connecting point between citizenship and global citizenship is to do with bridging the formal political and legal status of a national citizen with the global citizen's determination and ability to engage, as well as the attitudinal perspective that could be brought to that engagement. This is not to suggest that these two areas – citizenship and global citizenship – cannot be brought together, but if we are to come to terms with the nature of this educational framework there is a need for some precise discussion.

Citizenship, of course, may be seen in terms of identity (and our chapter in this book about identity (Chapter 5) explored this in detail). If we focus on issues about political and legal status, it is possible to argue that the most obvious alignment is with national citizenship. Other connections may be made between status and citizenship. As well as national citizenship, there may be dual citizenship (held of two states simultaneously) and layered citizenship (in federal constitutions and a few multinational communities) (Heater, 1997). If legal and political status can go beyond national boundaries would it then be possible, logically, to imagine a form of legal and political status that took the form of a world government? This may theoretically be possible but if we take this approach there would be significant implications to consider. Some argue strongly against the idea that world citizenship could be anything but an undemocratic nightmare (e.g. Miller, 2010). On the other hand, there are various bodies and individuals who argue for the development of such formalized structures that would allow for the status that currently resides in a nation state to be positioned globally. The Registry of World Citizens is long established and has many supporters but politically lacks influence (see http://www.recim.org/cdm/registry.htm). The World Government of World Citizens (http://www.worldservice.org/gov.html) led by Gary Davis has similar aspirations and is perhaps similarly regarded. Held (1995, pp. 279–80) is one of the relatively few academics who have developed a reasonably full account of what cosmopolitan governance could look like. In the long term Held envisages changes to both policy/governance and also to economy/civil society. In the former he argues in the long terms for such things as the entrenchment of cosmopolitan democratic law into a new Charter of Democratic Law, a global parliament, an interconnected global legal system (with the establishment of an international criminal court). For the latter he sees the possibility of pluralization of ownership and possession, investment priorities set through public deliberation and guaranteed basic income for all.

The above overlapping fault lines between formal legal and political status and perspectives on citizenship are powerful indicators of – and influencing factors upon – the nature of citizenship education. In order to make that connection between citizenship and education more explicit it is necessary to discuss a particular framework. Many different outlines have been used in different parts of the world and examples of those will be given below. But to choose just one national context for the moment we suggest that citizenship education is thought of as being related to three related elements: social and moral responsibility; community involvement and political literacy. These are the three things highlighted in the Crick Report (DfE/QCA, 1998). Each was explained:

> Firstly, children learning from the very beginning self-confidence and socially and morally responsible behaviour both in and beyond the classroom, both towards those in authority and towards each other . . .

Secondly, learning about and becoming helpfully involved in the life and concerns of their communities, including learning through community involvement and service to the community . . .

Thirdly, pupils learning about and how to make themselves effective in public life through knowledge, skills and values – what can be called 'political literacy', seeking for a term that is wider than political knowledge alone. (DfE/QCA, 1998, pp. 9–12).

The order in which these three elements occur is interesting. Crick was principally motivated by political considerations. He was an academic political scientist and philosopher and was actively engaged in political matters throughout his life (especially in relation to the UK Labour Party). He had been particularly prominent in developing political education and political literacy in the 1970s and in the 1990s under 'new' Labour led by Tony Blair he was to have his second chance. The communitarian agenda of Blair and the education minister (and former student of Crick), David Blunkett, and the widespread acceptance of social and moral imperatives meant that political literacy would be highlighted last. But Crick was genuinely concerned to focus on all three elements being involved in community-based initiatives in his adopted home of Scotland as well as elsewhere. Most of his ideas (beyond his classic work on politics – Crick, 1962) may be seen in a publication of the late 1970s (Crick & Porter, 1978) and in a collection of essays published in 2000 (Crick 2000). He wanted to ensure that a move was made from civics to political literacy, emphasizing a conceptual bedrock for the work and, perhaps in part in order to gain political support, titling it 'citizenship education'. In other words, he emphasized issues and ideas that affect people and are led by citizens, as opposed to learning about political structures related to constitutions and institutions. For some this has become confusing as 'civics' (about which Crick was dismissive in what he perceived as a boring and misleading focus on the so-called rules of the political system) and is used as a title in some parts of the world when actually a broader, more dynamic Crick-like citizenship education is being developed. It is also potentially confusing as citizenship began in the UK as something about which many were wary insofar as it was seen to emphasize a form of neo-liberal enterprise instead of a more diverse, inclusive and egalitarian approach (Kiwan, 2008).

Of the many issues about citizenship education, there are perhaps four key discussions. First, there is a debate about the relative weight to be placed on rights or duties (the former seen in terms of the liberal tradition; the latter relates more immediately to the civic republican tradition). Am I a citizen because I have rights (including the right to be left alone)? Or, am I a citizen because I do my duty for others – for my immediate neighbours, for the nation, for the globe? Second, the context or location of these rights and duties are fiercely debated. The key spectrum regarding debates about rights and duties is essentially concerned with the connection with institutionally framed considerations. The closer the connection with formal political and legal status, the closer, according to some, we come to moving beyond rhetoric and guaranteeing things. But, of course, the emphasis on status means that the everyday realities may be ignored. Some feminist perspectives, for example, may allow us more clearly to see the importance of power in everyday contexts as well as highlighting the need to be engaged with what is enacted by our elected representatives. Third, we need to ask what our citizenship is for. One of the most commonly quoted frameworks for this has been developed by Westheimer and Kahne (2004) with their emphasis on personally responsible and participatory and justice oriented perspectives. Finally, and getting very close to the practical circumstances of educational work are matters regarding implementation. Given the above, some prefer a very widespread and general approach in which ethos is vital. Others stress the importance of curricular activities often organized in discrete lessons that are explicitly titled 'citizenship'. There are opportunities (which are perhaps increasing) in some countries often in the HE sector for young people to engage in what is sometimes titled as 'global citizenship education' which are actually forms of volunteering (or, should we say 'voluntourism'?). The ways in which citizenship is characterized – as a central purpose of education and/or as a school (or college or university) subject and/or as something which is principally to with ethos and/or as an opportunity for some to engage often in places away from home – affects the ways in which it is implemented.

The above preferences and uncertainties about the characterization of citizenship are played out with students in schools and other educational contexts. We can see what is intended in specific contexts through official curricular statements. Canada does not have a national educational policy but some individual provinces have developed relevant curricula. In Ontario (see http://www.edu.gov.on.ca/eng/curriculum/secondary/canworld910curr2013.pdf) the civics syllabus highlights political inquiry and skill development; civic awareness; and civic engagement and action. In Australia there is an ongoing struggle about the development of the country's first national curriculum. 'Civics and citizenship' has been included focusing on knowledge and understanding and inquiry and skills. The content has been reviewed in light of political changes and it will be worth monitoring towards the final version to be implemented in schools (see http://www.australiancurriculum.edu.au/humanities-and-social-sciences/civics-and-citizenship/rationale). There have been several arguments in Australia over the Western focus and the reliance on a civics perspective (see the review by Anne Twomey, https://docs.education.gov.au/system/files/doc/other/review_of_the_national_curriculum_supplementary_material_0.pdf). In England a great deal of effort went into a framework which involved key concepts (democracy and justice; rights and responsibilities; and identities and diversity) key processes (critical thinking; advocacy and representation; informed and responsible action) and, lastly, a range of content to support the concepts and processes. Despite a wealth of evidence from the NFER and the independent government office for school inspections (Ofsted) as well as significant pieces of work by individual researchers (Whiteley, 2014) this has now been replaced by a curriculum that focuses on civics (knowledge of government and the legal system); volunteering; and managing personal finance.

Annotated bibliography

There is a wealth of material produced by the IEA cived programme and the ICCS. This major international research may be accessed at http://iccs.iea.nl/

Biesta, G. & Lawy, D. (2006). From teaching citizenship to learning democracy: overcoming individualism in research, policy and practice. *Cambridge Journal of Education*, 36(1), 63–79.

In this article there is a critique of what the authors see as an overly individualistic approach in which citizenship education is taught. There is an argument for research, policy and practice to engage more thoroughly with how young people actually learn.

The Crick Report, http://dera.ioe.ac.uk/4385/1/crickreport1998.pdf

The full title of the Crick Report is Education for Citizenship and the teaching of Democracy in Schools. It is the final report of the Advisory Group on Citizenship. It was commissioned by the UK government in 1997 and report in 1998. Its key ideas – citizenship education is essentially about social and moral responsibility, community involvement and political literacy – were highly influential in the development of citizenship education in many countries. Most obviously it informed the development of citizenship education as a National Curriculum subject in England but its influence was felt in Japan (see Ikeno, 2011); there were close links through networks such as citizED (www.citized. info) with colleagues who were leading the ICCS study (see http://www.iea.nl/iccs_2009.html) and there were clear connections to continental Europe (see Council of Europe http://www.coe.int/t/dg4/education/) and in various parts of South America.

Dewey, J. (1916). *Democracy and Education*. New York: Macmillan.

The philosophy stated in this book connects the growth of democracy with the development of the experimental method in the sciences, evolutionary ideas in the biological sciences, and industrial re-organization, and is concerned to point out the changes in subject matter and method of education indicated by these developments. There are twenty-six chapters covering education as a necessity of life, aims in education, and finally theories of morals. Throughout ideas about education as experience are important.

Marshall, T. H. (2014). *Citizen and Social Class* (London: Pluto Press).

Until the 1990s many people interested in political education and citizenship education did not focus strongly on the academic work of the sociologist T. H. Marshall. This was to change when governments focused more on citizenship. Marshall suggested that a rights perspective was important with civil, political and social (or welfare) rights developing, respectively in the 18th, 19th and 20th centuries. Marshall has been extremely influential but has also been criticized for being too optimistic, too British focused and too narrow in its exclusion of feminism, environmentalism and other things. It is important to read Marshall in the context of these critiques. A very interesting position has been developed by Dean (2014) who suggests that social citizenship can be positioned as global citizenship. For this to happen Marshall's thinking would need to be developed in terms of sociality (we rely on each other) and negotiation (there is a need to find a way in which these needs may be acknowledged or recognized).

Activities

Three activities are shown below in an attempt to illuminate Crick's recognition of three elements of citizenship education. (Of course, there is, as Crick intended, no hard and fast dividing line between these three elements but, broadly, the first activity shown below links most easily to community involvement, the second to social and moral responsibility and the third to political literacy).

1. In the following activity there is the opportunity to explore issues about the limits to engagement in charitable work. The relationship between citizenship and charity is contested. For some volunteering and charitable work is at the heart of good citizenship; for others it indicates only that rights of majorities are being neglected and that cheque book citizenship and 'clicktivism' needs to be balanced with or replaced by political engagement. The activity below is meant to allow for some consideration of these challenging fundamental issues as well as the perhaps more superficial considerations associated with choosing a charity to support.

   Answer the following questions to show the decision you would make and justify each response:

Choose a charity to support

- A very large charity with international reach supporting poor people's basic needs
- Small locally based religious organization that is working to support people's spiritual needs
- National political party that is campaigning to introduce laws that aim to make life fairer for people in that country

Explain your choice. . . .

Choose someone to ask for financial support

- Individual millionaire
- Business
- Family member

Explain your choice. . .

Choose an activity that you would ask for sponsorship

- Walk for 10 miles across rough terrain
- Make warm clothes to be sent to poor people experiencing cold climate
- Create and gather signatures for a petition to raise the profile of the connection between modern industry and global warming

Explain your choice. . . .

Choose a way of developing publicity

- Invite a speaker into a school
- Contact the local radio station
- Door to door calling to persuade people of the importance of your charity

Explain your choice. . . .

2. In the following activity questions are raised about a variety of matters including social and moral responsibility:

Review a media report about different communities living in tension. There are very many that could be chosen. An interesting example may be seen at http://www.independent.co.uk/news/world/europe/hungary-in-crisis-tensions-with-its-gypsy-population-threaten-to-rip-the-eastern-european-country-2307903.html. The article to be seen at the link we have provided is good for outlining the many different issues when communities live alongside each other. Diversity is of course always present in society and although there are challenges it usually brings *huge* benefits (socially, economically, culturally). But what is the 'right' thing to do when there is a clash of ideas and living practices? Is it worthwhile to identify what all people, irrespective of cultural values, should have access to and what they should be free from? Is it that simple?

3. In the following activity there is an opportunity to explore issues in relation to political literacy:

Votes at sixteen?

Should people be allowed to vote at sixteen? Think about some case studies from a range of countries (e.g. Austria – http://www.independent.co.uk/news/world/europe/austria-opens-the-polls-to-16-year-olds-943706.html). Think also about a global overview of ages at which people may vote (see https://www.theguardian.com/politics/datablog/2015/jun/18/votes-for-16-and-17-year-olds-where-else-outside-scotland). Here are some of the arguments for and against enfranchising 16-year-olds (table 9.1). Try to come to a decision about what you think and then discuss it with a friend or colleague.

TABLE 9.1 Arguments for and against enfranchising 16-year-olds

	16-year-olds should vote	16-year-olds should NOT vote
The developmental (age-related) argument	People are intelligent enough and mature enough at 16	Voting is not granted on the basis of intelligence or maturity. It is simply a best guess of when people are ready to engage in society
Enhancing engagement by increasing turnout	It will increase turnout (e.g. in the Scottish referendum)	Any gains in turnout are short lived (e.g. Austria, Brazil, Isle of Man). An argument to increase turnout may sometimes be used by politicians who want support for a very particular proposal
Tax	Young people pay tax indirectly when buying goods in shops and they can leave school and work	Young people buy goods in shops from a very young age. Very few 16-year-olds actually pay income tax

	16-year-olds should vote	16-year-olds should NOT vote
Demographics	The population is ageing and so we need to get young people into the habit of voting	Most things in society are becoming more restrictive – regulations mean that for example buying fireworks and cigarettes are more limited than previously. People at 16 do not tend to join the army, get married etc
Protection and autonomy	Young people need to be independent	Young people need to be officially recognized as being vulnerable. If not, they will soon be expected to fend for themselves as neo-liberal governments see them as another opportunity to exploit
Parity with other groups	It is important to ensure discrimination does not occur. Occasionally when this argument is made connections are made with the campaigns to enfranchise women	All young people are allowed to vote at the same age. There is no discrimination. It is inappropriate to compare an age restriction with a gender restriction

10

Social Justice

In 1980, Indira Gandhi as the first female prime minister of India, delivered a speech in which she identified social justice as one of the purposes of her government and education as the key tool towards achieving this purpose. Twenty years later, in a speech in 2000, Fidel Castro, president of the Socialist Republic of Cuba, highlighted that for 40 years his government had been committed to fight for social justice through educational policies. In 2009, the US secretary of education, Arne Duncan, explained 'I believe that education is the civil rights issue of our generation. [. . .] Great teaching is about so much more than education; it is a daily fight for social justice'. In a different context, we, in the introduction of this book, highlighted our commitment to global social justice. Examples of the relevance of social justice education, such as the ones above, can be found all around the world. Probably few people would openly disagree with the notion of social justice. But in our understanding, what each of us, including Gandhi, Castro and Duncan mean when we mention 'social justice' is likely to be very different. When claims are made establishing the links between 'global citizenship education' and 'social justice', the question is not only what 'global citizenship education' is but also what is 'social justice'?

In this chapter, we will outline different views about social justice education and how they relate to different approaches to global citizenship education.

Can we (and shall we) define social justice?

The first question to ask relates to the possibility and desirability of 'global' social justice: can we (and shall we) define a notion of social justice that can be globally used? As William Connolly wrote, 'without a set of standards of identity and responsibility there is no possibility of ethical discrimination, but the application of any such set of historical constructions also does violence to those to whom it is applied' (1991, p. 12). Applied to education, the question is: do we need and want a normative referent – an image of a utopian world – that guides our educational practices and the way we organize our education systems and institutions?

For some, it is essential to define what we could describe as a human notion of 'social justice'. If we do not define it how are we going to discriminate what is 'justice' from what is 'injustice'? For others, in contrast, a global ethics is impossible or unethical in itself. In his book, 'Whose justice, whose rationality?' (1988), the philosopher Alastair MacIntyre discusses how the notion of 'justice' is historically and geographically constructed and how a definition of justice always implies a set of assumptions that cannot be universalized to all human beings. In some ways, the simple act of defining social justice can be considered an imposition upon others who might have different understandings of what social justice means. In MacIntyre's understanding, attempting to construct a global notion of social justice is undesirable and unfair in itself. The dilemma is such that some have described the relation between 'social justice' and 'education' as an impossibility (Biesta, 2016): how are we going to have a social-justice orientated education if we cannot decide what 'social justice' means? And, if we do decide, are we failing in our commitment to social justice by imposing our views on 'social justice' onto others?

Dimensions on social justice and their links with global citizenship education

Even if we agree that social justice can be defined, the definition of this term is equally controversial. Within Western tradition, Michael Sandel identifies three different understandings of justice. For the utilitarians (e.g. Bentham, Mill), justice is understood as the greatest good for the greatest number of citizens. In this approach, laws should be made to privilege the greatest number of citizens. Liberals (e.g. Kant, Rawls) give primacy to the individuals. Certain individuals' rights -such as freedom of speech- are considered to be beyond the group's desires. Communitarians (such as MacIntyre or the same Sandel), instead, argue that individuals cannot be disconnected from the communities they belong to. Justice, therefore, needs to be defined in the context of each particular community. These three approaches, however, only represent Western understandings of justice. Non Western traditions discuss justice in different terms. In China, for instance, Li Zehou 李澤厚 draws upon Confucianism philosophy to criticize the notion of justice. Rather, he defends a sense of morality which is based on social harmony.

Unfortunately, it is impossible to explain here all the different approaches to justice that one could find worldwide. Rather, we have committed ourselves to discuss the three dimensions of justice that the philosopher Nancy Fraser (2009) identifies. These are: distribution, recognition and participation. We discuss each of these dimensions and their implications for global citizenship and education.

Distributive justice

Distributive justice refers to the principle by which resources and goods are distributed within society. According to John Rawls, considered to be one of the main theorists of distributive justice, a justice-orientated society would be a society in which all individuals have equal rights and liberties; and social and economic resources are equally distributed. In the educational field, we can think, for example, about all children having the right of being educated in school settings and the resources (e.g. the school) to ensure that this right is guaranteed. If, Rawls talks about 'equal distribution', there is a question, however, about how these resources can be equally distributed. In table 10.1, we illustrate different questions that emerge from the notion of 'equal distribution'.

In terms of global citizenship, social justice as distributive justice is particularly relevant if we consider the unequal distribution of resources in the contemporary world. Economic globalization is the force responsible for widening economic inequality, between the wealthier North and the poorer South and between the wealthier and the poorer in any state. If we understand global citizenship education in its qualification function, there is a question of whether teaching global competences to all students around the world is a matter of social justice. For some, the expansion of formal schooling worldwide will provide equal opportunities to all children. If students all around the world are taught global competences, they all will have equal opportunities to succeed in a globalized world.

For others, global citizenship education can raise inequality. Beyond the myth of equal opportunities, they argue, lies a human capital perspective in which human beings are seen as economic resources. In this respect, educating students about and for 'global competences' will only increase the inequality between the economic and political elites who have the power to decide what are the 'global competences' required and those who have to learn 'global competences' to attempt to secure a job. Only global citizenship education in its subjectification approach, they understand, can contribute to social justice by shedding some light on the unequal distribution of resources and other oppressive global structures.

TABLE 10.1 Different approaches to distributive justice

	Questions	Answer	Meaning	Example
Equal Distribution	What does 'equal distribution' mean?	Equality	All individuals receive the same resources	All the individuals need to pass the same exam in the same conditions
	Equity		Individuals receive different resources: there are greatest benefits for the least advantaged members of society	Some individuals have some adaptations in the exams. For instance, different questions and longer time
	If individuals receive different resources, what criteria do we use to decide matters about these resources?	Needs	Each individual receives resources in accordance with his/her needs	Students with special needs receive extra support
		Merits	Each individual receives resources in accordance with his/her merits	Students who demonstrate high performance receive extra support
	How do we distribute resources fairly?	Opportunities	Resources are provided so each individual has the same opportunities	Scholarships are provided to high performing students so they can have access to higher education
		Outcomes	Resources are provided so each individual, independently of his/her capacities and status, has the same outcomes	Scholarships are provided to minority groups so their presence in higher education is ensured
		Free access	All individuals have free access to the resources	Higher education is free for all students

Recognition justice

Recognition justice is based on the assumption that some identities and cultures, including their norms, values, and behaviours, are considered to be more valuable than others. An example of this is how in Western societies, caregiving and housework, traditionally associated with feminine roles, is often considered less valuable than paid employment which may stereotypically be associated with masculine roles. In this respect, recognition justice theorists attempts to fight against the misrecognition of some groups' identities, and cultural values.

Alex Honneth (1995) is one of the main philosophers of what has been called the 'politics of recognition'. He understands that our identity is constructed in relation to others. Consequently, if we want to understand what social justice means, we need to consider how the views of the others have an impact on our self-perception. Social justice, in Honneth's views, is about constructing alternative notions of 'valuable' that do not depend on dominant interpretations. In our previous example, if we misrecognize, using the dominant notions of what is perceived to be valuable, the work of someone who has spent her life in unpaid caregiving work, this might have a negative impact on the way this person perceives him/herself. Social justice, in this respect, is about considering alternative notions of 'valuable' and recognizing caregiving work as valuable.

Marion Iris Young is another key author of recognition justice. According to Young (2011), when we think about social justice, we need to consider ideas and issues not only in relation to individuals but also in relation to the groups to which these individuals belong. In society, she argues, we witness situations in which not only some individuals dominate others, but also certain social groups tend to dominate and marginalize other groups. Social justice, in Young's views, is about the freedom of groups from oppressive relations.

Recognition theory has been used by post-colonialist theorists to criticize global citizenship education in its socialization approach. In her text 'Five faces of oppression', Young (2011) defines cultural imperialism as one of the ways in which groups might be oppressed. She explains, 'The dominant group reinforces its position by bringing the other groups under the measure of its dominant norms. [. . .] Since only the dominant group's cultural expressions receive wide dissemination, their cultural expressions become the normal, or the universal, and thereby the unremarkable' (2011, p. 59). In this respect, if we consider global citizenship education through the lens of recognition theory, we can wonder whether a universalistic form of global citizenship is possible and desirable or whether, following Honneth's theory, alternative forms of global citizenship education should be considered.

Participatory justice

Participatory justice refers to the real possibilities of individuals and groups to politically participate in society and to have an impact through their political actions. Through participation, individuals and groups can have some opportunities of deciding what our societies should look like. In this respect, a lack of representativeness is considered to be an instance of political injustice.

Participatory justice has probably become more relevant now than ever. In her book 'Scales of Justice: Reimagining Political Space in a Globalizing World', the philosopher Nancy Fraser (2009) discusses how the acceleration of the globalization process has created some new forms of oppression. Fraser identifies three different ways in which a lack of representativeness might end in political injustice in a globalized world:

1. In the context of Young's (2011) work, Fraser understands that within the contexts of nation-states, representative democracies tend to benefit the interests of the majoritarian groups whereas minorities tend to be misrepresented.

2. The acceleration of globalization, Fraser explains, has contributed to a large amount of people living outside the borders of their nation-state. Immigrants, refugees, students and others lack representation in the countries in which they are living; and in some cases in their countries of origin. In certain cases, some people lack any national citizenship and therefore any framework that enables their representation.

3. Considering the absence of any global democracy, Fraser highlights how some individuals, because of their economic position or their national citizenship, have a larger impact in what happens in the world as whole than others. The lack of equal global political participation, in Fraser's views, challenges any possibility for global social justice.

In the context of Fraser's argument, participatory justice sheds some light on discussions about global citizenship itself. Citizenship, as we discuss in Chapters 7 and 9, is traditionally constructed in relation to nation-states that entitle their citizenry to rights and responsibilities. Quite often, one of these rights is political participation. When we consider 'global citizenship', however, one might wonder whether any global organization ensures this right (Held & McGrew, 2005). For some, the United Nations and associated institutions such as UNESCO protect the participatory right by emphasizing Human Rights. Global citizenship education, in this view, should promote participation using established mechanisms. We are here considering global citizenship education in its socialization function. Through global citizenship education, young people, for instance, should learn how to participate in the Youth Global Forums. For others, these institutions do not guarantee this right: they are un-democratic institutions by themselves and they do not put in place any measures to cover this right nationally and – even more obviously – globally. Global citizenship education, in this sense, can only contribute to the participatory dimension of social justice by challenging the structures, the forms and perhaps the institutions of global governance itself.

Conclusions: what would a social-justice orientated global citizenship education look?

The debates around social justice education are helpful to identify some key issues around global citizenship and education. First, is it possible and desirable to define a social-justice orientated global citizenship? Global citizenship, as social justice, is historically and geographically constructed and therefore, if we attempt to find a single definition for global citizenship we might fall into 'recognition injustice', considering some 'global attributes' more valuable than others. Second, who is entitled to decide what a social-justice orientated global citizenship education should look like? In other words, why are some people are entitled to have a stronger influence in deciding what is and what is not 'social-justice orientated global citizenship'? Third, if we consider alternative views on social-justice orientated global citizenship, how do we ensure that these differences will not enhance inequality? For instance, if, in an attempt to ensure that all languages are equally valued and preserved, each of us educate our children only in our mother tongue, are the children whose language is dominant (e.g. English, Arabic, Spanish) likely to have access to more resources? We suggested in the beginning of this chapter that although most people would defend social justice, social justice education can be considered an impossibility. Perhaps, as Biesta (2014) suggests, the only option left is to keep on asking the others 'what do you think about this?' and to let each of us answer this question.

Annotated bibliography

Fraser, N. (2009). *Scales of Justice: Reimagining Political Space in a Globalizing World*. New York: Columbia University Press.

Nancy Fraser discusses in this book her understandings about social justice and how the process of globalization has influenced her views. We find particularly illuminating the chapter 'Reframing justice in a globalized world'. In this chapter, the author begins by summarizing her views on the redistribution-recognition dilemma. This is followed by an in depth discussion around the participatory dimension of justice and the ways in which globalization is reframing participatory practices.

Harvard University (2011). *Episode 7 and 8. Justice with Michael Sandel* [video file] Retrieved from http://www.justiceharvard.org/2011/02/episode-07/#watch.

This episode is part of Justice, a Harvard online course in which Michael Sandel discusses justice, equality, democracy and citizenship. The website contains twelve episodes, forums of discussion and several other resources including links to the e-version of Sandel's book on justice. We recommend that you focus on episodes 7 and 8. In these episodes, Rawls' theory of justice is discussed in detail. The details provided online also includes a beginners' and advanced guide that can be helpful to better understand the main debates within Rawls' theory.

North, C. (2006). More than words? Delving into the substantive meaning (s) of 'social justice' in education. *Review of Educational Research*, 76(4), 507–35.

In this article, Connie E. North provides an exhaustive framework to conceptualize social justice. She draws upon the work of prominent Western philosophers and social theorists to different spheres and dilemmas associated with social justice. Particularly valuable, in our understanding, are the links she establishes between different approaches to social justice and different research findings and theoretical perspectives on education. Although the text does not outline the links between social justice, different views on global citizenship and global citizenship education, we feel that this article offers an in depth analysis of the field of social justice education in Western tradition.

Sant, E., Lewis, S., Delgado, S. & Ross, E. W. (2017). Social justice. In I. Davies, L. C. Ho, D. Kiwan, A. Peterson, C. Peck, E. Sant & Y. Waghid (Eds). *The Palgrave handbook of global citizenship and education.* London: Palgrave Macmillan.

Shultz, L. (2015). Decolonizing UNESCO's post-2015 education agenda: global social justice and a view from UNDRIP. *Postcolonial Directions in Education*, 4(2), 96–115.

In this article, Lynette Shultz, one of the authors of this book, uses a similar framework to the one presented in this chapter to analyse the global social justice approached assumed by UNESCO in the United Nations Declaration of the Rights of Indigenous People (UNDRIP). She first reviews the Education for All (EFA) agenda from 1990 to 2015 and later focus on the UNESCO's Post-2015 Education Agenda and the UNDRIP. Her analysis of UNDRIP can be understood as an example of how different approaches to social justice might be used to examine global policies and initiatives in global citizenship education.

Shultz, L. (2017). Equality. In I. Davies, L. C. Ho, D. Kiwan, A. Peterson, C. Peck, E. Sant & Y. Waghid (Eds). *The Palgrave handbook of global citizenship and education*. London: Palgrave Macmillan.

In these two chapters, the authors review different approaches to the notion of social justice at times of acceleration of the globalization processes. The first chapter ('Social Justice') examines the links between global citizenship education and social justice as framed in Fraser's text. In the second chapter ('Equality'), the author examines social justice through a decolonial lens and reviews the ontological assumptions that often underlie discussions on social justices.

Activities

The following activities aim to foster understanding on the different theories underlined in this chapter. However, whilet the first activity is more theoretically orientated, the second is more clearly related to practice.

1. The novelist Anne Enright has written an essay in which she discusses the burial (and re-burial) of an Irish rebel and patriot (https://www.lrb.co.uk/v37/n24/anne-enright/antigone-in-galway). She suggests that this situation is essentially 'Antigone in Galway'. She is making a link with the classic play by the ancient Greek Sophocles. There are many translations of the original play by Sophocles. You might like to look at the version by Seamus Heaney (*The Burial at Thebes*). In this play there are issues about whom one owes allegiance to. Given a choice would we do what we feel is right even if that contradicted the rules of the society in which we live? Would it make a difference to our decision if the rules had been agreed to fairly or unfairly? And what, exactly, would constitute fair or unfair agreement? If the majority of people decided on something, would that be enough to make us follow the law? What if most people in the world decided on something but that there was no formally constituted law to support that position? Reflect about these questions in relation to the theory discussed in this chapter.
2. In this exercise, we propose a debate of different views around social justice in a particular scenario.

This is a Music State School in Buenos Aires (Argentina). Until last year, teachers had organized a classical music contest each year. The student who won received a scholarship for musical material for the following year. All the students were allowed to participate. Last year twenty students participated. Among them were Elisabeth and Wayra. Elisabeth performed Handel's Ave Maria extraordinarily. Wayra, whose family arrived two years before from a little village in the Bolivian Andes, surprised the teachers with her own composition. Teachers agreed that among all the other students, Elisabeth's performance was exceptional. While considering Wayra's performance good, they did not know Andean music well enough to compare it with Elisabeth's. After a huge debate, they decided that Elisabeth would win. The teachers now consider revising the rules of the contest for the following year. Let's see what four teachers think about this.

>Rosa Ana – She suggests that they should employ someone who is more familiar with Andean music to recognize the importance of Quechua culture in American culture. This person could help to decide who should win.
>
>Ahmed – He mentions that Rosa Ana's suggestion would cost money and consequently it would reduce the scholarship. He proposes to redistribute the scholarship among all the students. Several families are considering leaving the Music school because they cannot afford the musical material.
>
>Maria – She considers that Wayra did not sing Classical music and this was a Classical music Contest. The rules of the contest should apply to everybody. This is a classical music school not a folk one. They should not change the contest for one student who did not read the rules.
>
>Marcelo – He comments that some students need help to understand what Western classical music is. Part of the budget of the contest should be allocated to provide extra help to these students.

Considering this scenario, organize a debate with your peers. In groups or individually, each of you will have to defend the position of one of these teachers. After the debate, discuss:

a) If you were one of the teacher of this school, what would be your proposal?

b) For each teacher, which/what dimension of social justice is he/she considering?

c) For each teacher, what are the links between their views and different approaches to global citizenship and global citizenship education?

d) Analyse your own views, which/what dimension of social justice are you considering?

e) What are the links between your views on this scenario and different approaches to global citizenship and global citizenship education?

11

Development Education

Development has a broad meaning that suggests progress and improvement. The term international development has applied this idea to tackling the significant differences in quality of life between countries. Generally, international development is about industrialized nations providing resources and support to improve conditions in countries facing significant issues around poverty and infrastructure. The Organization for Economic Cooperation and Development indicates that development aid totalled USD 131.6 billion in 2015. In addition to countries, there are large foundations and non-governmental organizations (NGOs) that conduct projects under the banner of international development. International development is also a key focus of the United Nations. While there are very important reasons for considering how to encourage quality of life around the world, the very premise that some countries are ahead and need to fund international development while others lag behind and need help speaks to a significant challenge in the field of international development. How do we tackle global inequality without reinforcing a sense of superiority of the 'haves' over the 'have nots'?

This chapter will review some general trends in international development and consider the overlapping and often contradictory theoretical paradigms shaping understandings of how to address global inequalities. Then, some key trends in education will be examined through two fields: *Education for Development* where education is a target for development and *Development Education* where students in countries considered 'developed' learn about international development.

Terminology

Social scientists use a variety of data sources to help determine where international development is needed. This includes economic measures such as the gross domestic product of a specific country and its average per capita income, and social and political measures such as literacy rates, life expectancy (including child survival and material survival rates), human rights provisions and political freedoms. Historically, various categories have been used to discuss and target international development. The idea of 'First World' and 'Third World' countries used an overt hierarchy which was eventually replaced by 'developed', 'un-' or 'underdeveloped' and 'developing' countries. More recently, the terms 'Global South' and 'Global North' have been used to recognize the fact that most of the power and resources in the world are held by countries and cultures originating in the North (e.g. Europe and the colonized North American countries). Another set of terms, 'global majority' and 'global minority' are also used to distinguish between those parts of the world that have the largest populations but experience highest levels of poverty per capita and the parts of the world with lesser populations where wealth and resources tend to be concentrated. All of these terms are imperfect, and while some can be important for recognizing significant inequalities, dichotomous terms can also hide the fact that there are experiences of wealth and poverty across the world.

More recently, the BRICS countries – Brazil, China, India, Indonesia, South Korea and Russia – have been called 'emerging economies' based on World Bank economists who predict that as a group, these countries will account for nearly 50 per cent of global growth by 2025. The BRICS countries and other organizations such as the non-governmental Qatar Charity are now also contributing to international foreign aid. As the sources of development aid widen and the need for development aid continues, there is an increased demand to research, analyse, propose and implement programs. An entire industry has been created to service international development. Given the recent global financial crisis and the continuing demand for development assistance, there is also a great deal of competition for funding and contracts among international development organizations.

Typology of theoretical approaches to international development

McCowan (2015) highlights the importance of understanding the theoretical underpinnings linking education and development. Government policies and teacher practice along with public understandings of the importance of education all draw on key assumptions about social justice, what counts as a good life, and what knowledge should be applied to address inequalities. He identifies five paradigms of development theory: liberal capitalist, Marxist, liberal egalitarian, postcolonial and radical. We will discuss some of these paradigms further in relation to global education in Chapter 13 but here we focus on how these paradigms help us to understand 'development'. While the categorization is neither exhaustive nor are the categories internally homogeneous, McCowan's (2015) typology provides us with an overview of the various theoretical frames interacting to influence the role of education in development.

1. Liberal capitalist paradigm

Background

After World War II, there was a great deal of policy work devoted to rebuilding economic growth in affected countries. As most of the powerful nations at the time ascribed to capitalism, it became assumed to be the best way to grow and sustain economies, and there was generally the sense that all economies would develop in similar ways. This corresponded with the idea of 'development economics' that focused specifically on how to improve and sustain economic growth in what were then referred to as 'Third World' countries. By the 1950s, capitalist, open-market principles defined how international development proceeded. In the 1980s and 1990s the capitalist focus re-emerged in what is referred to as neoliberalism. A key example is structural adjustment policies (SAPs) which were put in place in many of the newly independent nation-states of the Global South when they needed loans from organizations such as the World Bank and International Monetary Fund. SAPs outlined what nations receiving loans were required to do and resulted in significant reductions in public sector spending on education, enabling a role for private sector entities.

Main concepts

Modernization theory assumed that economic growth required a shift from traditional to modern ways of organizing the economy. Education was key as mass schooling was viewed to have modernized nation states in Europe and North America, and this could be applied to other regions which needed to 'catch up'. It thus very much created a deficit view of so-called developing countries.

Human capital theory specified aspects of modernization theory by explaining that investing in an individual's education would enhance their productivity and earnings while also enabling the nation-state to have a stock of skilled workers to promote economic growth. *Neoliberalism* is a newer idea building from the economic focus of modernization and human capital theories. It reinforces the idea that development is essentially economic growth and is achieved through 'market-based competition, minimal state intervention and individual entrepreneurship and initiative' (McCowan, 2015, p. 37). In education, it is tied to both a decrease in public funding of education and an increase in private sector provision and influence. As has been discussed in other chapters, contemporary processes of globalization have fuelled neoliberalism.

Critiques

The liberal capitalist paradigm has been critiqued for its exclusive focus on economic growth as the primary feature of development which effectively reduces key institutions in society (e.g. education, political structure) and other aspects of society (e.g. culture, spirituality, safety, environmental protection) to serving primarily an economic purpose. Also, there appears to be a relative lack of concern about equality resulting from the assumption that growing profits through an open-market will improve all aspects of society. This critique of neoliberalism reveals how modernization is assumed to be the single model for development applied all over the world and is based on 'Western' ideas. In this sense, it may reinforce rather than ameliorate unequal relations of power. Furthermore, such a view presents some countries as being superior to others while not fully accounting for the historical factors, including colonial abuses of power and exploitation of resources and human beings, that tie so called 'developing countries' to the fate of so called 'developed' countries.

2. Marxist paradigm

Background

In the 1960s and 1970s, questions that had been raised for a long time regarding the perceived lack of attention to inequality in the liberal capitalist approach began to become prominent. The work of Karl Marx became a touchstone as critiques proliferated pointing to the fact that as capitalism grew, so did economic inequality. A Marxist perspective suggests that not only has poverty persisted through capitalism, but that capitalist development and economic growth for some depends on the poverty of others. Marxist critiques challenge the assumption that continuous accumulation of capital leads to better life circumstances for all.

Main concepts

Dependency theory highlights that modernization theory essentially blamed poorer countries for their own lack of development. Instead, rich countries cause poverty and maintain it through establishing relations of dependency between richer and poorer nations. 'Core' countries benefit from the agriculture and minerals produced by 'periphery' countries. This theory has been popular in regions such as Latin America and has served as a basis for many contemporary critiques of global capitalism.

World systems theory, associated with sociologist Immanuel Wallterstein, adds that dominant capitalist centres maintain their position by involving peripheries and semi-peripheries into one global system that is interdependent and maintains those positions. He describes a world system as similar to an organism that has a life span within which some of its characteristics change while others remain stable as the organism itself lives on. The dynamics of how a world system develops are internal to the system. In this view, developed countries benefit the most from the integrated system because less developed countries on the periphery are constrained by a variety of structures. Accordingly, these countries will only get to the stage of accumulation of capital and of development that enables a reproduction of their subordinate status. Semi-peripheral states have characteristics of both core and peripheries. They experience more capital intensity than peripheral states as well as higher skill and wage levels. However, there is little movement upwards, and these semi-periphery states serve together as an intermediary that stabilizes the whole system. Wallerstein referred to the idea of *unequal exchange* whereby any surplus resource or capital from the peripheries or semi-peripheries goes back to the industrialized core so that capital is accumulated at a global scale, benefits the core the most, and maintains the overall system.

Dependency theory as applied to education led to the recognition of the large extent to which education systems in the Global South depended on former colonial powers. Some movements to interrogate the colonial systems of power have been expressed through the content and structure of school systems in the Global South. For example, in some contexts, movements were formed to honour local languages and knowledge systems by making connections with co-operativism and the realities of rural life.

Critiques and context

In the 1980s, development theory reached a stalemate amid the hostilities of the Cold War as neither global capitalism nor state socialism was apparently able to address poverty (McCowan, 2015, p. 41). Marxist critiques have been challenged for focusing too much on the state and social class, and in fact, some Marxist theorists challenged World Systems theory for not putting enough emphasis on the nation-state and class. Others challenged world systems theory for failing to fully account for all the scales of interaction. However, the main ideas connected to Marxist perspectives persist in, for example, the movements against global trade.

3. Postcolonialism

Background

The origins of a postcolonial critique of development are tied to a post-structuralist movement in the mid-twentieth century. This critique firmly interrogated the foundational premises of Western thought. It challenged the assumptions inherent to modernity such as the idea that all individuals are autonomous and questioned the extent to which its worldview is a universal world view. These critiques also challenged the idea that the Enlightenment principles underlying modernity – such as the basis of human development in progressing knowledge through empirical testing – had necessarily brought progress by highlighting how much oppression and injustice had been experienced under modernization.

Main concepts

Knowledge is contextual and contingent upon the context in which it is created. Post-structuralist theorists claimed that knowledge was neither universal nor objective nor neutral. Rather, dominant knowledge systems had been created through a set of historical and contextual factors. These taken-for-granted worldviews were revealed to be metanarratives that structured how societies understood and organized themselves and others.

Colonial dependency was a concept that developed from the poststructural challenge to universal knowledge and reality. It included the recognition that colonizers from the Global North had not only inflicted violence upon local peoples in various Global South contexts but had also forced them into a dependent relationship where their only way to exert agency was to use the colonizers' language and knowledge systems.

Post-development theories assert that the international system of donors and receivers of development aid reinforces colonialism. A new imperialism manifests in the dominance of countries in the Global North that persists despite countries in the Global South gaining official independence. Education serves an important role. It can help make the taken-for-granted assumptions holding up dominant worldviews and metanarratives of development visible and able to be challenged. This has also involved bringing forward indigenous knowledges and languages.

Critiques and Responses

Postcolonial theory is fundamentally about critique and enabling the interrogation and deconstruction of metanarratives that are supporting the continuation of unequal colonial power relations. While some see this as action in itself, others critique a lack of concrete set of actions. As has been discussed in other Chapters, the work of Walter Mignolo has helped to interrogate modernization and development as overarching metanarratives of development. As discussed in Chapter 8, he points out that there is a light side and a dark side of modernity. The light side includes ideas of never-ending forward continued progress. The dark side includes continuous colonialism, imperialism, and over-exploitation of resources and people. Mignolo (2011) asserts that the ideals that make up the light side of modernity are only possible because of the dark side. Colonialism is the process through which the link between the light side and the dark side becomes hidden. Postcolonial critiques, such as the work of Mignolo, challenge the good intentions of those seeking to help others through development aid. Andreotti (2014) refers to this as 'modernity's trick' where good, well-meaning people fail to recognize how in trying to help others by modernizing them they fail to interrogate or change the differently experiences of humanity and modernity including those attached to political affiliations, skin colour, class, gender and other distinctions. In this sense, from the perspective of postcolonial critique, Liberal Capitalist Theories and Marxist Critiques fail to fully account for or challenge the continuation of colonial systems of power.

4. Liberal egalitarianism

Background

Rights-based approaches to development became prevalent in the 1990s. They resisted a deficit view of those suffering from poverty, seeing those people instead as bearers of rights. This was a distinct change from the idea that they were receivers of charity.

Key concepts

Moral universalism: This paradigm shares with the liberal capitalist paradigm a basis in universalism with a strong assertion of the importance of individual freedom. However, it prioritizes moral universalism where human rights provide the central framework to guarantee a dignified life for all human beings.

Capabilities theory emerged at the turn of the twenty-first century as a change from seeing development as primarily economic and defined by outsiders to promoting a view of human beings as having a range of goals. It is associated with the work of Amartya Sen, Marth Nussbaum and Mahbub Ul Haq and promoted the freedom of people to have agency in their own life.

Community-based work connecting with local realities and grass-roots organizations also emerged as an influential and popular approach to international development.

Rights-based approach to education: Following in line with the other concepts, education was asserted as a set of rights including both the right to access and succeed in education and the assertion that education should empower individuals to know, exercise, and defend their rights towards enhanced efficacy and agency of individuals.

Critiques

The attempt to balance the primacy of the individual with the necessary redistribution of resources to enable more social justice is not only a challenge but also a potential paradox inherent to this perspective. Marxist theorists do not think this approach goes far enough to critique and change unequal systems of power and resource distribution and suggest that this approach merely makes the status quo slightly more palatable. Post-structuralist critiques focus on the fact that this is a lighter and perhaps brighter version of the same modernization metanarrative that causes the inequalities it seeks to address. Post-colonial critiques contribute that efficacy and agency are primarily constrained by colonial systems of power.

5. Radical humanism in education

Background

McCowan (2015) identifies a final group of theoretical engagements with development as those which do not share one coherent theory but rather focus on a set of principles relevant to education. A core theme is education is not a driver but the means of development. In this sense, learning is the most important means of emancipation.

Key example

Paulo Freire's work was rooted in his context in Brazil. In his seminal writing in *Pedagogy of the Oppressed* (1970), he drew on some elements of dependency theory and postcolonial theory while actioning those critiques to propose pedagogical practices. The work of Mahatma Gandhi could also be considered part of a radical humanist paradigm.

Key concepts

Dialogue was a central concept to Freire's work. He believed it was necessary to radically revise what it means to be educated and what it means to be a teacher or a learner.

Horizontal processes between teacher and learner focused on the importance of transforming the self through becoming critically conscious of the ways oppression functions. This was not simply about enabling learning, but had an explicit political purpose.

Critical consciousness would be the means and purpose of education. Becoming aware of systems of oppression would enable socially just ends: societal structures would become transformed. The participatory and horizontal nature of his pedagogical approach was influential in wider development activities.

Critiques and elaborations

Feminist theorists, among others, have pointed out the need to account for overlapping systems of oppression. Indeed, Freire's ideas have been adapted to a wider ranging approach to social oppression called 'critical pedagogy'. This approach has made some important gains through popular education movements in informal and adult education; however, in terms of influencing formal education, critics suggest that while it has had a significant impact in certain disciplines and certain groups of teachers, critical pedagogy has had marginal impact overall, and it is constrained given the resurgence of liberal capitalist approaches through neoliberalism.

McCowan (2015) acknowledges that this brief typology of theories of development influencing education is very generalized. It also represents only one way to consider the wide range of understandings and approaches to international development and the role of education therein. However, it is a helpful start to unpacking the various overlapping and even contradicting theories operating in current approaches. It is common to see strategy documents and educational materials that draw on human capitalist theories alongside rights-based approaches and acknowledgements of the importance of local knowledges and experiences.

Post-structural and postcolonial perspectives would suggest that this is because neither human capitalist nor rights-based approaches challenge the modern assumptions of the autonomous individual and assumed progress of applying rational and empirical thought to change society for the better. It is also important to recognize how, where, and why certain paradigms emerge more strongly and to remember that our ideas about what international development is, who needs it, and who is responsible for addressing global poverty and inequalities are tied to strongly held sets of assumptions that need to be recognized and critically reflected upon. More radical perspectives open up spaces to question and interrogate what otherwise can be seen as neutral and taken-for-granted ideas of 'helping' others in the world through development.

Education for development

Education has primarily served as a human capital function within international development programs and policies. Draxler (2014, cited in Weidman, 2016) notes that among key trends influencing international investment in education for development, there has been a significant focus on how education can promote national economic growth. Not only has this involved significant private sector influence, including by the World Bank, but there has also been an increasing use of large scale tests such as the Program for International Student Assessment (PISA) run by the Organization of Economic Cooperation and Development (OECD). These trends will be examined more fully in Chapter 13.

Goal 2 of the UN Millennium Development Goals (MDGs) was: Achieve Universal Primary Education. The target led to a large amount of international development work in education. According to the UN, enrolment rates in 'developing' countries reached 91 per cent in 2015. However, high levels of poverty and conflicts have continued to impact children's ability to go to school, and there are also significant disparities between rural and urban areas. Goal 4 of the SDGs is: Ensure inclusive and quality education for all and promote lifelong learning. It focuses on girls and boys not only accessing but completing free primary and secondary schooling by 2030. The focus is also on equal access to affordable vocational training, reducing wealth and gender inequalities, and ensuring access to higher education. Weidman (2016) sums up three key learnings from the experience with the MDGs that are brought to bear on the new era of education for development ushered in by the Sustainable Development Goals that replace them: '(a) reform and improvement of education are not a simple thing, (b) increasing enrolments does not necessarily mean increasing quality of outcomes and (c) problems faced are so complicated that simple, single-factor solutions no longer work' (p. 403). Importantly, while the MDGs targeted international cooperation to promote change in 'developing countries'; the SDGs apply to all nations. This is a change in a key paradigm within international development and allows for a focus on interdependence between nations. A key aim for education in the SDGs is improving quality of education.

Development education

While there are a variety of understandings of development education, generally it can be said to have originated in the 1970s as part of efforts to increase awareness in the Global North about and to gain support for international development initiatives. Through the 1980s and 19908s both policy-makers and practitioners – those in formal and informal education, including NGOs – saw how educational activities helped to promote awareness and understanding of international development. Originally, there was a focus on development education as transmitting information about international development because of a perceived awareness deficit on the part of people living countries in the Global North. Gradually this has shifted so that education is now seen as central to securing a more just world in both Global North and Global South contexts (Bourn, 2014, p. 8, drawing on Regan and Sinclair, 2006).

Bourn (2014) understands development education as a precursor and/or parallel concept to newer terms such as education for sustainable development and global citizenship education. He points out that these fields share an approach to learning and a general community of practice that draws on expertise and experience in both formal and non-formal education. Krause (2010) identified four main stages of development education: (a) public relations for development aid, (b) awareness raising for public dissemination of information, (c) global education focused on local-global interdependence, and (d) enhancement of life skills focusing on learning process and critical thinking (Bourn, 2014, p. 8). Bourn (2014) suggests that it is important to recognize the complexities and underlying pedagogical principles also influencing development education in the past two decades.

An important pedagogical distinction is the role of education as learning about the world and one's place in it versus education as campaigning for specific international development projects. In Europe, this has been a very strong debate because many organizations who have been involved in development education are primarily motivated by the need for significant and broad social change while other organizations wish to focus on campaign awareness and support. A key trend across countries in the Global North has been to emphasize global education as part of enabling sustainable development. Linking to the idea of global education enables a broader approach and focuses more specifically on learning goals (Bourn, 2014).

Bourn (2014) suggests a typology of four key themes defining recent work in 'development education':

1. Interdependence and interconnections: promoting the 'interdependent and interconnected nature of our lives [and] the similarities as well as the differences between communities and peoples around the world' (p. 21)

2. Voices from the Global South: ensuring their voices and perspectives are 'promoted, understood and reflected upon, along with perspectives from the Global North' (p. 21). A focus here is on moving beyond relativism to recognizing 'the importance of spaces for the voices of the oppressed and dispossessed' (p. 21).

3. Values-based approach to learning: Here there is an emphasis on 'social justice, human rights, fairness and the desire for a more equal world' (p. 21)

4. Linking learning and moral outrage: The influence of NGOs on the field focuses on tackling poverty and 'taking action to secure change' (p. 21)

The shift towards global learning and global citizenship education within the field represents an attempt to recognize and revise the dominant narratives underling the notion of international development. Indeed, a main critique of development education has been the tendency for it to reinforce rather than to revise the distinction between the 'Us' of the Global North who are modernized and have the moral duty to help and the 'Them' of the Global South who require help (Andreotti, 2006). This is a central paradox of international development that must be taken-up by global citizenship education: how to challenge inequalities without reinforcing them.

Annotated bibliography

Stein, S., Andreotti, V. D. O. & Suša, R. (2016). 'Beyond 2015', within the modern/colonial global imaginary? Global development and higher education. *Critical Studies in Education*, 1–21.

This article uses post- and de-colonial theories to consider how higher education is being included as a target for the SDGs. The authors analyse the 'Beyond 2015' campaign of the Association of Commonwealth Universities which intends to work with the SDGs. They argue that the campaign itself, despite aiming to enable a plurality of perspectives and voices, limits the capacity of voices from the Global South to offer critiques. The article raises questions about the role of higher education in education for development, and it also ends by raising some wider questions about what are the possibilities and limitations available to challenge mainstream development agendas.

United Nations Development Programme (UNDP). http://www.undp.org/content/undp/en/home/sustainable-development-goals/goal-4-quality-education.html

This is the main website for resources relating to Goal 4 of the SDGs. It contains information about the Goal and links to various projects being conducted by the United Nations Development Program to promote quality education around the world.

Unterhalter, E. (2014). Measuring education for the millennium development goals: reflections on targets, indicators, and a post-2015 framework. *Journal of Human Development and Capabilities, 15*(2–3), 176–87.

In this article, Unterhalter traces how education was targeted in the MDGs and considers the consequences of an inherent narrow framing of both the goals and indicators. She identifies some unintended negative consequences that came out of the MDGs related to education and suggests alternative indicators for education in the SDGs.

Activities

1. a. Compare the United Nations Millennium Development Goals to the United Nations Sustainable Development Goals.
   http://www.un.org/millenniumgoals/
   https://sustainabledevelopment.un.org/?menu=1300
   What are the main differences? Which theories of development and related concepts can you locate in each? Which theories seem to have influenced the move towards SDGs applying to all nations?

   b. Look specifically at the goals related to education in the MDGs and SDGs. How do they connect to education for development and development education?

2. Look up an international development project related to education or a development education project on the internet. This could be an initiative of an NGO or civil society organization, government, philanthropic organization or UNESCO. One example can be found at http://www.globalpartnership.org/country/malawi. Another example can be found at http://deeep.org/deeep-project/. Now find a further example of your own. What theoretical paradigms of development underpin the rationales and strategies of the project? What questions might be posed by a postcolonial, liberal egalitarian or radical humanist point of view?

12

Character Education

Character education is an important, powerful and increasingly recognized educational force. Any attempts to consider global citizenship without recognizing the perspectives of character educators would be at best a partial account. That said, character education is highly controversial and contested. It is particularly prominent in certain parts of the world (perhaps explicitly especially in north America and has links with Confucian-inspired forms of education in certain parts of Asia) and not so prominent in other areas (such as continental Europe). There are significant differences between many versions of global citizenship education and character education (as well as there being many points of contact and some overlap). In this chapter we highlight those connections and disconnections.

Character education is a diverse field but most of the leading proponents are essentially concerned with virtue as a

> trait or state of character of a person which is relatively entrenched. (McLaughlin & Halstead, 1999, p. 134)

Considered generally, it is admirable that this deep seated and vitally important part of our make-up as human beings is taken so seriously. Classic statements by those who have struggled for democracy and justice demonstrate the significance of this field:

> I have a dream my four little children will one day live in a nation where they will not be judged by the colour of their skin but by the content of their character. (King, 1992, p. 208)

Those aspects of character differ from place to place around the world but there are some fairly strong indications of what is regarded as central. In England (DfE 2015) character means:

- perseverance, resilience and grit
- confidence and optimism
- motivation, drive and ambition
- neighbourliness and community spirit
- tolerance and respect
- honesty, integrity and dignity
- conscientiousness, curiosity and focus

In the US Character Counts refers to the Six Pillars of Character:

- trustworthiness,
- respect,
- responsibility,
- fairness,
- caring
- good citizenship

The above are usually not presented as universal values but perhaps something of that is intended by character educators. In considering the nature of a good person they may be sketching what could or should apply around the globe.

However, the nature of character education has been discussed by other than policy makers and not only by those who are convinced of its worth. Indeed there are some who are rather wary about its purpose. Kristjánsson (2013) has written to try to rebut some of those challenges, arguing that it is not old fashioned, paternalistic, a form of religious education and so on. At times certain aspects of educational focus have appeared and then rapidly disappeared from the Department for Education (England) web pages, including a very positively worded emphasis on military ethos. Without failing to recognize the value of the armed forces and its many courageous personnel, for many teachers it seemed shocking that character education would be aligned with military ethos and that schools would be encouraged to promote this version of it. In light of these controversies it is necessary to explore some of the issues and aspects of character education and how they relate to global citizenship education.

First, it is high status. This is relatively unusual for a branch of social studies education. Successive US presidents (Clinton, Bush and Obama) have supported it. In 2014 the Senate unanimously accepted the following:

Resolved, That the Senate—

1. designates the week beginning October 19, 2014, as 'National Character Counts Week'; and
2. calls upon the people of the United States and interested groups—
   A. to embrace the elements of character identified by local schools and communities, such as trustworthiness, respect, responsibility, fairness, caring and citizenship; and
   B. to observe the week with appropriate ceremonies, programs and activities.
   (https://www.congress.gov/bill/113th-congress/senate-resolution/557/text)

In Singapore character and citizenship education is a key part of the work of schools (https://www.moe.gov.sg/education/syllabuses/character-citizenship-education).

> Our education system must . . . nurture Singapore citizens of good character, so that everyone has the moral resolve to withstand an uncertain future, and a strong sense of responsibility to contribute to the success of Singapore and the well-being of fellow Singaporeans.
> (Mr Heng Swee Keat, Minister for Education, Ministry of Education, 2012)

Character education has global influence with it being easy to see policy initiatives and networks in very many countries and including organizations (e.g. Character First http://characterfirsteducation.com/c/about.php) that operate across national boundaries. We need to consider whether character education has higher global status or higher status in many countries of the world than global citizenship education or whether it is a form of legitimated global citizenship education.

Second – and similar to many who promote global citizenship education – one of the key driving forces behind character education and which can be seen in some of the quotations given above is its wide-ranging commitment to transform society. Lickona (1994) argues for the need to build a moral society. Organizations such as character counts show the scale of the ambition:

> Effective character education involves helping schools build good kids – kids who demonstrate basic ethical values in their choices each day. But it

doesn't end in the schools. Parents and community groups must also get on board to be sure good character isn't only an on-campus activity. Ethical values must be reinforced everywhere, all the time.

This priority for morality makes the work of character education distinct from other forms of global citizenship education. Morality is the third point that we wish to consider in our description and discussion of character education. By emphasizing morality we are not suggesting that there is no connection with other forms of global citizenship. Hargreaves (1996, p. 33) has declared that: 'Active citizens are as political as they are moral; moral sensibility derives in part from political understanding; political apathy spawns moral apathy'. Crick (1962/1979, p. 25) asserted that:

> The more one is involved in relationships with others, the more conflicts of interest or of character and circumstance will arise. These conflicts, when personal create the activity we call 'ethics' . . . and such conflicts when public create political activity.

However, it is very important to take note of this key distinction between politics and morals. Crick made it very clear that he opposed the idea that 'values and rights are enough' for citizenship (Crick 2000, p. 123).

As well as discussing the place of morality as a key principle in global citizenship there is also an important issue regarding implementation linked at times to programmes of moral education or education in values. This issue of implementation is the fourth issue that we are discussing about the differences between global citizenship education and character education. There are key disagreements about how to develop character. Crick insisted that 'I do not believe that values can be taught – taught directly that is' (2000, p. 124). In England citizenship education is a National Curriculum subject; character education is not. But this issue of implementation is disputed as there are very many character education organizations that recommend teaching and learning resources (e.g. https://charactercounts.org/ccweek14-and-digcitwk-celebrate-them-together-oct-19–25/).

There are various ways in which character education resources are meant to work in the classroom. There are everyday scenarios in which students are asked to think about, for example, a friend who is about to take drugs, a shop in which the wrong change is given and so on. These link quite strongly with the sort of moral dilemmas that have been often used and are perhaps especially relevant to the sort of work (and controversies) undertaken by Kohlberg (1973). Some of these everyday scenarios are rather open ended; others are remarkably clear in their 'answers' with rewards of points for achieving the right answer. Some resources provide a good deal of work around exemplary role models. In this type of approach, a hero is chosen and students are asked to learn about him or her, express a sense of wonder and consider how that individual could be emulated. In Australia an example from history education would be Simpson and his donkey. This account is well known to most Australian students. The story focuses on a first world war event in which Simpson acted heroically as a stretcher bearer using his donkeys to carry the wounded. This approach of focussing on heroes is used in a variety of places. Soviet Russia, for example, ensured that Stakhanov was widely praised and that people were exhorted to follow his example for capacity for hard work. There is also the use of sources – usually literature – that have, supposedly, the capacity to improve. So, cheap thrillers, violent video games and pornographic novels would debase students, while classic literature such as the work of Jane Austen would improve. Of course, the debates over the quality of this material and its effects are conducted fiercely. It is not unusual to witness debates between politicians who see their favourite authors as providing the moral weight to help citizens.

Some of the debate about teaching materials also relates to what is the key area of dispute between global citizenship education and character education – our fifth point. To what extent is the 'right' answer required? This is a complex debate as few would wish to embark on an educational programme that was exclusively concerned with morality or declarations that there are no connections with morality. But some clearly want guidance to be direct and specific. Character education can be defined as 'any school-instituted program, designed in co-operation with other community institutions, to shape directly and systematically, the behaviour of young people by influencing explicitly the non-relativistic values believed directly to bring about that behaviour' (Lockwood, 1997, p. 179, quoted by Arthur, 2003, p. 8). This quotation is phrased very carefully. Many would agree with the determination to develop non-relativistic values, making connections with the global rights and duties discussed elsewhere in this book and avoiding a sort of social vacuum in which anything goes. It would be hard to argue that those who promote global citizenship education do not have a preferred view of what justice means and how it can be achieved. But certain character education groups are, strikingly, very insistent on what is the right thing to do and some of the examples that may easily be found from character education programmes are congruent with what Kristjánsson (2013) – see above – has attempted to rebut. For example, the resources produced by the Jefferson Center for Character Education (see http://passkeys.org/programs/jc_star_teaching.html) are in places very noticeably specific and often related to the self-imposition of rules established by those who are more powerful than students (e.g. 'be here'; 'be on time'). There would be very few teachers who do not wish their students to attend school but this Center has attracted criticism for its commitment to very specific concrete approaches:

> A huge, multiethnic elementary school in Southern California uses a framework created by the Jefferson Center for Character Education. Classes that the principal declares 'well behaved' are awarded Bonus Bucks, which can eventually be redeemed for an ice cream party. On an enormous wall near the cafeteria, professionally painted Peanuts characters instruct children: 'Never talk in line'. A visitor is led to a fifth-grade classroom to observe an exemplary lesson on the current character education topic. The teacher is telling students to write down the name of the person they regard as the 'toughest worker' in school. The teacher then asks them, 'How many of you are going to be tough workers?' (Hands go up.) 'Can you be a tough worker at home, too?' (Yes.) (Kohn, 1997)

The debates about character education will continue and we suggest that our five points (status, wide-ranging aims to transform society, focus on morality, issues about implementation and provision of right answers) will help in determining the nature of the relationship between it and the sort of global citizenship that we outline in the first chapter. At the moment there are many examples of global citizenship education and character education which make it possible simply to identify character as more concerned with morality in ways that expect individuals to conform to established norms.

Annotated bibliography

http://www.goodcharacter.com/

Extensive list of resources including a daily dilemma, guide for student action, service learning and so on. These materials are meant principally for a US context and there are many ways in which this sort of material could be of interest in many other parts of the world.

http://www2.cortland.edu/centers/character/index.dot

Center for the 4th and 5th Rs (respect and responsibility). This is the base of Thomas Lickona. He has been very influential in developing ideas and also in the production of practical teaching resources. Some of his recent work (see the link to the Jubilee Centre given above as well as on this site) is connected to sex and relationship education and character. There are interesting issues about debates over 'ideal' family structures and the morality that is assumed to be relevant to them.

Jubilee Centre – http://www.jubileecentre.ac.uk/

The Jubilee Centre at the University of Birmingham has very quickly established itself as the leading centre for character education in the UK and it already enjoys an impressively wide international reach. Nicky Morgan when Secretary of State for Education in 2016 (Conservative) and politicians from other political parties have expressed their support. There is a wealth of academic and professional materials on the site. Some of the academic materials includes conference papers (e.g. http://www.jubileecentre.ac.uk/1643/conferences/cultivating-virtues) but there are also very many practical resources for professional contexts, including, for example, a series of stories on knightly virtues. There are resources available for all phases of education.

Kristján Kristjánsson (2013). Ten Myths About Character, Virtue and Virtue Education – Plus Three Well-Founded Misgivings, *British Journal of Educational Studies*, 61(3), 269–87 doi:10.1080/00071005.2013.778386

This is a very interesting piece of work in which a supporter of character education addresses critiques of that initiative and suggests developing a more positive outlook. He argues that certain criticisms are unjustified. He says that character education is not unclear, redundant, old-fashioned, religious, paternalistic, anti-democratic, conservative, individualistic, relative and situation dependent. But he says that there are 'three better-founded concerns'. They are: historical ('there cannot be a serviceable social scientific theory of virtue or of its constitutive elements without significant input from philosophical virtue ethics, any more than there can be a reasonably developed philosophical theory of virtue without grounding in the empirical knowledge of how people actually think about virtues and the way virtues actually inform their character'); methodological ('the study of virtue and character lacks a clear empirical methodology', and as such he recommends that research instruments are developed) and practical ('we know very little about the impact of previous interventions in this field').

Activities

1. The annotated reading list shown above gives access to a great deal of practical material. There is a wealth of material around moral development. It may be the case that almost all material that is related to moral education is relevant to character education. Some analysis of the various guidelines associated with that would be useful. Some recent work at the University of York includes an investigation into the nature of

values education offered officially in Mexico, Spain, China and England. The values that seem to be highlighted across all four countries are:

Freedom
Human Rights
Prosperity
Democracy (participation)
Equality
Justice
Rule of law
Patriotism
Dedication/honesty/friendship
Harmony/tolerance/ civility(politeness)
Solidarity
Socioeconomic development/civilization
Respect for diversity/non-discrimination/non-prejudice
Intercultural understanding

In Mexico and Spain the Catholic Church emphasizes religion and individual moral choice. In China the communist party is heavily involved in the development of education policy. In England there is commitment to a parliamentary democracy, some recognition of diversity within a Christian tradition and a history of social class formation and consequent exclusion and uneven distribution of social capital. Very broadly what do you think the different contexts mean for the list of values given above? Following some general reading about these countries, working with others and being, of course, extremely careful not to enter into simplistic and unacceptable stereotyping what, for example, would a commitment to freedom look like in Spain as opposed to China? What would solidarity mean in Mexico as opposed to England?

2. In the article cited above by Kristjánsson, he suggests that it is very difficult to judge the impact of character education as 'no tried-and-tested instruments to measure moral character – on a naturalist–realist conception – seem to exist'. He then suggests a way forward:

I see no other way out of this predicament for current character educators and virtue researchers than to try to design their own tests for measuring virtue – or at least to search for eclectic multi-criterial combinations of already existing measures that work better in tandem than individually (cf. Kristjánsson, 2010, pp. 51–2). To complicate matters, such measures need to be age specific, as young people will exhibit different virtues at different stages of their moral development.

Lawrence Kohlberg researched the stages of moral reasoning. To do so he used what has been referred to as the Heinz dilemma. This dilemma is widely available on the internet. Heinz is the name of the main character of a story who has to consider what to do in light of wanting to secure a drug to be used by a sick friend. The six stages of moral reasoning go from doing (or not doing) something principally to avoid punishment to a complex consideration of what doing the right thing means in the context of adherence to a principle of justice. Kohlberg's work has been praised by some and criticized by others.

In this task you should review with others the Heinz dilemma and decide whether we already have the sort of instrument that would deliver what Kristjánsson wants. Do we have a suitable instrument to understand the impact of character education programmes? If no, what would we need to do in order to develop such an instrument? In order to do this well you would need to be able to work well together, being constructively critical and genuinely open to a range of views.

13

Global Education

Education, including but not limited to schooling, is increasingly becoming a 'global topic'. More than often, policy-makers discuss modifications in national curriculums, changes on education provision or approaches to higher education in comparison to what happens somewhere else or what has been recommended by an international globalization. As result of this, what is taught in schools, universities and other contexts of education is changing to offer a more global outlook. Examples of these are the expansion of foreign language education, the growing number of courses on global education in education degrees, and the increasing relevance of global geography on geography curricula. There is also a wide range of resources and academic papers on 'global education'. When teachers, academics and policy-makers write about global education, however, they discuss at least three different fields of study. For some, global education gathers different discourses on how education should look in an increasingly globalized world. This involves a discussion around what aspects of education should or should not be universalized. For others, global education refers to the ways in which global organizations have an impact on national educational policy-making. For a third group of academics, global education refers to the ways in which global perspectives are incorporated into the curriculum. In this chapter we seek to outline the main discourses in these three fields of study and the interlinks between them.

Global discourses on education

The term global education often refers to a particular approach to the school curriculum that emphasizes the content related to the world understood in a geographical sense, takes a holistic approach to the curriculum breaking down traditional boundaries such as academic disciplines, cultures and so on and pays particular attention to the affective dimension of the curriculum including issues on school and classroom climate.

Global education is a contested terrain. Torres (2015) identifies three main views concerning the limits and possibilities that the globalization process has in our lives and therefore in education. Each of these views would understand global education in a different way and would evolve into different teaching practices. For some, the sceptics, globalization has had a negative impact on education. They believe that education should be essentially a national or local topic. For others, the hyper-globalizers, the acceleration of the globalization process is beneficial for educational policy and practice worldwide. A third group, the transformationists, believe that while certain forms of globalization could bring more justice-oriented educational policies and practices, other forms of globalization contribute to an increasing inequality.

Each of these groups is highly heterogeneous. Indeed, there is a wide range of views on the possible benefits and problems that globalization brings to the field of education and how educational policy and practice should respond to this globalization process. Through a review of the literature (Pike, 2008; Spring, 2004), we identify seven major discourses around these topics. Following this, we discuss each of discourses and their links with different views on global citizenship and global citizenship education (table 13.1). We have outlined several of these discourses in Chapters 1, 2 and 11.

Taking a sceptical starting point, a discourse of neo-conservatism understands that one of the main functions of education is the socialization of new generations in national values. As Diana Ravitch (2006) posited, in the case of United States, for some, the key purpose of schooling is to teach 'patriotism'. Through this discourse, global education is only considered as a discussion of the national contribution to the global. In the area of history, for instance, neo-conservatives would promote a curriculum focused on discussing the contribution of the nation to world history rather than looking at world history in itself. Indeed, this discourse could initially be considered a national discourse rather than a global one. However, on certain occasions the similarities between 'national' values and the 'global' ones are evident. The links, for instance, between human rights and national values are strong in some Western countries. In this discourse, global citizenship is not an aim itself but may be seen in relation to the ways in which it mirrors national values and national forms of citizenship.

A neoliberal discourse is based on the principles of neoliberalism, the economic philosophy whose origins can be found in economic liberalism that we introduced in Chapter 1. Neoliberal theorists, such as Milton Friedman or Friedrick Hayek, understand that competition is (and should be) the driving force of economy. Barriers for competition, such as visas for travellers and workers and import/export taxes, should be removed. If there is to be any role

TABLE 13.1 Discourses on global education and their ideal global education curriculum

			Links with		Ideal form of global education (examples)		
Discourse	Underlying theories	Perspective on Globalization	GC	GCE	Global knowledge	Global skills	Global ethics
Neo-conservatism	Conservatism	Sceptics	–	–	Contribution of the nation	–	National values
Neoliberalism	Economic liberalism	Ultra-globalizers	Neoliberal	Qualification	Global perspective on knowledge	Flexibility and communication skills	Respect
Human capital	Human capital	Ultra-globalizers	Neoliberal	Qualification	Languages	Problem solving, Financial literacy	Responsibility
World culture	World culture	Ultra-globalizers	Humanist	Socialization	Human rights, sustainability	Conflict-resolution	Human Rights
Liberal	Political liberalism	Ultra-globalizers/ transformationist	Humanist	Subjectification	Knowledge of world cultures	Critical thinking, deliberation	Empathy
Radical	Marxism	Sceptics/ transformationist	Critical	Subjectification	Economic structures of domination	Critical literacy	Social Justice
Postcolonialism	Postcolonialism	Sceptics/ transformationist	Anticolonial	Subjectification	Political, economic and cultural structures of domination	Critical literacy	Social Justice

for the state it should be to promote competition. According to the neoliberal school, only competition ensures the improvement of any economic entity (such as a business but also a nation-state or a school) and only through competition will the whole economy prosper. Globalization, in this respect, is considered to be positive since it has enhanced the number of competitors and the contexts of competition. Applied to education, neoliberal theorists understand that schools and other educational institutions should be entirely privatized. Schools and other educational institutions such as universities should compete in the marketplace to be more attractive to students. Educational systems should compete with each other in order to encourage the spread of the 'best' educational practices. Global education, in this respect, relates to economic global citizenship and to the qualification function of global citizenship education.

Human capital discourse is based on the economic theory of human capital. Drawing from the early economic liberalism of Adam Smith and in the later work of Jacob Mincer, human capital theory understands that human beings, their knowledge and abilities, are resources that encourage the economic productivity of countries. An investment on education and, therefore, on human capital will eventually contribute to national economy. However, in contrast with neoliberalist theorists who initially would encourage the education of knowledge and skills that make each individual competitive in the global market, human capital theorists attempt to reinforce the education of knowledge and skills that makes a national economy competitive against other national economies.

The world culture discourse is associated with humanist approaches to global citizenship and with the socialization function of global citizenship education. In the basis of this discourse lies the world culture theory's assumption that world cultures are increasingly integrating into a single culture that embodies the essence of human values and norms. Global education, in this respect, is about emphasizing this world culture including human rights, democratic values, cultural diversity and sustainability. The expansion of a particular form of formal education (mainly schools) worldwide demonstrates and contributes to the increasing relevance of this world culture. This discourse emphasizes the connectedness, in terms of shared universal attributes of humankind and the interdependence of all people within the global system.

Drawing on the liberal tradition of political philosophy, the liberal discourse is also connected to humanist forms of global citizenship. Associated with a particular understanding of the subjectification function of global citizenship education, liberal theorists understand that global education can contribute to the education of autonomous, reflective and literate individuals. Supporters of this discourse understand that global education might offer students global and multiple perspectives that will allow them to look beyond their cultural meanings. Under this tradition, Martha Nussbuam (2002), for instance, identifies three abilities that can be promoted through global education: the ability to criticize one's own traditions, the ability to think as citizens of the whole world and the ability to be empathetic.

The radical discourse criticizes how globalization has accelerated economic inequality between and within countries. Drawing upon Marxist analysis, authors such as Wallerstein have developed the world systems theory. From a sceptical position, supporters of this theory criticize how the world is increasingly divided into two unequal zones – the rich countries and the poor ones. Through education and other cultural activities, the rich nations inculcate their capitalist and neoliberal values into the poor ones with the purpose of maintaining their economic power over them. Some radical theorists criticize how through global education people from poor countries are educated with skills and knowledge that will serve the economy of the wealthy nations. Some radical theorists, however, take a more transformativist approach and understand that alternative forms of global education that challenge structures of power and domination are possible and desirable. Global education, from this perspective, should be about uncovering economic inequality between the rich and the poor nations, emphasizing social justice, political activism and critical empowering pedagogy. By doing so, the radical-transformationists' views are associated with critical forms of global citizenship and with the subjectification approach to global citizenship education.

The postcolonialist discourse draws upon postcolonialist theories such as those developed by Fanon, Bhabha, Mignolo, Said and Spivak to criticize how globalization contributes to the worldwide imposition of cultural, economic and political agendas that benefit wealthy nations. By doing so, postcolonialist theorists argue, globalization is contributing to an increasing level of power held by some over others and at the same time destroying cultures, ways of lives and environments. Global education, including the expansion of schools worldwide, is contributing to the homogenization of the culture of the wealthy nations. Postcolonialists criticize how national history curricula worldwide often seem to present a single form of world history – the history of Western powerful men. Similarly to the radical discourse, some scholars (e.g. Andreotti, Shultz) take a transformationist view and understand that global education can contribute to the subjectification function of education by encouraging critical global citizens. In other words, they propose a de-colonized form of global education (table 13.1).

Global influences in education

International organizations (IOs), and more precisely, intergovernmental organizations (IGOs) such as the United Nations or the World Bank play an essential role in the distribution of these different discourses on global education.

Rutkowski (2007) identifies four different ways in which IGOs promote certain discourses on global education, essentially neoliberal and human capital discourses but also world culture discourses. In his views, IGOs promote these discourses through a construction of:

- Multilateral space for 'soft laws' to be formed. IGOs promote certain vague, imprecise a delegated laws that although the in theory allowed, they are not 'compulsory' and therefore, not brought into being. For instance, the UN's Universal Declaration of Human Rights specifies that 'everyone has the right to education' but it is not clear who needs to ensure this right or what are the consequences if this right is not guaranteed. Through the creation of these soft laws, IGOs, particularly the United Nations and UNESCO, promote, essentially, the world culture discourse. Views on global education, including what constitutes education, what constitutes knowledge, skills and ethics are universalized through particular understandings of education. As an example, UNESCO's policy, Education for All, promotes the schooling of children across the world from early years to secondary education.

- Means to directly implement policy through loans and grants. IGOs such as the World Bank offer loans and grants to various bodies (from countries to charities). The groups that share (or follow) the IGO's views on what education should be about (e.g. global knowledge and skills) are more likely than others to be awarded these loans and grants. For instance, Mahon (2010) reports how the World Bank, through strategic loans and grants, privileges the neoliberal discourse by encouraging private schools over public schools. This way of influencing national policy-making is often perceived as being highly problematic by post colonialist and 'radical' authors. IGOs are seen as implicitly imposing Western types of education systems that are not culturally sensitive and that do not benefit the interest of the local students

- Multilateral space to create and exchange policy knowledge. Some IGOs such as UNESCO are powerful entities that can organize international conferences, distribute educational resources and contribute to international educational research. Though all these activities, they might privilege certain discourses about global education over others. For instance, from 2013, UNESCO has organized periodic forums on global citizenship education. UNESCO's particular views on what a better global education would be like are discussed in the context of the forum as well as distributed through declarations and work documents.

- Expertise in measuring and evaluating educational policy. PISA, for instance, is a well-known international strategy of assessment that belongs to the OECD, an organization of countries that promote economic prosperity among its members. OECD promotes human capital discourse on global education through PISA. By creating a world-league table in which countries are ranked according to students' performances, the OECD selects areas of knowledge that are considered to be essential for national economies and the ways in which these areas are evaluated. From 2012, PISA includes evaluation on numeracy, literacy, science, problem-solving and financial literacy. Quite often, policy-makers across the world refer to PISA to argue how aspects of the national curriculum in their own countries should be expanded – usually without valuing humanities and social science subjects – to ensure national economic prosperity. International strategies of assessment such as PISA are often criticized by a number of scholars. A number of ethical questions can arise from the use of these evaluations. For instance, who benefits from these evaluations? Who has the ethical authority to decide what is a 'good' education system? Why are certain type of knowledge and skills considered to be valuable and others are not?

Conclusions

The field of global education is extremely complex and has strong links with the field of global citizenship. However, whereas global education focuses on analysing the ways in which education is universalized, including but not limited to the curriculum, and in discussing whether or not this universalization should take place, the field of global citizenship questions the type of citizenry that we, as a global society, should educate. In this respect, we feel as Davies, Evans and Reid (2005) argue, that the field of global citizenship education can bring together both traditions and shed some light to examine the present society, to discuss how a better society would look like and to analyse how we can move from our present to this more desirable future.

Annotated bibliography

Davies, I., Evans, M. & Reid, A. (2005). Globalising citizenship education? A critique of 'global education' and 'citizenship education'. *British Journal of Educational Studies*, 53(1), 66–89.

Davies, Evans and Reid discuss in this article the main similarities and differences between global education and citizenship education. Analysing the theoretical basis and the curriculum implementations of both traditions in England, the authors outline the strengths and weaknesses of each area and the possibilities for global citizenship education. Particularly relevant, in our understanding, is the clear differentiation that the authors establish between these areas. Whereas in other papers the use of 'global education' and 'global citizenship' seem to be unclear, in this paper, there is precise description of each of these areas in relation to the other.

GENE Global Education Network Europe. http://gene.eu/

This is the institutional website of GENE, the global education network Europe, the network of ministers and agencies with national responsibility for global education in European countries. The website gathers reports on the situation of global education, in particular, European countries such as Portugal, Finland and Poland. The website might be of particular interest to those who are interested in the ways in which global education is embedded in educational policies and curricula.

Schooling the World. http://schoolingtheworld.org/resources/educators/

This is the website of the documentary we identified in Chapter 4. In this website, a number of resources (primary, secondary and higher education) for educators are presented. The resources include teaching materials, videos and reports that can be used in a classroom context to discuss different issues related to global education.

Spring, J. (2004). *How Educational Ideologies Are Shaping Global Society*. Hillsdale, NJ: Lawrence Earlbaum.

In this book, Joel Spring discusses different discourses on global education. Focusing on most of the discourses that we have outlined in this chapter, the author presents a detailed account of the theoretical basis of each discourse as well as providing examples of practical implementations of the principles of each discourse in the global and national policies worldwide. The book is detailed and well documented and we consider it to be an excellent resource for those who are interested in the links between political and economic ideologies and their links with global education.

Standish, A. (2014). What is global education and where is it taking us? *The Curriculum Journal*, 25(2), 166–86.

In this article, Alex Standish analyses the development of global education in the last 50 years, considering the links with different political and economic ideologies and policies. Although the author focuses his work on a comparison of global education in the United States and England, the paper clearly illustrates different approaches to global education and it describes how these approaches are implemented in the curriculum and in educational practices. For those who are particularly interested in looking at global education from a curriculum design point of view, the last section of the paper is particularly helpful in highlighting different understandings of the meaning of global knowledge, skills and ethics.

Activity

In this exercise, we would like you to examine the underlying discourses on global education of different institutions by analysing some of their institutional documentation. Follow the links below and discuss, for each of them, which is the discourse on global education that emerges from the text.

- KEPA (2014). Enhancing Southern voices in global education. https://www.kepa.fi/sites/kepa.fi/tiedostot/julkaisut/enhancing-southern-voices-in-global-education.pdf.
- Reimers, F. M. (2014). Bringing global education to the core of the undergraduate curriculum, diversity and democracy, http://www.aacu.org/diversitydemocracy/2014/spring/reimers.
- Education Services Australia (2014) Global Perspectives: A framework for global education in Australian schools, http://www.globaleducation.edu.au/verve/_resources/GPS_web.pdf.
- OECD (2014) PISA Trifold Brochure http://www.oecd.org/pisa/aboutpisa/PISA-trifold-brochure-2014.pdf.
- UNESCO (2016) Education 2030. Incheon declaration and framework for action towards inclusive and equitable quality education and lifelong learning for all. http://unesdoc.unesco.org/images/0024/002432/243278e.pdf.
- World Bank (2011) Learning for all. Investing in people's knowledge and skills to promote development. Washington: World Bank. http://siteresources.worldbank.org/EDUCATION/Resources/ESSU/Education_Strategy_4_12_2011.pdf

Consider three documents presented above and identify the ways in which these IGOs can influence national educational policies and practices.

14

Peace Education

Global citizenship and issues of peace, violence and war are, of course, inseparably connected. Individuals and groups who wish to explore and establish global citizenship must be concerned with individual, interpersonal, structural and societal issues relevant to peace. Clauswitz, the philosopher of violence, may have believed that war is the continuation of politics by other means, but the poet Henry Disney is more likely right in his perspective that war is the failure of politics. If the attempt to achieve reconciliation of different interests leads to violence, then global citizenship is thwarted.

Peace education may be defined in various ways. A useful overarching statement is:

> [The] transmission of knowledge about the requirements of, the obstacles to and possibilities for achieving and maintaining peace, training in skills for interpreting the knowledge, and the development of reflective and participatory capacities for applying the knowledge to overcoming problems and achieving possibilities. (Reardon quoted by Tint and Koteswara Prasad, 2007, p. 24)

The disciplines and individual key thinkers that are drawn upon by peace educators are extremely diverse. Sen's (1989) capabilities approach (going beyond utilitarianism to emphasize the significance of being and doing in the achievement of justice) is attractive to some; the radical alternative schooling approaches led by A. S. Neill (1966) (himself inspired by Reich's psychological theorizing and a commitment to freedom) and the 'green' ideas that promote small, human-scale development of Schumacher (1973) and others are all relevant.

A key consideration often referred to by peace educators is the nature of peace and violence. Hicks (1980) has suggested that there are different forms of violence which may be broadly referred to as direct and indirect. Direct violence would include personal attack, involvement in terrorist outrages, war and so on. An absence of that would in Hicks's view allow for the achievement of negative peace. Indirect violence is largely seen as involving structural conditions of poverty, exclusion and marginalization and an absence of that would be seen as positive peace.

Hicks then uses these ideas to suggest that there are different approaches to peace education:

- *Peace through strength*: essentially seen as armed deterrence designed to ensure that superiority is maintained
- *Conflict mediation and resolution*: analysing conflict and making suggestions(and, crucially, being alert to the inequalities which may have led to the initial conflict)
- *Personal peace*: emphasizing empathy and cooperation
- *World order*: a global perspective which aims to link personal and global change
- *Abolition of power relationships*: raising awareness of structural violence and aligning oneself with all oppressed groups

As such, in light of these characterizations of peace, it is no surprise that there are various forms of peace education. Harris (quoted by Tint & Koteswara Prasad, 2007) refer to five main types:

1) Global Peace Education, which includes international studies, holocaust studies, and nuclear and disarmament studies; 2) Conflict Resolution Programs, which teach about mediation, negotiation, and various communication skills; 3) Violence Prevention Programs, which emphasize domestic violence, drug abuse, anger management, and the teaching of tolerance; 4) Development Education, which includes human rights education, environmental studies, and an emphasis on power, resource inequities, and structural violence; and 5) Nonviolence Education, which finds roots in the teachings and philosophies of Martin Luther King, Mahatma Gandhi, and other great peacemakers (p. 24).

There may be others that could be added to the list above. Hicks (1988, p. 8) suggests that aims of peace education include:

- exploring concepts of peace both as a state of being and as an active process
- enquiring into the obstacles of peace and the causes of peacelessness in individuals, institutions and societies

- resolving conflicts in ways that will lead towards a less violent and a more just world
- exploreing range of different alternative futures in particular ways of building a more just and sustainable world society.

Locked into the above discussion about positive and negative peace are issues about what might be seen as personal and/or public matters. The distinction between these things is often seen as crucial for determining the sort of work that could take place with learners. Some have suggested in certain aspects of – or, perspectives about – global citizenship that public matters should be the principal focus. Personal matters, so the argument goes, are not about things like citizenship, which is, at least in part, seen as being part of a legal and political status. Of course, the dividing line between the public and the private is not so straightforward and at least some aspects of peace education rely heavily on individual psychological and spiritual matters as well as interpersonal and societal considerations.

At the heart of much peace education is a view of the learner that is set against an alleged version of what currently exists in most schools. Learners are essentially seen as interacting in non-peaceful ways. Whitaker (1988) outlines his stance against a view as follows:

1. Pupils cannot be trusted to learn
2. An ability to pass examinations is the best criterion for selection and judging potential
3. What a teacher teaches is what a pupil learns
4. Knowledge is the steady accumulation of facts and information
5. An academic procedures, for example, the scientific method, is more important than the idea it is intended to investigate
6. Pupils are best regarded as manipulative objects, not as persons (p. 25).

He argues that instead of the above, a ten-point guide should be used as follows:

1. Emphasize learning how to learn
2. Learning is a journey not a destination
3. Pupils and teachers should relate to each other as people and not in terms of their roles
4. Priority should be given to the self-concept as the determinant of successful learning

5. The inner intuitive emotional and spiritual experiences of pupils should be regarded as vital contexts for learning

6. Encouragement should be given to divergent thinking and guesswork

7. Age specific learning should give way to variable and flexible age groupings

8. Greater attention should be given to the learning space with more attention to colour, comfort, personal space and privacy

9. Community education should be seen as an opportunity to break down the traditional association of learning with schools and institutions

10. Teachers should be regarded as learners too learning alongside the pupils they teach

The pedagogy of peace is a very important way of characterizing the nature of peace itself (e.g. see Hicks, 1988).

Critiques of peace education

It would seem difficult to disagree that peace is preferable to violence but as with much else to do with global citizenship there are several complex strands to consider.

It may be suggested that peace is not natural and it not helpful in the development of a better world. Of course, – hopefully – no one actively promotes war for the sake of it but it is commonly suggested, or at least implied, that struggle whether in political, economic or military contexts is necessary for the achievement of progress. Orson Welles's famous speech in the classic film *The Third Man* focuses on the Renaissance achievements of a society led by the violent Borgias with other more pacific places ('In Switzerland they had brotherly love – they had 500 years of democracy and peace, and what did that produce? The *cuckoo clock*.'). In fundamental terms these issues link with arguments about selfishness and altruism that are biologically determined or informed (Dawkins, 1976).

The purposes of peace and peace education are obviously relevant in political situations. During the 1980s, in many parts of the world, any attempt to ban nuclear weapons (e.g. by the Campaign for Nuclear Disarmament) was seen as a naïve ideological initiative which would not bring peace to the world. President Reagan pronounced that his additional arms-spending led successfully to the end of the Cold War. One seems close here to Orwell's discussion of Big Brother in the classic novel *1984* in that war is asserted to have the same meaning as peace. Interpretations of these matters, as might easily be imagined, vary hugely. But accusations of peace education as a form of politically inspired indoctrination have often been made (and have led to guidelines that are meant, variously, to restrict so-called dangerous teachers or to safeguard the professional work of those teachers). If the purpose of teachers is to educate *about* peace, to educate *through* peaceful means (even if they are working in an undemocratic environment of a school) and perhaps to educate *for* peace mean that these allegations are unlikely to ever go away completely.

There are concerns that peace education may simply lead to externally imposed outcomes. Much of this perspective connected to dependency theory – the idea that even if well-intentioned support offered by rich to poorer countries leads to a lack of autonomy and independence. There may be something to that thesis but it may not be entirely fair unless we suggest that organizations such as the Global Peace Foundation (https://www.globalpeace.org/about-us) should not, for example, continue its work in Cambodia. For the work of such organizations to be criticized we would need to see their workers imposing a foreign ideology and deliberately or unintentionally encouraging dependency, which weakens a country's ability to address its own problems. Some go even further and suggest that even if a poor country is helped, that supportive approach only indicates a failure to be patriotic as every other country is loved but one's own.

A critique which is related to the point about dependency (but distinct from it) is that peace education has tended to flourish in countries which have had to rebuild following significant defeats. Post–World War II Germany has seen good examples of peace education (see Duczek, 1984). At times this work in Germany was connected to educational and other programmes of de-Nazification. Germany's foreign policy is now criticized by some who feel that its leading position within the European Union has led to economically aggressive actions (perhaps especially towards Greece) but its adherence to peace seems still very strong. In May 2016, Germany (together with China and the UK) topped an Amnesty International poll to indicate a welcoming approach to migrants. Although Amnesty felt that this indicated a split between people and governments it is possible to argue that there is still a strong humanitarian impulse (https://www.amnesty.org/en/latest/news/2016/05/refugees-welcome-index-shows-government-refugee-policies-out-of-touch/).

Peace education can be seen very clearly in Japan. Avenell (2015) argues that in the immediate post-war period and especially during the American occupation until 1951, a victim culture was in evidence. In other words, the defeated had to learn their lessons. However, in the context of a developing economy and a national – and, crucially, international – engagement, a very different approach emerged. Opposition to the Vietnam War was just one of the factors that led to a changed perspective and which has helped Japan argue for peace through strength. Avenell argues that 'transnationalism in civic movements from the 1960s onward must be taken into account as a key variable in any explanation of the emergence of civil society in contemporary Japan' (p. 380). We should not state these things too strongly. The 2016 elections in Japan, which strengthened the position of Prime Minister Abe, may be seen to assist the development of military capability. In the context of territorial disputes in the South China Sea, we cannot be sanguine about the prospects for peace or for peace education.

A final critique to be considered here is that peace education lacks rigour. Perhaps the most well-known critics taking this line are Cox and Scruton (1984). In a very trenchant criticism, they argued that peace education is merely an excuse for political posturing. It is not immediately obvious why issues of war and peace should be regarded as being intellectually less demanding than other things. Perhaps attachment to the bureaucratically established single academic disciplines means that interdisciplinary work is less highly regarded. It is more likely that accusations were being made about peace educators' political intentions. Scruton elsewhere (Pike & Selby, 1986) attacked global education and wrote passionately about education and indoctrination. It is perfectly possible, of course, for all those who consider peace education (and indeed education of any sort) as an attempt to engage in influencing learners' views of the world. Whether there is any more evidence of peace educators doing this in inappropriate ways as opposed to, say, historians who are firmly committed to particular political positions and political parties remains a moot point.

What essentially is revealed by a consideration of these issues, approaches and debates is that global citizenship is intrinsically linked with peace education. Continued exploration of the precise nature of this connection is needed to ensure that peace is clarified and achieved across the globe.

Annotated bibliography

Avenell, S. (2015). Transnationalism and the evolution of post-national citizenship in Japan. *Asian Studies Review* 39(3), 375–94.

Japan is sometimes, erroneously, represented by Japanese people as well as by outsiders as a culturally homogeneous and a national entity that is unusually separate from others. This article discusses the impact of transnational work which meant that activists in Japan moved from a victim status as a result of oppression by the state and industry to a more confident and outgoing sense of self.

It is well worth looking at the work of Lynn Davies. Three books in particular are:

Davies, L (2004). *Conflict and Education: Complexity and Chaos.*
London: Routledge.

Davies, L (2008). *Educating against Extremism.* Stoke-on-Trent:
Trentham books.

Davies, L (2014). *Unsafe Gods, Security Secularism and schooling.* Stoke-on-Trent: IOEPress/Trentham books.

In these books Lynn Davies explores many issues about peace and conflict, making very good use of debates in feminism and referring to struggles to ensure fair and just resolution regarding the rights and identities of diverse communities.

Peace Education Foundation. http://www.peace-ed.org/

This is an US-based organization with an internationalist outlook (some of the materials are in Spanish and French as well as English). It contains practical resources as well as a discussion of ideas and issues in a series of research papers.

Pike, G. & Selby, D. (1988). *Global Teacher, Global Learner* (1988).
London: Hodder and Stoughton.

This is a rather old book but an excellent resource. It is packed with very good educational activities that are of great educational value and that actually work. But there is also an excellent overview of the aims of global education. Many of those aims link directly with the aims of peace education. There are several key areas: systems consciousness; perspective consciousness; health of planet awareness; involvement consciousness and preparedness; and process mindedness. As one might imagine, this work has been strongly criticized by the opponents of global education and peace education – it is (supposedly) academically weak, politically motivated and so on. But it is well worth reading, and the opportunity to try out the activities leads to great fun as well as worthwhile professional work.

Tint, B. S. & Koteswara Prasad, G. (2007). Peace education in
India: academics, politics and peace. *The Canadian Journal of Peace and Conflict Studies* 39, (1–2), 23–37.

In some ways one might imagine India to be centrally concerned with peace education. The life and work of Gandhi play an important part in the life of the country. But he is not viewed positively by all, and this article points to the dearth of activities around peace education. It does, however, announce the establishment of the Centre for Peace and Conflict Resolution Studies (CPCRS) in 2003 at the University of Madras.

Activities

1. There are various fables that can engage children and adults and can lead to some high-level discussion. Aesop's fables are easily available. One example is shown at http://www.taleswithmorals.com/aesop-fable-the-town-mouse-and-the-country-mouse.htm. In this story, the town mouse invites the country mice for a meal. The town mouse has fine food available. But during the meal dogs begin to bark. The mice run away with one shouting, 'Better beans and bacon in peace than cakes and ale in fear.' A discussion about this should bring out issues to do with the different types of peace (avoidance of conflict; achievement of basic and preferred living standards; limits to toleration; possible action against aggressors and so on).

2. The following is ambitious but, if practical circumstances allow, it should give rise to some very interesting and valuable work. We advise great care towards ethical matters. You would not, of course, want to do anything which might put someone in a difficult position. You may wish to review ethical procedures that are used by academic associations to check that your actions are appropriate. Developing insights into conflict in different parts of the world gives students an opportunity to understand the nature of conflict and how particular differences might be resolved. On the basis of existing contacts and with the knowledge of the limits that are sensible for your own particular context, make contact with people in two countries. Ask those people, separately, to do three things: (a) describe a current public conflict (it might be about a disagreement over government policy, an argument with another country, a story about interference in a celebrity's personal life or another matter); (b) highlight three possible ways in which agreement could be reached; (c) choose one of those three methods and explain the reasons for the judgment. Now each of the people who are not from the country where the dispute is taking place are allowed to do two things: ask questions for clarification; make a suggestion about how the dispute could be resolved. The person in the home country has to come up with a response to the questions and suggestions. All participants are now encouraged to find a common agreed way forward.

15

Diversity Education

On 7 January 2015, twelve people were killed in Paris (France) by two individuals who identified themselves as belonging to al-Qaeda's branch in Yemen. Eleven of the victims were journalists working in the satirical newspaper Charlie Hebdo. Charlie Hebdo has repeatedly published caricatures of Muhammad the Prophet and jokes on Islam considered by some as an example of hate speech (Brooks, 2015). All around the world, people demonstrated their support to the victims and to the 'right of speech' through the slogan *Je Suis Charlie* (I am Charlie). In France, the French constitution (the declaration of rights of the man and the citizen) states in its article 11, 'The free communication of thoughts and of opinions is one of the most precious rights of man.' In this respect, for some, the attack was considered not only an attack against the lives of journalists but an attack against the French community denying one of their most precious rights. The slogan *Je Suis Charlie*, however, was immediately followed by another slogan: '*Je ne suis pas Charlie*' (I am not Charlie). At the same time of condemning the violent action, critics of the satirical newspaper also appeared around the world. For example, the US columnist Roxane Gay (2015) wrote, 'Murder is not an acceptable consequence for anything, [. . .] Yet it is also an exercise of freedom of expression to express offense at the way satire like Charlie Hebdo's characterizes something you hold dear – like your faith, your personhood, your gender, your sexuality, your race or ethnicity.'

These two different reactions illustrate some of the debates on citizenship and diversity. The question of diversity is at its base a question of how different communities can live together without oppressing one another and how individuals in some occasions struggle to be members of different communities when their values and rights are in opposition.

Diversity and forms of diversity

Scholars often attribute three key meanings to the concept of diversity (Cooper, 2004; Taylor, 2012). First, diversity describes complex social realities where communities coexist and where individuals might simultaneously belong to more than one community. Second, the concept of diversity brings into discussion the relationship between groups – including but not limited to the relation between majorities and minorities – and the consequences of this relation on issues on equality, justice, discrimination and power relations. Third, diversity involves consideration of how these realities and relationships can be 'valued, assessed and managed' (Taylor, 2012, p. 1). Diversity education, in this respect, focuses on how educational policies and practices respond to this social complexity and its consequences.

Discussions on diversity – understood as the relationship between groups – are complex and need to be contextualized. Majority and minority groups, dominant and non-dominant groups can be different in different settings. For instance, whereas Muslim citizens belong to a minority and non-dominant community in Denmark, in Algeria, they are the majority and the dominant group. But, there is much diversity within the Muslim community. For example, in Algeria, the Shia community represents only 1 per cent. Diversities can be multiple and often overlapping.

In each context, the institutional powers decide, which non-dominant and minority communities need to be particularly considered to be given specific representations and rights. For instance, the South African Constitution was the first constitutional law that specifically acknowledged diversity in relation to sexual orientation. In a wider context, the universal declaration of human rights explicitly mentions race, colour, sex, language, religion, political or other opinion; national or social origin, property, birth or other status.

Diversity and citizenship

The debate on diversity and citizenship is mainly a debate about how to ensure that citizens can simultaneously be part of different communities without challenging the existence of the communities themselves and without failing to act appropriately in oppressive situations. Quite often, this includes discussions on how individuals might be integrated into the national community without having to renounce their membership to a minority cultural group (e.g. religious, ethnic and language). A feeling of common citizenship, Kymlicka (2011) argues, is essential for the social cohesion of the national community. To exist, communities require a minimum of common/shared aspects – a minimal universalism (Olssen, 2004) – but in which that 'minimum' is contested. On the one hand, if communities allow each group within the community to keep their own rights and values, there is a question of the survival of the wider community. Individuals might stop identifying themselves with the large community because they feel they do not share anything with the other members. This can challenge social cohesion and to an extreme, the community itself. If, on the other hand, communities demand that individuals renounce their other traditions, values and identities in order to share the community's rights and values, dominant values can be imposed and a process of oppression might occur. Kymlicka (1998) refers to integration as a 'two-way process' where the dominant society must also adjust and become more open and just towards minorities.

Different philosophical and political traditions have different understandings of how this balance between shared-non-shared should be kept. In the following, we review four main approaches to this discussion considering their implications for education and for global citizenship education.

- 'Segregationist' approaches (Joppke, 2007) or what Banks (2008) calls 'differential exclusion' draws upon ethnic understandings of the community to approach diversity. The basis of this approach is the assumption that citizenship is associated with biological heritage. The borders between those who are included and those who are excluded in the community are established when one is born, giving little scope for the inclusion of the others. Critics of this perspective understand that the limits between segregation and institutional forms of racism, ethnocentrism, extreme nationalism and religion fundamentalism are blurred. Segregationist views on education would encourage the creation of different schools, curricula and policies for different communities even within the same state. In the example of Apartheid South Africa, for instance, four school systems coexisted in the same country, one for each of the four racial groups the society was divided into: White; Black; Indian; and Coloureds. It is unlikely that those who agree with segregationist approaches to diversity would support education for global citizenship. At most, we understand that those people would promote exclusive forms of global citizenship in which only the members of the original community would be welcomed.

- In the liberal assimilationist approach, citizenship refers to the relationship between the individual and the state where all individuals are expected to be equally treated under the law (Kymlicka & Norman, 1994). Through this approach, individuals are expected to renounce those values, views and traditions that are contradictory with the national ones in order to be fully integrated in the national community. Although for those who hold alternative views on citizenship this was always problematic. A consideration of different forms of social diversity (e.g. class and gender) recognizing issues on recognition justice (see Chapter 10), and the increase of cultural diversity in most contemporary societies has made more visible some of the controversies associated with the assimilationist approach. In education, policies following the liberal assimilationist approach have attempted to integrate students into national forms of citizenship. This includes, for instance, the immersion in the national language and national values. In England, the Department of Education, as part of the counter terrorist agenda decided to promote 'British Values' in schools. British Values, explicitly described as 'Democracy, tolerance for other faiths and beliefs, individual liberty and the rule of the law' are often perceived as an attempt to 'assimilate' students belonging to the Muslim community into liberal secularism (Arthur, 2015). Indeed, as Ahmed (2012) explains, 'The difficulty for liberals is that individual autonomy rests on truths they consider to be 'self-evident' and universal. Whilst liberalism argues that reason must challenge dogma, many non-western peoples challenge non-negotiable liberal truths as dogmatic and oppressive' (p.728). The liberal assimilationist approach has certain similarities with some humanistic forms of global citizenship. The basis of these forms of global citizenship contains two different assumptions. First, that global community requires a set of shared aspects – a minimal universalism – to be constituted as community and to allow sense of belonging and participation of the citizens. Second, only those who accept and integrate these shared aspects including rights, duties, shared interpretations and knowledge (e.g. human rights and international languages) are considered global citizens. Critics of this approach would challenge the idea that the constitution of these shared aspects necessarily create or reinforce power relationships between those whose rights, culture and traditions, are appropriated as global and those who are not.

- Multiculturalism draws upon liberal egalitarian and communitarian philosophy to highlight that groups as well as individuals should be entitled to rights. In contrast with the liberal assimilationist approach, multiculturalists understand that a legal or minimal citizenship (few shared aspects) is the only way to avoid situations of oppression. Citizens would mainly be members of their near communities and the links with wider communities (e.g. the state) would be through their rights/duties relationship as individuals and through their group rights. In this school of thought, Marion Young (1989) understands that members of minority or oppressed groups will only be included in the wider community if their group membership is considered. A 'differentiated citizenship', Young argues, is necessary. In this respect, three types of group rights should be considered (Kymlicka & Norman, 1994): special representation rights, self-government rights and multicultural rights. Particularly relevant for education, multicultural rights would include public support for non-dominant languages education and ethnic studies in schools. Multiculturalism has strong links with cultural approaches to global citizenship. Diversity is highly valued and there is an attempt to be respectful and welcoming to all communities. Some critics of this form, however, highlight how Western rights (e.g. Human rights) remain as the essential common aspects imposed everywhere else. Other critics, instead, emphasize how a minimal citizenship based on this approach is unlikely to create the necessary global cohesion to be able to talk about a global community. Through multiculturalist ways of approaching diversity, these critics argue, the different communities are kept isolated and they coexist rather than contribute to the larger community.

- Pluralist theorists, such as Robert Dahl, argue that power in society is distributed among a number of groups in competition. For them, the balance of majorities and minorities is in constant movement. For instance, someone might be in 'power' if we consider his economic status, but might belong to a religious minority, who might be oppressed. In this respect, majority and minority, dominant and non-dominant values, rights and understandings, would compose (and perhaps compete) in the larger community. Critics of pluralism often emphasize that pluralists are too optimistic in terms of power distribution. Power, they argue, is often concentrated in some hands and some forms of power – such as economic power – are more relevant than others. Within the pluralist approach, two different approaches are in evidence. Liberal pluralism, drawing on the work of Rawls, Habermas and Arendt, understand that different communities could participate in a deliberation process that would end in defining a set of shared values and understandings and therefore in a more harmonious community. Agonistic pluralists such as Chantal Mouffe, instead, argue that pluralism cannot be dissociated from conflict and so the community should offer spaces and institutions where this conflict might take place. In relation to global citizenship, in both cases there is a demand for global spaces of discussion. However, whereas liberal pluralism can be associated with some humanistic forms of global citizenship, agonistic pluralism is more likely to be associated with critical global citizenship. In terms of education, although both forms of pluralism would support the existence of education settings (e.g. schools) where students from different communities are educated together, these forms of pluralism approach diversity education and global citizenship education in different ways. For the liberal pluralists, diversity education can be understood as democratic education in the way Parker (2008) describes. This is through a process of deliberation in which students attempt to identify and solve controversial issues. The agonistic pluralist, however, suggest that students should not learn how to solve controversial issues but rather how to live with this controversy. For the agonistic pluralists, diversity education is associated with political education in which students learn how to respect the adversary at the same time as fighting for their own demands (Ruitenberg, 2009).

Conclusions: a diverse global community

Discussions on the global community necessarily involve a debate on how diversity should be tackled in this global community. A global community requires a minimal universalism that keeps the whole community together but what is and what should this minimal be, is highly contested. Advocates of some humanistic and critical understandings of global citizenship would argue that this minimal universalism should be composed by ideas on global social justice, equality and concerns on the threats to the world community, such as environmental, health and peace issues (Banks, 2008). Education for global citizenship should contribute to the reinforcement of the global community through ESD, peace education and social justice education. All these concepts, nevertheless, are controversial as we have highlighted in previous chapters. If diverse views on these ideas are integrated within this minimal universalism, there is a risk of weakening the shared values. If, instead, some views are privileged through, for instance, Human Rights, there is a risk of attempting to impose dominant understandings (e.g. Western ones) on non-dominant communities.

Multiculturalist theorists' views on global citizenship would defend a more minimal form of citizenship. The challenge here is whether this would contribute to a global community or only to the coexistence of the communities within the globe. If students are taught to feel solidarity and respect for the others rather than with the others, the challenge is to accept shared responsibility and to contribute together through global engagement (Osler & Starkey, 2003). Global multiculturalism is also challenged for its relativism. By ignoring situations of oppression and inequality, there is a risk of contributing to pre-existent power relations (Andreotti, 2011).

Pluralist views on diversity are associated with critical forms of global citizenship and, in our understanding, with subjectification approaches to global citizenship education. Here there is an understanding that the global community should be constituted through the contributions of all communities in the globe. Educational settings, in this respect, could be understood as spaces where these contributions are negotiated or disputed. For instance, students from different communities could be encouraged to discuss how the global community should look like. Whereas liberal pluralists would expect students to reach an agreement, agonistic pluralists would expect a permanent discussion. In the first case, the challenge is in reaching agreements that equally satisfy different communities. In the second case, there is a risk of falling into never-ending discussion on problems requiring immediate decisions (e.g. global warming).

Annotated bibliography

Banks, J. A. (2008). Diversity, group identity, and citizenship education in a global age. *Educational Researcher*, 37(3), 129–39.

James A. Banks analyses in this paper different contemporary ways of facing diversity education. The author establishes clear links between these forms of diversity education and different approaches to citizenship education. We find particularly interesting the discussion around globalization and diversity education. The author examines the ways in which globalization has had an impact (e.g. migrations) on formal education contexts and how diversity education might shed some light to discussions around global citizenship and global citizenship education.

Edmunds, J. (2013). Human rights, Islam and the failure of cosmopolitanism. *Ethnicities*, 13(6), 671–88.

In this article, June Edmunds examines the way in which present forms of cosmopolitanism accommodate non-Western cultures. In particular, she focuses on how Muslim communities can be included/excluded from discourses and policies on European cosmopolitanism. She discusses several European examples including Germany, Italy, Belgium, France and UK and she concludes that secularist cosmopolitanism tend to exclude European Muslims. She argues for the need to look at some forms of Islamic cosmopolitanism to identify ways in which global forms of citizenship might be more inclusive.

Soysal, Y. & Wong, S. (2013). Diversity from within and without: comparative notes from France and Japan. *Multicultural Education Review*, 2(1), 77–92.

This article represents a good example of how national policies can be examined through the lens of diversity education. The authors compare diversity education as encountered in the curricula and textbooks of history and citizenship education in Japan and France. The examples illustrate two different ways of approaching diversity with France tackling diversity in a context of complex dynamics between postcolonial, national and European citizenship; and Japan understanding diversity in the global – and to a lesser extent – national context.

UNESCO (no date) Cultural Diversity. Available online at http://www.unesco.org/new/en/education/themes/leading-the-international-agenda/education-for-sustainable-development/cultural-diversity/ (15 March 2016).

In this website, UNESCO gathers different resources associated with cultural diversity worldwide. Along with a description of UNESCO's approach to diversity education, the website has links to different UNESCO policies and reports including information about minority languages; and the links between cultural diversity and biodiversity. We find the website particularly useful to identify worldwide case studies in which different approaches to diversity can be examined and considered.

Activity

In this chapter, we propose you analyse how different countries face religious diversity in school settings. Although the most controversial case is probably France, which in 2004 banned any sign of religious affiliation in any public schools (including the Muslim hijab), other countries have taken varied approaches to religious diversity. In this respect, we would encourage you to read the article by Smith (2007) and to examine the approaches taken by France, Turkey, the UK and Uzbekistan. More precisely, we would encourage you to consider:

- What type of diversity does the article consider?
- What are the minimal common aspects that each country has considered appropriated?

- What is the approach to diversity education that each country has taken?
- In which ways does each particular country relate to discussions on global citizenship education?

Smith, R. K. M. (2007). Religion and education: a human rights dilemma illustrated by the recent 'headscarf cases'. *Globalisation, Societies and Education*, 5(3), 303–14.

16

Education for Sustainable Development

Many young people today were introduced to the idea of sustainable development through learning about the Millennium Development Goals (MDGs) mentioned in Chapter 11. Developed in 2000 as part of the UN Millennium Declaration, they set a deadline of 2015 to reduce poverty in so-called developing nations. Recently, the Sustainable Development Goals have replaced the MDGs and apply to all nations. Target 4 focuses on quality education. In sub-target 4.7 sustainability and sustainable development are featured along with global citizenship:

> By 2030, ensure that all learners acquire knowledge and skills needed to promote sustainable development, including, among others, through education for sustainable development and sustainable lifestyles, human rights, gender equality, promotion of a culture of peace and non-violence, global citizenship and appreciation of cultural diversity and of culture's contribution to sustainable development.

Sustainable development and education for sustainable development (ESD) are ubiquitous terms today. They are used by many organizations from non-governmental organizations (NGOs) and civil society organizations (CSOs) to multinational corporations, among many others. This chapter focuses on how the work of the UN and its related organizations has shaped the discourses of sustainable development and ESD and has influenced their prominence today. This chapter is divided into several subsections. First, we look at how sustainable development is linked with ESD and how ESD has evolved as an international discourse and area of debate. Next, we look specifically at some tensions within the field of ESD including its conflation with environmental education and the role of indigenous perspectives. Finally, we consider how ESD relates to global citizenship education.

Sustainability and education for sustainable development: history and debates

One of the most common definitions of sustainability is from the Bruntland Report of 1992: 'development that meets the needs of the present without compromising the ability of future generations to meet their own needs' (World Commission on Environment and Development, 1992, p. 41). The report sought to address the fact that so-called undeveloped countries experienced poverty and environmental degradation. The concepts of sustainable development and ESD are deeply connected to the different approaches to, and critiques of, international development, education for development and development education reviewed in Chapter 11.

Building from the Bruntland Report's concept of sustainability, the term ESD can refer to 'a set of processes, pedagogies and practices which seek to ensure that education systems are responsive to, and prepared for, current and emerging sustainable development challenges' (Mochizuki & Bryan, 2015, p. 5). The UN declared 2005–14 the UN Decade of Education for Sustainable Development (UNDESD). The aim was 'to integrate the values inherent in sustainable development into all aspects of learning to encourage changes in behaviour that allow for a more sustainable and just society for all' (UNESCO, 2006, p. 4). In this section, we provide a brief timeline to review some of the main milestones and challenges in the evolution of sustainable development and ESD through UN processes. We draw on the reflections of Hopkins (2012) based on his direct involvement as a contributor to the UN's work in ESD. We then look at the critiques and continued points of tension inherent to ESD.

- 1972: World Conference on human environment in Stockholm

The 1972 conference in Stockholm was the first international meeting addressing pollution and environmental degradation. Outside the buildings housing the meetings, the conference was met by protests by NGOs and civil society groups, including a strong presence of indigenous peoples, demanding action on issues ranging from pollution to civil rights. A group of scientists who had also gathered raised warnings about population growth, increased pollution rates and continued unfettered use of natural resources.

The World Conference in Stockholm began important conversations and led to governments starting to have some policies regarding environmental protections, with some even creating ministries for environment. However, according to Hopkins (2012), there was no significant progress in environmental legislation in the decade following. He attributes this to a push-back against environmental regulation from the private sector, as multinationals continued to move into and expand their work in developing countries. The growing rift in equalities between 20 per cent of the world's population living in the Global North and 80 per cent in the so-called developing world prompted the UN to initiate a commission of experts representing various regions of the UN under the lead of Gro Harlem Brundtland (then prime minister of Norway).

- 1982: Submission of the Brundtland Report, our common future: Sustainable development used as a key concept

By using the term sustainable development, the commission called for economic development that would last over time and not compromise future generations:

> If large parts of the developing world are to avert economic, social, and environmental catastrophes, it is essential that global economic growth be revitalized. In practical terms, this means more rapid economic growth in both industrial and developing countries, freer market access for the products of developing countries, lower interest rates, greater technological transfer, and significantly larger capital flows, both concessional and commercial. (World Commission on Environment and Development, 1987, p. 89)

The critiques of the liberal capitalist paradigm reviewed in Chapter 11 can be applied to the way that development is framed in this excerpt where economic growth is positioned as the main or only way to improve the situation. Based on the acceptance of world leaders from close to 200 countries, the UN proposed a global implementation plan to adopt the recommendations of the Brundtland Report (Hopkins, 2012).

- 1992: The United Nations Conference on Environment and Development in Rio de Janeiro
- Main outcome document: 'Agenda 21: An action plan for the twenty-first century' (United Nations, 1992) included specific conventions on biodiversity, climate change, forestry and desertification as well as a declaration of principles of sustainable development. 'Chapter 36: Education, public awareness and training' included ESD.
- Drafting the Earth Charter began as part of the lead up to the Rio conference as an intended universal declaration and was continued afterwards.

At the 1992 Rio Conference, often referred to as the Earth Summit, the term sustainable development became accepted internationally. Almost all the nations of the world participated in the conference, and Article 21 (United Nations, 1992) set a new course for international development. However, critics point out that using the term sustainable development as a basis for the conference did not offer anything new and continued rather than questioned a growing neoliberal agenda (Castro, 2004). Trade liberalization was promoted alongside environmental protection measures without fully grappling with the mutually reinforcing relationship between growing corporatization and environmental degradation. A key idea of the conference was that countries in the Global South needed help to train people to achieve sustainable development. Thus, a problematic underlying assumption positioned marginalized or 'periphery' nations and peoples in a deficit view: 'developed countries are to provide technical assistance, and the indigenous people and communities are to be trained in sustainable development' (Castro, 2004, p. 199).

Importantly, the Earth Charter was an attempt to address a recommendation in the World Commission on Environment and Development for a universal declaration to frame sustainable development work. The drafting and adoption of the Charter did not happen at the Rio conference and was redesigned as a civil society initiative after the conference. There was a world-wide participatory consultation process, and the Earth Charter was written and published in 2000. It affirmed three key pillars of sustainable development: social, environmental and economic wellbeing. The Earth Charter continues as a civil society movement; however, it has not been formally adopted as a universal declaration.

Education was mentioned across the Chapters of Article 21, but was a main focus of Chapter 36. Hopkins (2012) notes an important decision was made in the lead-up to the Rio conference that ESD was to be a systemic approach not an add-on subject. Hopkins (2012) suggests a major flaw from the ESD perspective was that the conference focused mostly on scientific understandings of environmental issues at the expense of other social and political factors tied into sustainability issues. Consequently, environmental educators ended up the main supporters and leaders of Chapter 36 despite the wide range of education fields and subject areas required to address the issues included. He notes a lack of engagement with Ministries of education and laments the formal education systems generally turned their backs on ESD due to budget cuts, the rise in popularity in large scale monitoring systems and already bursting curricula content.

- 2002: World Conference on Sustainable Development in Johannesburg ends with decision to make 2005–14 the UN Decade of ESD (UNDESD).

- 2009: Bonn hosts World Conference on ESD where engaging formal education systems in ESD is a focus.
- 2012: UN Conference on Sustainable Development in Rio establishes the SDGs framework established with ESD included in Goal 4.7.
- 2014: UNESCO World Conference on ESD in Nagoya sets up the Global Action Plan on ESD to scale up concrete actions and contribute to the SDGs.

Since the turn of the 21st century, ESD has become a major focus of United Nations work highlighted by the decision to make 2005–2014 the UNDESD. It is thus important to consider the benefits and limitations to conceptualizing and applying the idea of sustainable development to education.

Fonesca de Andrade (2011) wrote a reflection on his participation in a UNESCO young people's forum that ran in parallel to the 2009 Conference in Bonn. As a Brazilian representative, he found some significant contradictions. He noted too much focus on reducing poverty in so-called developing nations of the Global South without a critical view as to on going the generation of wealth and consumerist cultures in the Global North. His reflection highlights that these tensions persisted despite the transformative intentions of the UNESCO (2006) work. Therefore, a main risk and challenge in the use and application of the term sustainable development is the tendency for it to suggest change while avoiding the political nature of the actions that could actually address the roots of sustainability issues. Importantly, as Hayward (2010), points out: 'our sustainability crisis is a complex, multifaceted series of dynamic problems that we cannot address independently. In this sense, our sustainability crisis is also a deep political crisis' (p. 9). Because the SDGs have only recently been adopted, only time will tell if the shift to a focus on all nations being accountable for change will addresses this critique.

Similarly, Huckle and Wals (2015) reviewed the materials created in support of the UNDESD. They note the strong emphasis on change and acknowledgment of growing global problems. However, 'shifts in values, lifestyles and policy within prevailing forms of society, [were seen to be] sufficient to put global society on a sustainable path' (p. 491). They found there was a positive spirit in a vision that everyone should be able to access education that provides the opportunity to contribute to a sustainable future through positive transformation of society. Yet, again, there was a lack of analysis as to how politics and power relations would have to shift in order to transform societies and enable sustainability.

Rathzel and Uzzell (2009) warn that the concept of sustainable development is a policy negotiation term used where there are concerns around how to enable economic growth and acknowledge environmental protection. They warn against assuming a neutral application of the concept of sustainable development to education, particularly if the goal is to promote lasting and systemic change. They suggest that the original policy-focused idea of sustainable development actually conceals deep value conflicts in communities in order to find policies that can encourage economic development. Thus, they suggest that ESD inherits this tendency that works against true transformative learning.

Another key tension has to do with short-term indicators and long-term potential for ESD. Vare and Scott (2007) argue there are at least two different, if complementary, approaches conflated into the idea of ESD. One promotes informed, skilled behaviours and ways of thinking that meet short-term goals, whereas the other is more about building a capacity to critically engage with research and explore the contradictions and challenges of living sustainably. They warn that the tendency is to focus on the first in isolation of the second.

ESD and environmental education

As Hopkins (2012) pointed out in his critical reflection on the pre- and post-Rio 1992 process, ESD was first taken up largely by environmental educators (based in science and geography). An important concept was contributed in 1996, when Wackernagel and Reis promoted a tool that provided a graphic account of how much physical space is necessary for a given population in terms of manufacturing, distribution, consumption and waste (Hayward, 2012, p. 143–4). The idea of the 'ecological footprint' caught on as a good way to illustrate how the ecological system cannot keep up with the rate of material consumption and use of energy. It effectively raised awareness and enabled discussions about other ways to measure human consumption (e.g. carbon and water footprints).

The ecological footprint inspired another educational concept: the ecological handprint. Where the footprint focuses on one's negative impact on the environment, the handprint focuses on what individuals can do to change their footprints. This example is a case in point regarding the pedagogical tensions inherent to ESD. Hayward (2012) points out that the handprint can certainly promote a positive impact of engaging students in their local communities to make significant behavioural changes such as increasing recycling. Yet, she warns, 'there is also a risk in celebrating the power of local action that we overlook the ways that the actions of individuals are constrained and mediated by a wider context, including their social institutions, cultural norms and economic institutions' (Hayward, 2012, p. 146). She suggests that it may be more effective to promote youth to use a variety of methods to target various levels of local, national and international decision making:

In an era of global environmental change, effective, collective citizen action will require careful thought about the way we use our hands to effect change to ensure we are not simply displacing or obfuscating the problems, let alone making things work. Before rushing to leave our handprint, we need time to reflect on the possible consequences of our actions, listening carefully to all voices, including children. (Hayward, 2012, p. 147–8).

Hayward (2012) argues that it is important to bring together underlying principles of environmental education together with those of citizenship education. This would encourage a link between learning about environmental issues and taking action from within students own contexts to promote change. She also argues that young people must be at the centre of creating a vision of sustainability: 'This is easier said than done. Most Anglo-speaking democracies don't really want to think about children or adolescents at all, let along rethink our ideas about ecology, democracy or citizenship from their point of view' (p. 13). Often environmental and citizenship education are 'separate silos'; however, bringing them together 'recognises that citizenship is not only legally-defined membership of a political community, but also a state of belonging, feeling affiliation and participation in communities that can extend across national borders and acknowledge intrinsic value of the non-human world' (Hayward, 2012, p. 13).

ESD and indigenous perspectives

Another important critique of sustainable development and ESD has come from a variety of indigenous perspectives through a concern about the Western-centric perspective at the root of the very notion of sustainable development. Chapter 4 provides more information about the importance of de-colonial processes and frameworks. A suggested resource in Chapter 4, Schooling the World, speaks to the ways formal schooling is intrinsically linked to colonialism. Ironically, there are many instances around the world where children are removed from environments in which they learn to have a sustainable relationship with nature in order to send them to school. Then, there is much effort at deciding on the right curriculum that will teach them to have a sustainable relationship with nature, while making it increasingly difficult for them to do this. Thus, an important area of research in the field of ESD is a re-centring of indigenous knowledges and ways of being in formal and informal education settings. This section considers two examples of many.

First, Mokuku (2012) outlines the work in Lesotho where there have been significant initiatives in relation to ESD. These include the addition of ESD concepts and theories to the formal curricula including 'a holistic view of the environment; action competence as a goal for environmental education; integration and infusion of environmental issues across subject disciplines; a thematic approach to teaching and school environment policies; and outdoor learning' (p. 160). Another important initiative has included promoting critical reflection among teacher educators as to what is a 'Lesotho-centred meaning of ESD' (p. 160). Mokuku (2012) laments that these developments have had a limited capacity to develop a contextualized meaning of ESD in Lethoto and calls for a stronger focus on indigenous African-centred worldviews. Such an approach would further emphasize interconnectedness, harmony, balance and holism and reveal indigenous knowledges: 'Mainstreaming these concepts in our ESD discourse could unleash untapped potential, and engender a new consciousness and unanticipated ways of envisioning a sustainable future' (Mokuku, 2012, p. 170).

A second example is the continued debate about how to involve 'traditional ecological knowledge' in ESD across contexts. Reid, Teamey and Dillon (2002) highlighted the importance of traditional ecological knowledge (TEK) in ESD, recognizing a Western-centric bias. They noted that it is often outsiders who conceptualize ESD and how TEK could be added: 'While TEK tends to be associated with the diversity of knowledge, innovations and practices that indigenous communities hold about the biophysical, socio-economic and cultural-historical aspects of their local environment, it is also often defined in opposition to (Western) modern, scientific conceptions of knowledge' (p. 113). They suggested that educators who do not identify as indigenous can consider TEK in their understandings of ESD by starting from the position that there is not a coherent definition of TEK. This leads to a pedagogy of what we do not know: 'Do we – and perhaps, more importantly, *why* and *where* do we – inquire what lies beyond our terminologies, thinking, and assumptions about ecological knowledge and sustainability in environmental education?' (Reid et al., 2002, p. 130). This is an important departure from the trend of either not including indigenous perspectives in ESD or including them merely as a novelty and/or as a type of local mysticism (O'Donoghue & Russo, 2004).

Overall, a general project of de-colonizing ESD through de-centring neoliberal and Western-centric approaches and re-centring on indigenous ways of being and ways of knowing is an area of research growing in prominence and importance. In a 2014 special issue of the journal *Environmental Education Research* on land education, scholars provide a range of perspectives on the important ways 'the ongoing colonization of land and peoples are in fact embedded within educators' and researchers' practices and understandings of (environmental) education around the globe' (Tuck, McKenzie & McCoy, 2014, p. 1).

ESD and citizenship education: linking to GCE

Building from the critique of a lack of fulfilment of the transformational potential of ESD, there has been a push to emphasize its ties to citizenship education. Bringing together environmental education and citizenship education 'recognises that citizenship is not only legally-defined membership of a political community, but also a state of belonging, feeling affiliation and participation in communities that can extend across national borders and acknowledge intrinsic value of the non-human world' (Hayward, 2012, p. 13).

In a similar vein, based on their review of the UNDESD, Huckle and Wals (2015) suggest that global citizenship education should be central to ESD (p. 493). They promote the concept of Global Education for Sustainability Citizenship through four dimensions:

- The *scale* dimension focuses on how individual and collective actions have impacts on humans who live far away and on non-humans: 'students should recognize that a focus purely on individuals' values and lifestyles serves to depoliticize and privatize a very political and public issue, and thereby contributes to the reproduction of the status quo' (p. 494).

- The *ethics* dimension encourages students to 'consider their own behaviour, and that of others, in relation [to] issues of justice/injustice; right/wrong; rights/obligations; and sustainability/unattainability' (p. 495). This involves moral development and looking at human rights and different ways of contributing to cultures of peace.

- The *relational* dimension considers how ideas like sustainability and citizenship represent a variety of values and interests. Media education raises awareness of how sustainability issues find their way into our lives: 'Links to social movements and school students in other parts of the world, via social media, should enable them to understand how concepts of sustainability and citizenship are changing under the influence of such movements, and how dialogue across space can engender global solidarity' (p. 495).

- The *political* dimension encourages students to examine the structural causes of issues of the environment and development. This also enables them to consider reforms and radical approaches to change as they study and engage with various actions by government and non-government organizations and civil society movements.

There are strong links between the contested history and present of ESD and GCE. At the heart of both are key tensions around who is seen as developed or developing and as helper and helpee, and how to challenge those binaries in order to promote a notion of interdependency that is at the core of our earth's sustainability crises.

Annotated bibliography

http://earthcharter.org/discover/the-earth-charter/

The Earth Charter is an ethical framework for building a just, sustainable and peaceful global society in the twenty-first century. It started as a UN initiative and was later taken on as a civil society initiative. The drafting included consultations with people all over the world. The website of the Earth Charter Movement includes a history of the drafting of the Earth Charter, the Earth Charter itself, and links to various programs and initiatives around the world using the Earth Charter as an inspiration.

https://www.viacampesina.org/en/

The website of La Via Campesina, an international peasants movement, provides an example of a civil society movement bringing together peasants, small and medium sized farmers, landless peoples, women farmers, indigenous people, migrants and agricultural workers from all across the globe. The website includes an overview of the movement itself, its mission to oppose corporate driven agriculture, and provides materials about news updates from their partners, their conferences and publications.

Environmental Education Research, Volume 21, Issue 3

This is a special issue that explores how environmental education is shaped by the political, cultural and economic logic of neoliberalism. Articles cover a range of topics from ecotourism to urban planning, community organizing, higher education and critical environmental education. By focusing on the political aspects of ESD and covering perspectives from both the Global North and the Global South, the special edition both contests neoliberalism's conceptions of economic growth and hyper-individualism while suggesting alternative ways of imagining the connection between the environment and building just communities.

Hayward, B. (2012). *Children, Citizenship and Environment: Nurturing a Democratic Imagination in a Changing World*. Cornwall, UK: Routledge.

In this book, Hayward draws on experience with young people in New Zealand whose lives were immediately touched by poverty and social inequality alongside devastating earthquakes. She uses data from her research with these children to argue for a bridging of environmental education with citizenship through the SEEDS approach: Social agency, Environmental education, Embedded justice, Decentred deliberation and Self-transcendence. The book combines strong theoretical critique with insightful research and promotes concrete ideas for educators.

Activities

1. In what ways has ESD inherited and/or challenged the critiques of development discussed in Chapter 11? Make a mind map linking the theoretical paradigms of development (liberal capitalist, Marxist, liberal egalitarian, postcolonial and radical) and their critiques with the key mile stones and debates in the evolution of sustainable development and ESD reviewed in this chapter.
2. In their opening editorial to a special issue about the UNDESD, Nambiar and Sarabhai (2015) promote a turn towards GCE to help fulfil the transformative potential of ESD:

   The critical contribution that the global citizenship approach makes is in providing a uniting and galvanizing principle for ESD by seeking to identify skills, values and approaches that are essential for sustainable development in a conceptual framework that is amenable to implementation across formal and informal education systems and at all levels. By seeking to re-politicize people along global lines through high-lighting skills needed for [sustainable development], [GCE] is capable of bringing the radical change agenda implicit in ESD in a universally accepted way. (p. 2)

   Critically consider Goal 4.7 of the SDGs that starts off this chapter in light of Nambiar and Sarabhai's (2015) claim above. To what extent are ESD and global citizenship mutually reinforcing or distinct as educational agendas? Select one or two examples of developments in the history of ESD (and corresponding tensions/critiques) outlined in this chapter and consider to what extent a global citizenship approach would contribute to 'the radical change agenda implicit in ESD in a universally accepted way'.

PART THREE

Key Issues in Research and Practice in Teaching and Learning about and for Global Citizenship

This part of the book contains five chapters: research; curriculum; community; teaching and learning; and, evaluation. In this section of the book we get closest to practice (although all of the book indicates the sorts of things that may be done by professionals and others). We explore what we know on the basis of research and scholarship, what is used to frame professional engagement, what specific pedagogical approaches are used (and could be used) and how we can begin to make sense of the ways in which judgments are made about the quality of educational work. By the end of this section of the book you will have consolidated your understanding of key ideas and reflected on the ways in which global citizenship education may be developed and reviewed.

17

Research

In this chapter, we review some of the research that has been conducted on global citizenship and education. As we were writing these lines, we conducted a search on an academic search engine with the terms 'global citizenship' *and* 'education' in English, Spanish and French. Unfortunately, we were unable to review articles written in any other language. We obtained 30,958 results from which 16,860 had been written from 2010. We assume that if we have included other terms usually used such as 'cosmopolitanism', 'world citizenship' or 'planetary citizenship', we would have obtained an even larger number of results. We felt it was impossible for us to review in this chapter all these articles. Instead, we committed ourselves to the task of reviewing a sample of 100 of these articles. We only reviewed articles published in academic journals or books between 2005 and 2017 that specifically refer to empirical research studies. We focused on reviewing studies examining global citizenship education as encountered in policy documentation or in formal educational contexts (primary, secondary and higher education). Finally, we only analysed those studies that convey an overall picture of the research field we have examined.

Research on policy, curriculum and other forms of written documentation

Research has been conducted to examine how discussions on global citizenship are included in the national curricula of different countries. Kennedy (2012) using data from the International Civic and Citizenship Study (ICCS, 2009) conducted in thirty-eight countries suggests that national rather than global perspectives continue to dominate civic education curricula worldwide. In a review of European policies, Philippou, Keating and Ortloff (2009) conclude that global citizenship education is a secondary or supplementary concern built on top of national approaches to citizenship education. A similar situation seems to take place in United States. At least in Virginia, standards are devoid of any cosmopolitan influence (Journell, 2010). In Central and South America, some countries such as Colombia emphasize global citizenship as an additional layer to national citizenship whereas others, such as Cuba, seem deliberately to avoid discussions on global citizenship (Sant & Gonzalez, 2017). In Hong Kong, Kwan-choi Tse (2007) presents a situation where global, national, local and ex-colonial discourses compete to gain curricular supremacy.

Researchers have also examined the way global citizenship is portrayed when discussed in the curriculum. Global citizenship is presented essentially in relation to social-justice principles and/or global capitalism. In some cases, these discourses are integrated. This seems to be the case in the Philippines and the United Kingdom (Camicia & Franklin, 2011; Marshall, 2009; Oxley & Morris, 2013). In other cases, global citizenship is essentially associated with a particular discourse. In the United States, global citizenship is often related to issues on national security and global capitalism (Philippou, Keating & Ortloff, 2009). Similarly, in Singapore, global citizenship is essentially presented as a way of promoting the country as an international hub for education (Daquila, 2013). In contrast, in Hong Kong and Ecuador, global citizenship is constructed through discourses challenging injustice, discrimination, exclusion and inequality (Chong, 2015; Sant & Gonzalez, 2017).

Some researchers have also examined the ways in which global citizenship is presented in textbooks. After an examination of 500 worldwide textbooks, Buckner and Russell (2013) concluded that there are major similarities in the ways textbooks look at global citizenship education. Worldwide textbooks, they argue, often mention human rights, international events and contents emphasizing international interconnectedness. In contrast, after their comparative analysis of English, German and Swedish textbooks, Wermke, Pettersson and Forsberg (2015) suggest that there are major differences in the ways textbooks from different countries approach global citizenship. For instance, German textbooks seem to present global citizenship as a threat whereas English textbooks relate global citizenship to multiculturality (Wermke et al., 2015).

Research on primary and secondary education

There is a limited body of research exploring what happens in primary and secondary schools in relation to global citizenship education (Myers, 2010). Research conducted in Northern Ireland, England, Catalonia and the United

States suggest that students do not tend to identify as global citizens but rather they privilege their national or cultural affiliations (Meyers & Zaman, 2009; Reilly & Niens, 2014; Sant et al., 2016). Indeed, in the United States, a case study of sixty-five secondary students suggested that a third of the students might perceive these forms of citizenship as being in conflict (Myers, 2010). This study also revealed that students essentially understood global citizenship as moral global citizenship, with students thinking that global citizenship is about having a moral commitment to improve the world. In contrast, in Spain, researchers found that most primary students often understand global citizenship in relation to environmental issues (Benedito-Vidagany, et al., 2016).

Researchers have particularly focused on investigating how international students understand global citizenship. In the United States, Myers and Zaman (2009) compared global and national affiliations between immigrant and dominant-culture students. The authors concluded that whereas students from immigrant background favoured universal positions, dominant-culture students privileged their national affiliations. In contrast, in Australia, some research suggests that international students reinforce their national affiliations when they are abroad (Matthews & Sidhu, 2005). International students do not feel more 'global' but they adopt some sort of 'flexible citizenship'. This is, they 'use material and symbolic resources to position themselves to maximize advantages under circumstances where choices constitute and straddle economic, national and geopolitical power dynamics' (Matthews & Sidhu, 2005, p. 60). A reason for this is that, as suggested by the authors, international secondary students often feel excluded by local students and, in practice, limited communication is established between both groups.

There is relatively limited research on how global citizenship is included in schools' practices. In the United States, Parker (2011) concluded that public schools adopting 'international education' often approach global citizenship from contradictory approaches. Although a discourse of national security dominates professional contexts there are competing discourses on global perspectives, cosmopolitanism and international student body (Parker, 2011). In the UK, schools have introduced a global dimension to the curriculum (including forms of global citizenship education) in a wide variety of ways including curriculum initiatives, school clubs, awards and schools councils (Bourn & Hunt, 2011). In the Canadian province of Saskatchewan, teachers seem to include many notions related to global citizenship education – such as globalization and multiculturality – although they do not necessarily associate these topics with global citizenship education in itself (SCIC, 2016).

There is considerable research exploring how teachers perceive global citizenship education. The way teachers understand global citizenship is likely to be different in different parts of the world. In the United States and in England, teachers associate global citizenship with notions of cultural diversity (Osler, 2011; Watson, 2015). In the Netherlands and Germany, by contrast, teachers understand global citizenship in relation to a universal morality (Ortloff, 2011; Veugelers, 2011). Some research suggests that Chinese, Canadian, English and Northern Irish teachers are enthusiastic about teaching global citizenship education (Larsen & Faden, 2008; Lee & Leung, 2006; Osler, 2011; Rielly & Niens, 2014; Yamashita, 2006). By contrast, US teachers are likely to be less enthusiastic than others (Rappoport, 2010).

Teachers face a number of barriers when they attempt to include global citizenship education in their practices. Teachers in the United States, China, Northern Ireland and Canada report they have a lack of conceptual and pedagogical knowledge to know how to teach global citizenship education (Larsen & Faden, 2008; Lee & Leung, 2006; Rappoport, 2010; Rielly & Niens, 2014; Yamashita, 2006). US teachers, for instance, tend to rationalize unfamiliar concepts related to global citizenship with more familiar concepts (Rappoport, 2010). In Ontario, although the civics curriculum and the standards for teaching are global citizenship education-friendly, teachers still have to interpret the prescribed curriculum imaginatively in order to justify teaching about global citizenship (Schweisfurth, 2006). Teachers in China express how exam-orientated curricula constrain the inclusion of global citizenship education in their practices (Lee & Leung, 2006). Teachers in Canada and in Northern Ireland report a lack of time and resources to include global citizenship in their practices (Larsen & Faden, 2008; Rielly & Niens, 2014).

Research on higher education

There are a larger number of research studies conducted in higher education settings. However, it is important to highlight that most of this research has been conducted in English-speaking countries. In a review of previous research and policies, Haigh (2002) highlights the increasing level of interest on issues on internationalization of higher education being caused by two factors: economic outcomes from international students and the attempt to make higher education graduates globally competitive. In England, the extent in which each higher education course incorporates global citizenship education depends on the institutional strategy (Lunn, 2008). Studies investigating academics' views also suggest that the ways global citizenship education is included in particular courses in Ireland, Australia, New Zealand, Netherlands, South Africa, Colombia and the United States, depends on the area of study and the commitment of particular academics (Clifford & Montgomery, 2014; Lunn, 2008; Sawir, 2011; Trahar, 2011).

In his review, Haigh (2002) also identifies a wide range of strategies used by universities in their attempt to promote global citizenship. This includes teaching of foreign languages, encouragement of abroad experiences, employment of international staff, incorporation of global perspectives in the curriculum, creation of new courses associated with minority groups (e.g. black studies) and creation of spaces where international and local students can interact. Among these strategies, the impact of abroad experiences (including exchange programmes, the students education placements and service-learning in other countries) on students' understanding and knowledge about global citizenship is probably one of the most thoroughly investigated fields. Hong Kong students with experiences abroad have positive attitudes towards global citizenship education (Chui & Leung, 2014). In contrast, US-educated Koreans hold higher levels of national identity than their peers educated in Korea (Cho & Chi, 2015). Research conducted in the United States suggests that experiences abroad do not necessarily help students to develop deeper levels of intercultural competence (Dolby, 2007; Root & Ngampornchai, 2012). Although there are contradictory results about the impact of the time abroad on students' learnings and understandings (Horn & Fry, 2012), research suggest that abroad experiences are more influential to British and US students when these experiences are structured and when they combine an academic focus with more experiential situations (Horn & Fry, 2012; Tarrant, 2010; Tarrant, Rubin & Stoner, 2014).

Previous research has also examined the opportunities for global citizenship education in local settings. Some studies have investigated online collaborations between students from different parts of the world (Harshman & Augustin, 2013; Patterson, Carrillo & Salinas, 2011). Such collaboration, the researchers argue, offer great opportunities for global citizenship education (Harshman & Augustin, 2013; Patterson, Carrillo & Salinas, 2011). Similar optimism can be found in the research conducted by Montgomery & McDowell (2009) in the United States. For the authors, the contact with international peers might enhance global citizenship education. In contrast, research conducted in the UK suggests that local students do not necessarily interact with international students and therefore the potential benefits for both are lost (Peacock & Harrison, 2009). In this respect, two small-scale studies, one in the UK (Spiro, 2014) and the other in the United States (Coryell, Spencer & Sehin, 2013), highlight that to be meaningful, the contact between students from different backgrounds needs to be structured and articulated through a collaborative community of learning practices, sharing similar teaching and learning goals. Caruana (2014) and Woolley (2008) in two other small-scale British projects suggest exploring students' identity through cultural biography and storytelling (Caruana, 2014) and through an exploration of their own spirituality (Woolley, 2008) as a way to re-conceptualize global citizenship. Miller (2013) and Bamber and Hanking (2011) in two other British case studies, highlight how university students can enhance their understanding of global citizenship through structured activities involving academic content and service learning with international communities in local settings.

A few researchers have analysed the effect of making changes in the higher education curriculum. Studies undertaken in the UK (Brookes & Becket, 2010; Jones & Killick, 2013) and Australia (Breit, Obijiofor & Fitzgerald, 2013) highlight the need for staff development in order to include global citizenship education in the higher education curriculum. After their experience of de-Westernizing the curriculum, Breit et al. (2013) also understand that a global citizenship approach requires not only the incorporation of new content but also the reconceptualization about the entire teaching and learning experience.

Other scholars have conducted qualitative research exploring how higher education students perceive global citizenship. In research examining how 642 university students worldwide understand global citizenship, Parmenter (2011) highlights that students associate global citizenship with self-transformation, engagement with the international community, connectedness and human-bigness. Parmenter (2011) also highlights that students who manifest a higher engagement with environmental issues are more likely to identify themselves as global citizens. Research conducted in Hong Kong found that Hong Kong university students essentially perceive global citizenship in its economic dimension (Chui & Leung, 2014). In contrast, students from Manchester (UK) seem to understand global citizenship in relation to the economic dimension but principally in relation to the cultural dimension, including notions of diversity, identity, interconnectedness and mobility (Prowse, 2013).

There is a group of studies investigating how pre-service teachers understand global citizenship and whether they are willing and ready to include global citizenship education in their practices. In Europe, Spanish pre-service teachers understand global citizenship in relation to Human Rights and equality (Colomer Rubio, Campo Pais & Santana Martin, 2016). In England, trainees related global citizenship to notions of culture, the global, tolerance and diversity (Davies & Fülöp, 2010). Hungarian pre-service teachers, in contrast, understand global citizenship in relation to the EU, (foreigners and immigrations (Davies & Fülöp, 2010).

Research conducted in Turkey, England, Wales and Ireland highlight that pre-service teachers are interested in including global citizenship education in their prospective practices (Berna & Aytac, 2012; Holden & Hicks, 2007; McCormack & O'Flaherty, 2010; Robbins, Francis & Elliott, 2003). In the case of Turkish student teachers, this willingness seems to be shaped by whether or not they speak a foreign language and by their daily internet use (Berna & Aytac, 2012). In England and Wales, the trainees' main teaching subjects mediate their attitudes towards global citizenship education (Holden & Hicks, 2007;

McCormack & O'Flaherty, 2010; Robbins, Francis & Elliott, 2003). Although student teachers are essentially willing to teach global citizenship, researchers also highlight that they don't feel confident to include global citizenship education in their practices and they don't understand it as a priority in the curriculum (Holden & Hicks, 2007; McCormack & O'Flaherty, 2010; Robbins, Francis & Elliott, 2003).

Conclusions: possible gaps in the research field of global citizenship education

At the time of writing this chapter, we feel that there is a considerable corpus of research examining global citizenship education. In some contexts, where higher education institutions have demonstrated a clear economic interest in promoting global citizenship, the volume of research is, indeed, highly extensive. Our review suggests that researchers have investigated how to promote different forms of global citizenship (mainly neoliberal and humanistic) through different pedagogical strategies. We feel, however, that most of these studies discuss the impact of pedagogical strategies in terms of immediate consequences. In contrast, there is a lack of longitudinal studies observing how students' understanding and knowledge about global citizenship is (or, is not) influenced by educational practices over longer periods. More ethnographic and mixed-methods research studies could be conducted to understand these possible changes and continuities.

In most primary and secondary settings, policy-makers and – perhaps as a consequence of this – researchers have privileged national rather than global approaches to citizenship education. Studies on primary and secondary schools often investigate global citizenship education as a secondary concept related to wider approaches to global education or citizenship education. Therefore, there are a number of research gaps including how primary and secondary students across the world understand global citizenship, what is happening in classrooms and how teaching and learning practices can contribute towards a more social-justice orientated global citizenship. Furthermore, if global citizenship education is to have a place in formal education, there will also be a need to examine how pre-service and in-service teachers can be supported so they can include global citizenship education in their practices.

Most of the reviewed studies have been conducted in the United States and in the UK. We understand that a reason for this can be our language limitations and our accessibility to resources. However, there is also a possibility that global citizenship – at least the term itself – is only relevant to educational research in some countries or regions. If this is the case, the issue at this point becomes an ethical one. Researchers working in these countries might want to carry on examining what happens in their local context. But there is a question of to what extent we can talk about global citizenship education unless we consider this a worldwide project. Researchers can also decide to investigate (perhaps in partnership with other colleagues) what happens everywhere else. But there is a risk that this can be perceived as an 'imposition' of ideas. To overcome this dilemma, we recommend researchers to work (or carry on working) to investigate whether the same or similar ideas are covered using different terminology or if, ideas on global citizenship are, in themselves, only framed by certain understandings. In this respect, we feel international teams are essential in order to guarantee that different understandings are not lost in translation. To be 'global' – if we understand 'global' in inclusive terms – the research on global citizenship education needs to carry on examining points of encounter but also points of conflict between the ways across the world students, teachers and policy-makers understand the world and their role within it.

Annotated bibliography

Ethical Internationalism in Higher Education Research Project. http://eihe.blogspot.co.uk/

This website is the research project website of the 'Ethical Internationalism in Higher Education Research Project' a research project funded by the Academy of Finland. The website includes various materials such as an overview of the methodology used by researchers, questions on ethics, description of the partners involved and outputs of the research. The researchers define the website as being a 'repository of non-confidential documents related to the EIHE project and to serve as a hub of communication among project partners, advisors and potential collaborators'. We feel that in addition to this, the website has a strong educational potential. It offers multiple opportunities for you to explore the different aspects of a research project in global citizenship education.

Hahn, C. L. (2016). Pedagogy in citizenship education research: a comparative perspective. *Citizenship Teaching & Learning*, 11(2), 121–37.

In this article, Carole Hahn presents an extensive review of research conducted in the area of comparative civic education. We feel the article provides a clear overview of what happens in research on citizenship education particularly in English-speaking countries and it can be helpful not only to understand the links between national and global forms of citizenship education but also to identify possible areas of research that could be further developed in the case of global citizenship education.

Activity

We would like you to review one of the studies we have discussed. You can base your selection on your own areas of interests, your course of study, access to the articles or in any other criterion you consider relevant. In particular, we encourage you to conduct an in-depth reading of the research study considering the following guiding questions:

a. What approach to global citizenship is taken by the researchers?
b. What approach to global citizenship education is taken by the researchers?
c. What is the context and what participants took part in the research?
d. What method(s) has been used to collect and analyse the data?
e. What are the conclusions of the study?
f. To what extent do you think the results of this study can be universalized to other contexts?
g. In which ways does this research shed some light on your own questions about global citizenship education?

18

Curriculum

Global citizenship is not commonly found on students' timetables. It is not usual for an explicitly titled subject 'global citizenship' to be given a particular slot. But, of course, a form of global citizenship education is always present and those who deny it either failing to understand what goes on in schools and other educational institutions, or are disingenuously attempting to portray schooling as something that is neutral. It does, as a curriculum matter, receive from time to time, high profile attention from policy makers and others (DfID 2005; OECD 2016). As education generally, and schooling in particular, is always by definition concerned with issues of power and justice (about who understands what and who gets access to scarce goods) the inevitability of a form of global citizenship education is clear. The key is to decide whether or not we wish that education to be professionally informed or whether we wish to leave it to chance (the latter would in practice mean allowing those who are already powerful to present their own perspectives as, supposedly, obvious common sense).

We need to establish a definition of curriculum if we are to be able to relate it to global citizenship education. A rather old but nevertheless useful definition is shown below:

A school's curriculum consists of all those activities designed or encouraged within its organisational framework to promote the intellectual, personal, social and physical development of its pupils. It includes not only the formal programme of lessons but also the 'informal' programme of so-called extra-curricular activities as well as those features which produce the school's ethos, such as the quality of relationships, the concern for equality of opportunity, the values exemplified in the way the school sets about its task and the way it is organised and managed. Teaching and learning styles strongly influence the curriculum and in practice they cannot be separated from it. (DES, 1985)

The above makes it clear that a curriculum is concerned with more than just content. Indeed many curriculum specialists have suggested that it is possible to characterize curriculum as involving a rationale (why are we doing it); a plan for implementing it (what would we like to do) and the effects of it (what is actually being achieved). These things will then be seen in terms of content and style giving appropriate attention to what has become known as the hidden curriculum (Jackson 1968). In other words, what is learned by the ways in which learning is organized and experienced. All of these things provide a way of thinking about whether or not we have global citizenship education.

Smith (1996/2000) organizes part of his discussion about curriculum in terms of transmission (what content is used), product (what do we achieve), what is the process used to encourage learning) and praxis (a development of the process model but with a particular commitment to emancipation). The really fascinating part of Smith's discussion is his connection with the big ideas or purposes behind these different aspects. He suggests that there are four key groups that show the key perspectives about curriculum. These groups can be easily related to the different purposes of education that we discussed in Chapter 2. First, he considers the liberals who value knowledge often for its own sake. These people wish to see students engaging with the best that has been thought and done. A case is often made for that best to be recognized in the form of, for example, the study of classic literature. This transmission (cultural and otherwise) is often associated with a liberal position and in its emphasis on reason seen as being high status. Its most explicit forms are to be seen in expensive independent schools and elite universities where a commitment to pure reason is extolled and where certain forms of knowledge are valued (some might say that an example of that framing of high status knowledge restricted to a few could be seen in the teaching of ancient languages). Transmission is often presented as something that is a neutral and intellectually exacting process whereas it has obviously become entangled with connotations of cultural elitism. At times the work of Plato (especially in The Republic) is cited to connect this approach with certain types of learners. In Plato's terms the men of gold may see the fire directly whereas others will only see the shadows that are reflected on the cave wall. Smith (1996/2000) provides a second type in his reference to the scientific curriculum makers. In this case commitment to what is needed in society is strong. This need may not be developed only in the form of training but it is associated with managerial approaches and vocational education (whether those vocations are for the professions or for less well-paid trades and enterprises). The connection between education and the economy is often made explicitly by a scientific approach. The third group referred to by Smith are the developmentalists. This group focuses on the needs of the child. At times this is emphasized by referring to the classic *Emile* by Rousseau but also to many more modern progressives such as John Holt (1964/1977) and others. Finally, Smith refers to the social meliorists who see schools as a major agent of change in society. Education for this group is about helping people to understand society and to develop the skills to achieve social justice. It is immediately obvious that all four groups link directly with global citizenship. The strength of looking at curriculum models in this way is that purpose is prioritized over content. It enables thinking not just about whether global content has been included or whether global citizenship is likely to be achieved; instead we are confronted with the challenge of identifying what sort of global citizenship do we want (elitist; economic; child-centred; political). While it is likely that no one would wish to exclude completely any of these approaches (few would wish to exclude classic literature, ignore the economy, deny the rights of children or pretend that there is no link between schools and society) individuals will have their preferences and those choices indicate the nature of the global citizenship education that is to be promoted and, perhaps, (in the context of pressures from policy makers, parents, exam boards, students and so on) implemented.

Controversies

Given the different perspectives identified above controversy has never been far from discussions about curriculum. A few examples of these disagreements provide an insight into what people have argued about. These examples give some sense of what could be taught as well as indicating what is really being taught even when those aims have not been explicitly identified.

In relation to curriculum that is supposedly appropriate for different types of global citizens there have been many indications of social and economic status. When using contemporary documentation, the intended purpose in relation to the social groups may be hidden. That is not always so obviously the case. As an example of the inequalities that may be imposed through schooling, nineteenth-century policies are fascinating:

> We shall call these the Third, the Second, and the First Graded education respectively . . . It is obvious that these distinctions correspond roughly, but by no means exactly, to the gradations of society.
>
> First Grade. . . This class has no wish to displace the classics from their present position in the forefront of English education.
>
> Second Grade . . . parents consent to give a higher place to Latin on condition that it did not exclude a very thorough knowledge of important modern subjects, and they would hardly give Greek any place at all.

> Third Grade . . . belongs to a class distinctly lower in the scale . . . The need of this class is 'very good reading, very good writing, very good arithmetic'.
> (Schools Inquiry Royal Commission, Taunton Report, 1868, pp. 15–21)

In global citizenship education we would hope that work is appropriate for all and that when differentiation occurs it is achieved equitably and without discrimination.

In arguments about economics national policy makers are often determinedly fixated on wealth creation (with all that may mean for unequal distribution). A very clear example of this may be seen in the statement of the then secretary of state for Education, Michael Gove, in 2011 when launching a review of the National Curriculum in England,

> We have sunk in international league tables and the National Curriculum is substandard. Meanwhile the pace of economic and technological change is accelerating and our children are being left behind. The previous curriculum failed to prepare us for the future. We must change course. Our review will examine the best school systems in the world and give us a world-class curriculum that will help teachers, parents and children know what children should learn at what age. (Gove, 2011)

Those who promote global citizenship education often do not develop their rationale on the basis of wealth creation. But those advocates are often highly enterprising and creative people and economic and cultural diversity is a challenging and valuable target.

Perhaps the most striking arguments about the purposes of schooling – and this of course relates directly and immediately to global citizenship – are related to issues of morals and virtues. It seems that any subject or knowledge form is likely to be seen as controversial:

- The state of Tennessee had passed a law making it unlawful to teach evolutionary theory in any state-funded educational establishment. John Scopes was a high school teacher who, financed by the American Civil Liberties Union intentionally violated the Act. At his first trial a jury found Scopes guilty. Eventually on appeal, Scopes was cleared on a legal technicality, but the statute remained in place and was not repealed until 1967. Although, in 1968, the Supreme Court of the United States ruled such legislation as illegal, the controversy lingers on.
- Arguments have been made by some for teaching creationist theories alongside ideas about evolution. In 2008 Professor

Michael Reiss, director of education of the Royal Society (and an ordained Church of England clergyman), had to resign for advancing such a view.

- In the 1960s and 1970s there were attempts to introduce new or 'modern maths'. One French university professor, Roger Apery, suggested in February 1972 that: Pornography, drugs, the disintegration of the French language, upheavals in mathematics education, all relate to the same process; attacking the central parts of the liberal society. (L'Express, 6 February 1972)

How can global citizenship be expressed in a curriculum?

In order to consider how global citizenship might be recognized it is necessary to discuss the frames of reference that are used when developing curriculum. There are strong links between this section and some of the points made in the chapter in this book on Global Education. We highlight here five aspects that are usually highlighted in curriculum construction and we show below what they might mean when applied to global citizenship:

- Knowledge – is global content to be highlighted? Are concepts the defining framework and, if so, of what sort? Generally, educators will refer to substantive concepts which are very closely aligned with content (e.g. in history lessons a teacher might focus on revolution, war etc.); and procedural concepts which show how a subject is studied and practised (so, to use the history example again a teacher may focus on evidence, causation, chronology, interpretation and so on). The choices for global citizenship content and concepts may be seen in the statements produced by authors such as Westheimer and Kahne (2004) and Oxley and Morris (2013).

- Balance – what would a balanced global citizenship programme look like? Would we 'balance' economics with politics, culture with morals or is there another framework?

- Breadth – how wide would our curriculum be framed? Would we include the full range of perspectives and subject matter? Would we in each of the fields mentioned above mention everything? Surely that would be impossible. So, how do we choose what to include? Would we return to the frameworks of liberals, scientists, developmentalists and social meliorists referred to above?

- Coherence. Once we have made our decisions about the above, what holds it all together? Is it acceptable to opt for an avowedly political purpose? Would it be coherent if we were to include all possible perspectives (even if only in limited ways) Is it appropriate to consider subjects as forming the best approach to achieve coherence or are there are areas of knowledge that global citizenship can be attached to? At times the commitment to traditional subjects such as history, maths, science and so on may stand in contrast to an approach in which there are areas of experience (e.g. personal, social and emotional development; language and literacy; mathematical development; knowledge and understanding of the world; physical development; creative development). Would a curriculum be more coherent and would global citizenship education be more likely to be present if we were to frame things in terms of areas of experience rather than subjects?

- Continuity and progression – how might we frame material as being suitable for learners of different ages and abilities? Do we rely on a notion that some content is harder than others? Is the abstract really more difficult than the everyday? Very young children seem to be fascinated with things of the imagination which might be relying on the abstract. Do we need to consider issues of questions used (e.g. open and closed), accessibility of material (with attention, for example, to language level), questions framed (e.g. comprehension, analysis)? And should the skills that we expect be seen as transferable or are they essentially intertwined with the content under consideration (e.g. comprehending history may be very different from comprehending science).

Does a national curriculum support global citizenship?

The existence of a national curriculum may at least initially seem contrary to ambitions for global citizenship education. The boundaries and concerns of a nation state may seem to be the principal focus rather those of a more connected world. This may well be the case as often we can see curricula established that focus on national history, national literature and so on. But it is worth considering the justifications that are often provided for national curricula. These usually include the ambition to: establish an entitlement for all pupils; establish standards that can be used to set targets and measure performance; promote continuity and coherence; promote public understanding of and confidence in the work of schools (http://www.nc.uk.net). These four factors were used in the late 1980s in England to justify the establishment of the first National Curriculum and something very similar is being used now as the first national curriculum is being introduced into Australia (see www.australiancurriculum.edu.au). There are of course criticisms about a national curriculum, some of which apply directly to an exclusion of global citizenship education. State control of knowledge means that flexible professionalism disappears as teachers become technicians, there is massive bureaucracy and competitiveness which in most circumstances leads to most students being branded as losers. But the key point is to decide not whether the structure that is used to establish the curriculum (whether it be nationally framed; dependent on federal states such as in the US or where there is local decision making as in Finland) but rather whether in any geographical area there is a commitment to global citizenship. For some the contradiction between state and globalism mean that a national curriculum will always be problematic; for others a commitment to globalism is simply part of multiple loyalties that individual countries as well as other policy making contexts should be able to work within.

Who are the key stakeholders?

The discussion above about the connections (and possible disjunctions) between a national curriculum and global citizenship education as well as other considerations about the nature and purpose of the curriculum, connects with issues about who should be in control of what is taught and learned. Essentially, there are three sorts of debates which we have deliberately shown below in stark terms. These three arguments reveal in practice only false dichotomies but we hope that we this sort of presentation is useful for considering the sorts of discussions about curriculum.

The first debate is sometimes seen as relying on experts as opposed to the general population. The nature of who counts as an expert shifts depending on context. In England David Cameron argued in August 2015 that: 'I want the power to be in the hands of the head teacher and the teachers rather than the bureaucrats'. Michael Gove insisted that 'people in this country have had enough of experts' (Mance, 2016). These two quotations are very different in that in the former there is recognition of competing expertise; whereas the second seems, bizarrely, to reject all expertise. But this suspicion of all experts or of certain types of expert perhaps relates to the second area of discussion or debate which is concerned with the political and social motivations for comment as opposed to perhaps what is felt to be a common sense attitude of what works. This has many interesting implications for how discussions including those in the media are conducted. In an attempt to achieve balance perhaps everyone (or, at least those who are regarded as rightfully having a voice in a particular debate) – whatever their expertise or motivations – is allowed to have an equal say in the resolution of difficult and complex matters. This leads perhaps to a very curious sort of balance which in matters of public policy is very hard to resolve. Often those who are seen by established organizations (such as the media) as having an obvious right to contribute may not actually be representative or even particularly knowledgeable. Finally, the nature of discussions about curriculum goes to the heart of our consideration for – and characterization of – the nature of childhood. Notwithstanding debates about lifelong learning it is the case that most people who attend schools are young. Is it the case that those people who, by definition, have less experience than others should be protected and have decisions taken for them? Or, are school students currently citizens – not citizens in waiting – who should have power now?

Assessment

Assessment is a complex and multifaceted topic. In this section of the book we wish to give a simple indication of its importance by highlighting that curriculum is not separate from assessment. Rather we feel that there is an integrated approach that needs to be considered across teaching, learning and assessment. Global citizenship educators may wish to consider the ways in which assessment should be positioned given the choices outlined above about the different possible purposes of curriculum. Four dynamic relationships need to be acknowledged. First, summative assessment (the final grade) may be differentiated from a formative judgment. The latter does not emerge from a single test and the main purpose of formative assessment is to aid further learning. But there is overlap between the formative and summative and unless we are to abandon completely the ways in which society makes use of assessment data, we may when promoting global citizenship education usefully engage in the creation of ways to review learning. Second, traditional forms of assessment focus on individuals but there is increasing emphasis on work produced collectively. It is sometimes simplistically assumed that global citizenship education is more obviously aligned with collective work but there is room to recognize a variety of actions. Third, it is important when promoting global citizenship education to reflect on the frameworks that are being used, of which there are three principal approaches: norm (students are compared with each other); criteria (students are judged according to how well they meet declared objectives); ipsative (students are compared against their own progress). It is unlikely that any of these three frameworks may be used independently of the others and that all may be used positively in global citizenship education. Finally, a wide variety of techniques should be used in reporting (self-assessment, co-reporting and report from a teacher) as well as employing a sufficient level of 'bilingualism' in order to be able to communicate effectively and inclusively with different audiences (parents and carers; fellow professionals; and so on).

Annotated bibliography

Davy, I. (2011). Learners without borders: a curriculum for global citizenship. International Baccalaureate. http://www.godolphinandlatymer.com/_files/IB/B309322691ABF031CB793E9DDA47FE3A.pdf.

In this paper Davy outlines some principles and key considerations about developing a curriculum for global citizenship education. It is published by the International Baccalaureate and as such there are important issues to consider in relation to the development of a syllabus that might be enacted in an international school as well as mainstream state schools.

Smith, M. K. (1996, 2000) 'Curriculum theory and practice': *the encyclopaedia of informal education,* www.infed.org/biblio/b-curric.htm.

In this paper Smith writes very clearly about the different types and purposes of curriculum. Some of the ideas discussed above are taken from this paper. Smith's comments about liberal, scientific, developmental and social meliorist positions are very valuable indeed.

Activities

1. Draw up a timetable for year nine school students (aged 14–15). The students will be attending school during Monday through Friday, arriving at school at 9.00 am and leaving at 3.30 pm. They will have 40 minutes for lunch and a 20-minute break in the morning. Be prepared to justify your timetable in terms of what sort of purpose it has; how it is likely to be successful in teaching and learning and assessment; and who would be consulted.

2. Most of this chapter has dealt with issues relevant to the construction of the curriculum. Of course, it is also extremely important to consider the ways in which global citizenship education is taught and learned. There is material in many of our chapters about teaching and learning. You might want to consider the following questions about progression and differentiation. Progression refers to making things increasingly complex to provide an appropriate challenge for learners. Differentiation is about providing material that is suitable for all learners, whatever their learning styles. Consider the following two questions: (a) what makes material challenging for students?; (b) how can material be made accessible for students who have a range of learning styles? Think about the amount of material to be learned; the type of skill to be targeted (comprehension, analysis, evaluation etc.); the type of data to be used (low or high language level; statistics; pictures etc.); the type of question to be asked (closed, open etc.). Think also about the possibility of giving all students the same task in a way that would allow for different levels of achievement to be recognized; and providing different tasks for learners whom a teacher feels are at different levels of achievement. Choose an activity from any textbook for global citizenship and make that activity harder; and then make it easier. Review what you did and ask whether your approach is fair. Ask yourself if one of the aims of global citizenship education should be for all students to achieve the same outcomes or whether it is acceptable for different levels of achievement to be recognized? It is very unlikely that a simplistic approach would be appropriate but, generally, how can we provide progression and differentiation in a way that is appropriate for justice in the classroom?

19

Community Action

In February 2011, a Facebook group entitled DemocraciaRealYa (RealDemocracyNow) appeared on the internet. The group was supported by several small groups criticizing the economic and political situation in Spain and demanding changes as people voted in their local elections. The group created a twitter hashtag #democraciarealya. In a few days, this hashtag appeared in more than 600,000 tweets of accounts registered not only in Spain but also in Brazil, Indonesia, Mexico, United States and others. The movement, known internationally as the Spanish revolution, directly inspired the worldwide cascade of Occupy protests including, but not limited to the Occupy Wall Street (United States), Occupy Central (People's Republic of China), Occupy Melbourne (Australia), Occupy Nigeria (UK) and Occupy Bogota (Colombia). The Occupy protesters campaigned for a reduction of social and economic inequalities worldwide. This example illustrates the complexity of any form of community action undertaken by the citizenry worldwide. It shows how local demands can easily become global demands, how comments and actions in the digital world crystallize in community actions in the physical world, how traditional and new forms of political participation interact in complex dynamics of communities and actions. In this chapter, we attempt to shed some light on this complexity by discussing actions that can be undertaken in global and other communities.

In Chapter 9, we discussed that community involvement together with political literacy and social and moral responsibility are the three dimensions of citizenship education outlined by the Crick Report (DfE/QCA 1998). In this chapter, we focus on providing an overview of the meaning of the term 'community action' and the different types of community actions, their challenges and possibilities.

Citizenship and participation

Discussions on citizenship and citizenship education often involve a strong consideration of participation. It is worth noting here that the terms community action, participation and engagement are often used indistinguishably in the literature. Here, we follow the framework created by the Swedish political scientists Ekman and Amnå to discuss political participation as a wider concept including individual and collective forms, attention (involvement) and action (engagement) as forms of participation.

Participation, in our understanding, becomes 'global' not for the form of the participation but rather for the purpose of participating. For instance, whereas participating for environmental issues can easily be considered 'global', whether or not becoming a representative in a youth city council is 'global participation' is a matter of debate. Similarly, while volunteering in a refugee network can be contextualized within global citizenship education, it is very hard to imagine that any sort of racist protest would be understood as pursuing the purpose of any form of global citizenship with which we are concerned.

The links between participation and citizenship are usually a matter for discussion and debate. Participation can be considered a citizen's right, a citizen's duty, a citizen's virtue or the combination of any of these. Participation is associated with representative or direct forms of democratic government. Participation is also understood as a way to generate consensus (e.g. via a deliberative process) or as a way to generate conflict (e.g. participants posing demands to the government). There is also a question of what exact forms of action or non-actions are considered to be 'community actions' (see Ekman & Amna, 2012). For some, participation includes conventional, representative and governmental forms of action such as voting, being elected and engagement through political parties. For others, by contrast, participation includes a wider range of actions – including direct, nongovernmental and even illegal actions – such as demonstrating, online protesting, occupying spaces, etc. Some people have considered whether forms of non-participation (e.g. refusal to vote) can actually demonstrate radical forms of being politically engaged.

In what follows, we gather different types of community actions and discuss the challenges and possibilities of each of them.

- Formal political participation: Electoral activities are probably the most traditional forms of engagement in contemporary Western societies. Electoral activities include any form of participation associated with representative democracy: involvement with political parties, voting and becoming a political representative. In non-global forms of citizenship education, there is a wide range of electoral activities including participation in children and youth councils or discussions with political representatives. In some national contexts, formal political participation has been put into question by some groups on the understanding that party democracy has democratic deficits. Further, in the global context, the relevance of electoral activities seems to be questionable. There is no such thing as a global institution of governance in which representatives are voted for by the world citizenry. Although some IGOs, perhaps mainly the United Nations, is considered to be the closest we have to this sort of global institution, representative participation in the global community is quite obscure. Citizens do not directly vote for their representatives at the UN. Instead, representatives are selected by the national governments following different procedures. Even those who argue for global institutions of government and for political forms of global citizenship recognize that at present IGOs have democratic limitations (Held, 2005). In the particular case of global citizenship education, key activities are, for instance, simulations of the United Nations (Kirkwood-Tucker, 2004) or the participation in the UNESCO Youth Forum (http://en.unesco.org/9th-unesco-youth-forum).

- Civil participation: Civil participation refers to activities within the civil society sphere; these are activities without links with institutional forms of governance. There are different forms of civil participation:

  - Social involvement can be understood as paying attention to or showing interest in political and social issues. In the global context, this can include having a sense of belonging to the global community, being interested and following media on international and global politics and having the perception that global issues are important. Although being socially involved seems to be a pre-requisite for any further act of participation, involvement can be challenged for not having any sort of impact in itself.

  - Civic engagement may involve contributions to charities and volunteering. Particularly relevant, for global citizenship education, are international forms of volunteering. Volunteering quite often involves international service in which the participant crosses national borders to volunteer, usually for humanitarian or ecological purposes. There is a wide range of views on international volunteering, which in our understanding, respond to different views on global citizenship (Hartman & Kiely, 2014). If we consider the discussion on the Chapter 11, certain approaches to international volunteering and service-learning are considered to be transformative and social-justice oriented whereas other approaches may be considered to be patronizing, charity-focused and as new forms of colonization. Civil engagement, in general, often raises concerns among those who understand that through volunteering, the participants do not challenge the structures that reproduce patterns of injustice. By volunteering to teach abroad in places where there is a lack of qualified teachers, for instance, only the immediate problem is tackled, but not the underlying issue that generates the problem in the first term.

- Activism: Activism involves (legal and illegal) protest activities aimed at challenging institutional and majoritarian forms of governance and lifestyle. Activism, regardless of the local, national or global focus, involves activities such as demonstrations, civil disobedience, strikes, boycotting, or occupations. It also may involve participation through societies, forums, cooperatives, trade unions and other similar things. Examples of global forms of activism include the participation in the Million mask march, engagement through Greenpeace, the Occupy movement, participation in the World Social Forum (https://fsm2016.org/) or the social involvement with global cooperative practices: democratic cooperatives, microcredit societies and local food production. We are aware of a limited number of activist forms of participation being used in the context of citizenship education, for instance, through demonstrations in which teachers and students join to demand changes in educational policies (Sant, 2015; Ross & Vinson, 2014). While some would understand the links between activism and education as particularly engaging and educational, others wonder to what extent students are directly led (and perhaps used) by their teachers. In addition, since activism may include legal and illegal forms of actions (Ekman & Amna, 2012), projects linking activism to global citizenship education might have to be extremely careful in ensuring that work is completed ethically.

A particular form of activism is digital activism. The internet and more precisely social media have been highlighted for their participatory potential across national borders. Examples of this includes online sites to create and sign petitions, the use of twitter and other sites of micro-blogging (e.g. during the Arab Spring) or the use of impacting images through media and social media (e.g. the photography of Aylan Kurdi and the subsequent twitter hashtag campaign #refugeeswelcome). There is a discussion, however, about the democratic nature of these communication activities (Loader, Bromen & Xenos,

2014). For some, social media and the use of the internet enhance the opportunities for participation for everybody. Sites such as twitter or change.org are free to use and most people have the opportunity to start global campaigns, to contribute to global causes, and to tweet global hashtags. The internet offers opportunities for digital, physical, conventional and non-conventional participation as illustrated in the example we have discussed in the introduction to this chapter. For others, the impact of these communication activities is less relevant. They are, for some, 'light' forms of engagement. Communication campaigns on the internet are usually brief and their impact is often limited. Concerns have also been raised about the unequal accessibility to technological resources or what has been described as the digital divide. Age, socio-economic status, nationality, place of residence among other factors condition whether or not people have access to new technologies and to the participatory potential associated with this.

Service-learning: community action and education

In most citizenship education and global citizenship education projects, there is an expectation that students, through education, will become more involved in their communities through any of the types of participation previously discussed. Citizenship education usually encourages students' participation in their communities, within and outside schools and other educational settings. In educational theory and practice, community actions are usually assembled under the umbrella of community service or service-learning activities. According to Wade (2008), in community service projects the learning element is weaker or absent. In contrast, in service-learning projects, the service necessarily involves learning activities associated with the actions undertaken. For instance, whereas in community service students might volunteer to clean up an environment, in service-learning it is expected that students will volunteer at the same time as learning, for instance, about global warming. In our understanding, in the context of global citizenship education, community actions are preferably to be included in service-learning activities as discussed by Wade (2008).

But service-learning activities, particularly abroad, have received strong criticisms. In the line of what we have outlined for the case of volunteering activities, service-learning abroad can reinforce the existing power relations and stereotypes of the students:

There has been growing dissatisfaction among many people both inside and outside the service learning movement since the 1990s, particularly when it comes to the issue of whether service learning truly serves communities. In the worst cases, analysts saw poor communities exploited as free sources of student education. Others worried that the 'charity' model of service learning reinforced negative stereotypes and students' perceptions of poor communities as helpless. (Stoecker & Tyron, 2009, p. 3).

Indeed, service-learning activities can be connected with different forms of global citizenship education. Furco (1994) reviews a set of service-learning activities and argues that different activities have different purposes. Although we want to highlight that, in our understanding, sponsors and participants usually pursue several of these purposes simultaneously. Furco's typology is helpful to consider service-learning through the eyes of global citizenship education.

- Related to the qualification dimension of global citizenship education are:
  - Academic purposes: For some, the purpose of community activities is to enhance academic learning. For instance, through participation in a Global Youth Forum organized by the UNESCO, students can learn about UNESCO's procedures.
  - Economic purposes: Some community activities aim to provide students with knowledge and skills that will make them more employable. For instance, some students participate in international service-learning to learn languages that will help them to find a better job. Other students might be involved in local charities to gain job experience.
- Related to the socialization dimension of global citizenship education are:
  - Social purpose: In some occasions, the purpose of community activities is social cohesion. Activities that gather different members of the community often promote sense of belonging with this community. For instance, international volunteering quite often attempt to create some sort of belonging to the global community by bringing people from different parts of the world together.
  - Moral purpose: Some community activities attempt to enhance certain values and attitudes. For instance, schools sometimes organize food drive campaigns for international charities. These activities mainly attempt to enhance students' attitudes and values such as empathy or sense of responsibility.

- Political purpose: Community activities aim to promote students' participation. The understanding is that through participation in community actions, students might learn how to participate and might feel more inclined to participate in the future. For instance, the EU organizes a youth parliament with the aim to encourage young people's involvement with EU institutions.

- Related to the subjectification dimension of global citizenship education are:

  - Individual purpose: Some community activities encourage students' self-reflection and awareness. For instance, university courses may offer volunteering activities embedded in their educational programmes. Education students, for instance, may spend part of their degree courses in school settings. In these activities, there is usually an expectation that students will reflect on their prospective professional role. We understand that whereas on some occasions these activities are linked to the subjectification view on global citizenship education (e.g. self-awareness), on other occasions, the qualification function is privileged through the learning of skills considered to be valuable for the world of work.

When associated to the socialization function of education, different types of service-learning activities attempt to educate (socialize) different types of citizens. Westheimer and Kahne (2004) developed a well-known typology considering how different types of community service activities would contribute to the education of different types of citizens. They identified three types of community service activities:

- Personally responsible citizenship: Some community activities, often associated with formal political participation and sometimes civil participation activities, attempt to educate an honest, hard-working, self-disciplined citizen who will act responsibly in her community. These activities usually include recycling, contributing to food drives, or giving blood. In the context of global citizenship education, some of these activities would probably focus on educating a neoliberal global citizenry whether others would probably aim to educate a humanistic citizenry who would essentially engage through civic engagement and formal politics.

- Participatory citizenship: Some community activities aim to prepare students to engage participants in their communities essentially through civil participation activities. This implies an education on the work procedures of government and community based organizations and participatory skills (e.g. how to run a meeting, organize a campaign, etc.). Whereas, for instance, a responsible citizen would contribute to a campaign, the participatory citizen would organize this campaign. These activities could probably make a contribution towards some humanistic forms of global citizenship.

- Justice orientated citizenship: A third group of community activities is particularly focus on analysing the underlying social, economic and political injustices and in acting, using any form action, against them. Although these activities might be associated to any of the forms of participation previously discussed, activism is particularly associated with the education of justice orientated citizenship. As described by Westheimer and Kahne, 'if participatory citizens are organizing the food drive and personally responsible citizens are donating food, justice oriented citizens are asking why people are hungry and acting on what they discover' (2004, p. 241). In the global context, justice-orientated citizens would probably respond to critical and anticolonial forms of global citizenship engaged with different types of political participation.

Conclusions

Community actions are, in our understanding, essential components of any global citizenship education projects. However, we believe that embedding community actions in the curriculum or as part of a global citizenship education project requires careful consideration of different issues. First, we understand that different forms of participation offer different possibilities and challenges that need to be considered. Beyond the ones highlighted in this chapter, other issues such as the age of the participants or the context of the project need to be examined. Second, following the work of Westheimer and Kahne (2004), we understand that different service-learning activities might educate different types of citizenry. In the context of global citizenship education, we believe that different types of global service-learning activities are associated with different functions of global citizenship education and therefore promote different types of global citizenry.

Annotated bibliography

Amnesty International Campaigns. (https://www.amnesty.org/en/latest/campaigns/).

This website gathers together various worldwide Amnesty International Campaigns. The website provides an updated list of present Amnesty International Campaigns and includes a wide range of resources such as videos, case studies, photos, blogs, letters, reports and articles. The website also offers the possibility to search on different topics (e.g. education, children, censorship and women's rights) and to different regions and countries. Particularly interesting is, in our view, the educational resources that the NGO provides in relation to topics such as asylum-seekers, human rights and political activism.

Hartman, E. & Kiely, R. (2014). A critical global citizenship. In M. Johnson & P. M. Green (Eds). *Crossing boundaries: tension and transformation in international service-learning*. Sterling, VA: Stylus Publishing.

In this chapter, Hartman and Kiely examine three different global citizenship education projects promoted by US higher education institutions. Following a review of the literature in which they contextualize the links between global citizenship education and study abroad programs, the authors investigate three projects conducted in Tanzania, Bolivia and the United States. The chapter is particularly outstanding in illustrating how different forms of civic engagements are related to different understandings of global citizenship and different approaches to global citizenship education. Drawing on the Westheimer and Kahne's (2004) typology, the final table in the chapter summarizes these different approaches in a very accessible way.

Loader, B. V., Vromen, A. & Xenos, M. A. (2014). *The Networked Young Citizens*. New York: Routledge.

This book explores the links between social media-based community action and young people's political engagement. Following an introduction in which the editors explore the main challenges and possibilities of social media for political participation and civic engagement, the book is divided into three different sections. In the first section, the ways in which social media is presently used in the context of youth political engagement is discussed considering examples from Sweden, the Unites States and others. In the second section, examples from Australia and UK illustrate possible ways in which social network can enhance community action in the context of citizenship education. In the final section, the political impact of social network is considered looking at different examples around Europe.

Activities

1. In the first activity, we would like you to examine the spoof music video created by a Norwegian group calling itself Radi-Aid. You can find the video here: https://www.theguardian.com/world/2012/nov/19/radi-aid-charity-single-africa

Watch the video and discuss with others the following questions:
   - What types and purposes of 'global participation' is the video parodying?
   - What approach to 'global citizenship education' is the video parodying?
   - What are the implicit critiques of the video?
   - After discussing these questions, write your own reflection on the participatory nature of the video itself. Would you consider the video in itself a global participation? And if so, what type of action?

2. Now, we would ask you to work in collaboration with other students to design a community action campaign aimed to promote global citizenship among higher education students. If possible, we wish to encourage you to work cooperatively (face to face or virtually) with students from another university. Although we suggest that you take this activity as a real opportunity of participation, different levels of involvement, in relation to different levels of resources, and commitment, are expected. You can promote the form of global citizenship you feel more comfortable with, you can design the type of community action you prefer and whether or not you bring this into reality. Once the campaign has been designed, we would like you to reflect on the following questions:
   - What type of global citizenship did you promote?
   - What approach to global citizenship education did you take?
   - Did the action involve community service or service-learning?
   - What type of community action did you design?
   - What was the purpose of the community activity?
   - What are the possibilities and challenges of your campaign?
   - Is the type of community action designed coherent with the approach to global citizenship you wanted to promote?

20

Teaching and Learning Methods in Global Citizenship Education

In the previous chapters of this book, we have discussed key questions, concepts, dimensions and frameworks associated with the global citizenship education project. We have also explored the research conducted in the field and the possible links between global citizenship education, the curriculum and the community. However, those of you who are particularly interested in the practicalities of this project might be wondering how educators can include global citizenship education in their practices. In other words, how global citizenship can be taught and learnt.

In this chapter, we provide a general overview of different approaches to global citizenship education and we identify some documented examples of teaching and learning practices for each of them. We want to be particularly cautious about these examples. As we have highlighted before, there are different understandings of global citizenship and therefore, different understandings of what global citizenship education should consist of. Whereas certain teaching and learning practices can be considered 'good practice' for some, others might consider these educational practices challenging, problematic or even un-ethical. This is why, in this chapter, we do not attempt to identify what works in the field of global citizenship education but rather to map different practices that are presently taking place worldwide and to associate these practices with different approaches to global citizenship and education.

Global citizenship education as a cross-curricular theme

Global citizenship education can be incorporated in the school curriculum through a holistic approach. Schools may include the promotion of global citizenship among their principles and values. Through activities that take place across different subject areas (e.g. interdisciplinary projects), in extra curricula time (e.g. school clubs, trips and exchanges), aspects of the organization of the school (e.g. school assembly) or professional development activities for the staff, (Think Global, n.d.; https://globaldimension.org.uk/resources/browse/), schools often aim to promote active citizenship, global and political literacy, cultural awareness, 'global' values and sense of belonging. We now examine some examples to illustrate this approach.

The holistic approach often emphasizes the action dimension of citizenship education (Nelson & Kerr 2006). Probably the most well-known example is the organization of the school through assemblies and school councils that promote democratic forms of governance (see e.g. http://www.education.vic.gov.au/school/teachers/management/Pages/schoolcouncil.aspx?Redirect=1). Quite often schools might choose to encourage values such as solidarity and social justice while supporting a globally oriented active citizenship. In Spain, schools often organize 'book collection drives' in partnership with NGOs that will later send the books to other Spanish-speaking countries. In Ireland, Trocaire (https://www.trocaire.org/), the overseas development agency of the Catholic Church, distributes collection boxes together with education materials to schools around the country (Bryan 2013). There are also numerous examples of schools organizing donations for NGOs with the purpose of building new schools often in Sub-Saharan Africa, Southern Asia or Latin America. Although the explicit purpose is often to enhance students' solidarity, in the context of what we have discussed in the Chapter 11, some might see these practices as patronizing.

Other schools emphasize the links between active citizenship and political literacy. In the line of critical and social forms of global citizenship, Amnesty International, for instance, gathers 'taking action' projects (Amnesty international UK, 2014) (https://www.amnesty.org.uk/actions). In these projects, school communities, class communities or school clubs can be involved through a range of activities, including signatures, letter collections and thematic weeks. In Canada, schools worked in partnership with university centres and NGOs to discuss youth views for global citizenship education (National Youth White Paper on Global Citizenship, 2015) (http://www.takingitglobal.org/images/resources/tool/docs/Global_Citizenship.pdf). In Colombia (and in a number of other countries), schools can be involved in the Model United Nations initiatives, a simulation of the UN General Assembly (Naciones unidas, n.d.) (http://nacionesunidas.org.co/modelos/). In this later case, the aim is to teach students the procedures and structures of an already existent global institution of governance.

On other occasions, the emphasis might be in the promotion of cultural awareness, intercultural competence and some sort of global (or transnational) sense of belonging. There are numerous examples of two or more schools working in partnership towards these aims. As an example, the British council supports school partnership among schools all around the world (British Council, 2015) (https://schoolsonline.britishcouncil.org/partner-school). The EU promotes 'school twinning' among European schools through the Comenius programme (https://www.etwinning.net/en/pub/index.htm). Examples of these school-twinning activities include the 'Rainbow village' where students from France, Greece, Italy, Poland, Romania, Turkey, Slovakia and the United Kingdom develop intercultural competence (Rainbow village, 2015) or a project where Spanish, Romanian and Polish students actively engage in 'saving the planet' (Rico, Dominguez, Ferreira & Coppens, 2012). Usually, these activities involve the creation of international groups of students working together (online or face-to-face via exchanges, school trips or meetings) in the pursuit of certain educational aims. The links of these activities with different understandings of global citizenship will depend, we believe, on the educational aims associated to each project. In our examples, whether 'saving the planet' project seems to rely on sustainability-based approaches to global citizenship, the 'Rainbow village' probably reinforce cultural forms of global citizenship.

Global citizenship education integrated into other subjects

Global citizenship education can also be integrated into 'mainstream' subjects. In a number of countries, the departments of education, higher education institutions and NGOs have developed guidance to encourage teachers from different subject areas to include global citizenship education in their practices. In Scotland, the Education Scotland website offers a number of resources to learn global citizenship across the curriculum (Education Scotland, n.d.) (http://www.educationscotland.gov.uk/learningandteaching/learningacross-thecurriculum/themesacrosslearning/globalcitizenship/). Similar resources have been developed by the Australian government (Australian Government, n.d.) (https://www.globaleducation.edu.au), Oxfam Hong Kong (Oxfam, 2016) (http://www.oxfam.org.hk/en/globalcitizenshipeducation.aspx), US UNICEF (UNICEF United States Fund, 2015) (http://www.teachunicef.org/teaching-materials/topic/global-citizenship) and the Universitat de Barcelona (Gonzalez, 2015) (http://hdl.handle.net/2445/34623). All these resources tend to identify possible contributions of different subject areas to the education of the global citizenry. In the following, we summarize some of these contributions for the areas of social sciences, languages and STEM (science, technology, engineering and mathematics).

Social sciences

Social sciences and some humanities (essentially history and geography but also politics and anthropology) are usually pointed out as the subject area the links between global citizenship and the disciplines are more explicit. Social science or social studies subjects are usually the context where students discuss controversial global issues such as world poverty, migrations and violent conflicts. There are examples of Portuguese students examining migration over long time periods (Barca, Castro & Amaral 2010; Gaudelli 2017), Spanish students examining walls, frontiers and borders in different times and spaces (Santisteban, Pages & Bravo 2017), British students discussing modern and old forms of slavery (Arthur, Davies, Kerr & Wrenn 2003) and Australian students discussing world trade (Oxfam Australia, n.d.) (https://www.oxfam.org.au/get-involved/how-schools-can-get-involved/resources-for-teachers/term-two-features-resource-fairtrade/). Particularly relevant for our purposes, there are examples of students and teachers from different parts of the world working in partnership in online forums to discuss local and global controversial issues (GTP, n.d.) (http://www.ict-edu.nl/gtp/wat-is-gtp/). In all these cases, they work through controversial issues with aims to develop critical literacy, argumentative reasoning and often, support for values such as equality and social justice.

In the particular case of history education, some authors suggest that world history can promote global sense of belonging (Levstik 2014; Sant et al. 2015). Through the construction of global narratives, students can learn history as 'ongoing story towards the achievement of a peaceful, just, and fully democratic world in which students are identified as the future – and perhaps the present – characters that need to decide what exactly a 'peaceful, just, and fully democratic world' is, how to accomplish this world, and when the story is complete' (Sant et al. 2015, p. 356). Other authors understand history education as particularly helpful in order to generate empathy and peaceful dialogue. For example, competing narratives on the same historical event have been presented to Palestinian and Israeli students to enhance peace and other global values (Adwman, Bar-On & Naveh 2012). For others, history can help students to trace their own existence in time and space. In Brazil, curricula recommendations suggest activities such as the development of students' genealogical trees with the purpose of understanding diversity as constitutive part of their societies (Sant & Gonzalez, 2017).

Geography education has the potential to challenge pre-deterministic views on the links between social context and physical spaces (Gaudelli 2017). For instance, 'up-side down' maps can be used to problematize the ways we often understand the world (Segall, 2003). Geography – and other science education – can also be the context where ecological forms of global citizenship education are promoted. Besides the use of ecological issues as controversial issues, there are a number of examples where different technologies are used to examine human interaction with the environment. Google earth has been used as a tool towards environmental literacy (Environmental Literacy and Inquiry Working Group at Lehigh University Group 2015) (http://www.ei.lehigh.edu/eli/index.html).

Languages education

Languages education (including 'native' and foreign language education) is often understood as essential for the education of the global citizenry in three different ways. For those defending economic forms of global citizenship, languages are essential to allow communication, employment, and mobility. Those defending cultural forms of global citizenship argue that languages education should aim to generate intercultural citizenship and to make a contribution towards a global community. In contrast, those defending critical forms of global citizenship understand language education as a way to critical examine interpretations and assumptions.

In the particular case of ('native') language education, it is expected that students will learn how to critically examine texts. There are examples of resources helping French-speaking students to examine African conflicts through the analysis of radio texts (De Mol 2007). There are also numerous examples of resources in which students examine the media cover of immigration and refugees' crisis (Aragon, Bittencourt & Johnson, 2011). Language education can also contribute towards active forms of global citizenship by helping students to build their civic skills. In Egypt, students were encouraged to develop and share videos online (Gomaa, 2014). The use of social media as expression and civic tool has also been examined in India and South Africa (Shatel, 2017). International Amnesty offers numerous resources helping students to write letter to local, national and global institutions of governance. Finally, through literature, students can also learn to put themselves in someone else's shoes. Some educators have used children's literature to discuss global citizenship (Bradbery, 2012). Similarly, the Brazilian educators Vanessa Andreotti and Mario De Sousa designed a set of materials called 'Learning to read the world through other eyes' (2008).

Foreign languages education has often been understood as a key aspect of the education of the global citizenry. Economic global citizenship is often encouraged through exchanges where students are expected to develop their linguistic competence. In foreign language education, students not only learn linguist competence but also can learn about others. Regarding cultural forms of global citizenship, students are frequently required to inquire about other countries (Perkins & Pearson, 2016). In other cases, teachers aim to promote mutual understanding and some sort of sense of feeling to the global community. There are multiple cases of teachers using chat, Skype and other telecollaboration activities (Guth & Halm, 2010; Dooly, 2015). Argentinean and Italian higher education students, for instance, have worked together to examine, share and compare particular aspects of their local environments (Porto, 2017). Foreign language education can also be used to challenge the dominance of a particular language (i.e. English and Spanish). Reading dual language books might be a way to break down some stereotypes and assumptions and to put two languages as equal (Naqvi, Thorne, Pfitscher, Nordstokke & McKeough, 2012).

Science, technology, engineering and mathematics (STEM) subjects

In a review of the links between STEM subjects and global citizenship, David Geelan (2017, p. 507) writes, 'many of the challenges that will face students at all levels of education in the future they will inhabit have two features in common: they have a scientific or technological dimension and they are no respecters of state boundaries'. Science education, he argues, should prepare the citizens of the future 'to review current efforts and approaches' and to face these challenges.

Besides the ecological perspective (that we have already mentioned in relation to geography), there are a number of ways science education can help students to face these present and future challenges. Maths and science education can help students to critically examine numbers and data. Oxfam UK, for instance, has activities where students are expected to use probability to analyse whether or not The World Cup is a fair game (Oxfam UK, n.d.) (http://www.oxfam.org.uk/education/resources/the-world-cup-a-fair-game). The purpose here is not only to ensure that students develop scientific literacy but also to examine ways in which science and values interact. Science education can also be the proper context for students to develop solving-problem skills that require science knowledge. A group of students in Singapore, for example, participated in a simulation where they were expected to research and suggest solutions to ecological, social and cultural problems (Lim, 2008). Science education can also be helpful to protect students 'from charlatanry' (Geelan, 2017). Students can learn how diseases spread and the importance of vaccination to stop plagues (British Council, 2016). Finally, technological subjects can help the students of the present to create product and technologies that will one day enhance human life. The NGO 'Practical action' offers a set of teaching resources to encourage students to learn ways technology can challenge poverty, including the Wind power challenge or the Floating garden challenge (Practical action, n.d.) (http://practicalaction.org/stem).

Global citizenship education as a subject

At the time of writing this chapter, we are not aware of any country where global citizenship education is explicitly included as a subject. Citizenship education, in contrast, is present as an independent subject in a number of countries. In the 2009 ICCS study (Schulz, Ainley, Fraillon, Kerr & Losito, 2010), eighteen of the thirty-eight countries reported providing civic and citizenship education as a specific and compulsory subject. Among these eighteen, only the Russian Federation did not have any emphasis on the global dimension of citizenship education.

Citizenship education has often been understood as the confluence of political literacy, community engagement, social and moral values (Davies, Evans & Reid, 2005). In all these aspects, citizenship education can contribute towards global citizenship. For instance, there are examples of resources addressed to promote students' participation in the local, national and global context (Sant & Perez, 2013). The Association for Citizenship Teaching has a number of resources addressed to develop political literacy (Association for Citizenship Teaching, n.d.) (http://www.teachingcitizenship.org.uk/democracy-government-politics-economy/political-literacy). In many cases, citizenship education has also been the context where global education resources have been used. Multiple IGOs and NGOs have other resources aimed to promote peace, equality, (Manos Unidas, n.d.; Equality and Human Rights Commission, n.d.) (http://www.unjuegopeligroso.org/) (https://www.equalityhumanrights.com/en/lesson-plan-ideas) that are often recommended to be used as part of the citizenship education curriculum.

Conclusions: different approaches, different strengths and weakness in the education of the global citizenry

Each of the three mentioned approaches (global citizenship as a cross-curricular theme, global citizenship integrated into other subjects or global citizenship education as a subject in itself) has, in our understanding, its strengths and weakness. Although, considering the scope of this chapter, it is impossible for us to discuss these issues in depth; we would not like to finish the chapter without identifying at least some of the implications arising from each of these approaches.

Global citizenship education as a cross-curricular theme is often considered the most natural and coherent way of educating the citizenry. When school structures, processes and ethos are coherent toward democratic forms of citizenship, it is more likely that students prefer practicing democracy rather than learning about citizenship. However, there is a risk that by not having an allocated time in the curricula and by offering activities that often are voluntary and not-assessed, global citizenship education is lessened and might easily disappear or become inappropriately characterized. Furthermore, some might feel that if in-school global citizenship education projects are left in the hands of non-prepared citizenship/global specialists, there is a risk of falling into stereotypes, patronizing and other similar attitudes.

In contrast, if global citizenship education is integrated into other subjects, it seems likely that each subject specialist might make a more sophisticated contribution. This second alternative encompasses two risks. First, unless teachers collaborate, students might perceive the global citizenship curricula as fragmented. Second, specialist teachers can be more interested in the discipline content (e.g. history) than in the potential contribution of their discipline to other aims (e.g. history for global citizenship) and leave global citizenship education merely as an anecdote designed to illustrate something which is perceived to be more important.

Some of these challenges could possibly be overcome if global citizenship education was a subject or if the global dimension of citizenship education subjects was emphasized. In both cases, global citizenship education would be guaranteed allocated time in the curricula; specialist teachers would construct a coherent global citizenship education project and some sort of assessment that would reinforce the relevance of the subject. However, the experience of citizenship education – being in constant threat in a number of countries, with little time allocated to it in the curriculum and small numbers of specifically qualified teachers – tell us that we are far from having a strong 'global citizenship education' subject in most countries.

Annotated bibliography

Davies, I., Kiwan, D., Ho, L. -C., Peck, C. L., Peterson, A., Waghid, Y. & Sant, E. (Eds) (2017). *The Palgrave Handbook of Global Citizenship and Education*. London: Palgrave Macmillan.

This handbook provides a detailed account of some of the issues we discuss in this textbook. Particularly interesting for the purposes of this chapter, the section 'Key issues in learning and teaching about global citizenship' of the handbook covers a number of subject areas and discuss how these areas can contribute towards global citizenship education. More precisely, contributions are made in relation to language, science, geography, history and drama and examples are provided from a number of countries including Argentina, Italy, Japan, Chile, Australia, Spain and the United States.

Gaudelli, W. (2016). *Global Citizenship Education: Everyday Transcendence*. New York: Routledge.

This book represents an excellent resource for those interested in looking at how global citizenship education could look in practice. The author, William Gaudelli, is well-versed in the fields of global citizenship, social studies education and in the education of social studies teachers. This knowledge of the theoretical and practical field derives into a book in which critical guidance – is provided about how global citizenship education can be taught and how teachers could be trained to include global citizenship education in their practices.

Think Global (n.d.). The global dimension: the world in your classroom. Retrieved from https://globaldimension.org.uk/resources/browse/

Think global is a UK-based charity that aims to promote global learning. In their website, the charity offers links to numerous resources related to the education of the global citizenry. The website is particularly helpful for primary and secondary teachers. It allows searches for subject, age range and topic. Furthermore, the search engine also allows users to look for resource and can be used cross-curricularly such as teaching materials to prepare school assemblies, awards, audits and so on.

The different links included in this chapter often direct to websites containing multiple resources that could be used for global citizenship education.

Activity

Think about a school you know. It can be the school you work in, the school you would like to work at, the school you attended as a student, the school your children attend or any other school. Select one of the partnership projects you might find in the Erasmus Plus:

(https://www.etwinning.net/en/pub/connect/browse_people_schools_and_pro.htm) or in the British Council website (https://schoolsonline.britishcouncil.org/partner-school/partner-by-project/testimonials) or one of the resources you can find in the global dimension website (https://globaldimension.org.uk/) and discuss the following questions:

a. What activities does the project involve (exchanges, online collaboration, etc.)?
b. What is the approach of the project/resource (cross-curricular, integrated or citizenship as subject)?
c. What are the links of this project/resource with the curriculum of the country/state where the school is settled?

d. What aspects of global citizenship education are emphasized?
e. What type of global citizenship is this project promoting and why?
f. Assuming the aim of the project is to promote this type of global citizenship, what are the strengths and weakness of the project in the pursuit of this aim?
g. What are the challenges and opportunities of participating in this project?
h. What are the challenges and opportunities of participating in this project?

21

Evaluation

Evaluation is widely accepted and practised; it is centrally relevant to many different perspectives about global citizenship education; and it is complex and intensely controversial. We discuss below some of the very many challenges about conducting evaluation in ways that are congruent with the developing what we see as a valid characterization of global citizenship education.

In very broad terms, evaluation simply means considering what an initiative means and whether it has value. It is not the same as assessment: that term is often used to refer to the measuring (formatively or summatively) of the level of achievement reached by individual students. A discussion about assessment of global citizenship education may be seen in the chapter on 'curriculum'. Below are the explorations of what happens when education systems are evaluated and how that connects with global citizenship education. There are increasing emphases on international evaluation but as will be shown below the purposes and processes of such work may not be congruent with the ideals of those who promote global citizenship education. One of the activities towards the end of the chapter asks you to design an evaluation that is congruent with global citizenship education.

The purposes of evaluation may include the following:

- Effectiveness – we want to ensure that we do more good than harm
- Efficiency – we need to use scarce public resources to maximum effect
- Accountability – there must be transparency of what is done and why
- Trust – we want to help ensure/restore trust in government and public services

The data relevant to such work is readily available. There are now large national data sets which may be compared and there are data which have been collected by various international bodies using internationally agreed methods. Examples of the latter include the Organisation for Economic Co-operation and Development (OECD) which manages the high profile Programme for International Student Assessment (PISA).

> The Programme for International Student Assessment (PISA) is a triennial international survey which aims to evaluate education systems worldwide by testing the skills and knowledge of 15-year-old students. (https://www.oecd.org/pisa/aboutpisa/)

OECD also produces Education at a Glance which reports on

> the state of education around the world. It provides data on the output of educational institutions; the impact of learning across countries; the financial and human resources invested in education; access, participation and progression in education; and the learning environment and organisation of schools. (http://www.oecd.org/edu/education-at-a-glance-19991487.htm)

The International Association for the Evaluation of Educational Achievement (IEA) manages Trends in International Mathematics and Science Study (TIMSS) and Progress in International Reading Literacy Study (PIRLS) (see http://timssandpirls.bc.edu/). There are also frameworks to bring together the various projects. There is a Network of Networks Impact Evaluation (NONIE) which brings together various groups including the OECD's Development Assistance Committee's Evaluation Network, the United Nation's Evaluation Group, and the International Organization for Co-operation in Evaluation.

The evaluations undertaken by these international bodies are of clear, obvious and vital significance for reflecting on issues about achievement. It would be extremely unhelpful for our understanding of global citizenship education if we were not to know what these surveys provide about basic or fundamental areas of knowledge. And it is extremely interesting that new developments are occurring in these international surveys that highlight global issues and perspectives (see https://www.oecd.org/pisa/oecd-proposes-new-approach-to-assess-young-peoples-understanding-of-global-issues-and-attitudes-toward-cultural-diversity-and-tolerance.htm).

We also wish to draw attention to the particular focus on the evaluation of civics and citizenship across a wide range of countries. Since the 1970s the IEA has been concerned to explore civics and citizenship with the most recent International Civics and Citizenship Study (ICCS) data gathering taking place in 2016. ICCS has recently introduced work about global citizenship as well as nationally oriented frameworks (see http://www.iea.nl/fileadmin/user_upload/Studies/ICCS_2019/ICCS_2019_Brochure.pdf and http://umc.minedu.gob.pe/wp-content/uploads/2016/04/IEA-ICCS-2016-Framework.pdf). A summary of the work being undertaken by ICCS with some contextual information is given below:

> ICCS 2016 is the second cycle in the framework of the International Civic and Citizenship Education Study (ICCS), and the fourth project conducted by IEA in this area. This comparative research program investigates the ways in which young people are prepared to undertake their roles as citizens.
>
> ICCS 2016 will report on students' knowledge and understanding of concepts and issues related to civics and citizenship, as well as their beliefs, attitudes, and behaviors. For countries that participated in ICCS 2009, the study will also monitor trends in civic knowledge and engagement over seven years. As in the previous cycle, ICCS 2016 will collect a rich array of contextual data about the organization and content of civic and citizenship education in the curriculum, teacher qualifications and experiences, teaching practices, school environment and climate, and home and community support. Optional regional/thematic modules may also be established to explore specific topics of common interest. (http://www.iea.nl/iccs_2016.html)

Results of the 2009 ICCS study can be seen summarized at http://www.iea.nl/iccs_2009.html and in more detail in a range of publications (e.g. Ainley et al. 2013). In very brief summary it can be said that almost all countries do something to provide civics and citizenship; twenty countries that we are included in the survey have it as a specific subject; knowledge and skills are regarded as important but active participation is not widely accepted in teaching programmes. Girls tend to have more knowledge than boys. Social and economic status and an open classroom climate are positively associated with higher levels of knowledge (although in many countries levels of knowledge seem to be declining). Most respondents to the survey are committed to a form of democracy.

The above is meant to indicate that there is a good deal of evaluation work taking place and that it deserves careful consideration. It would not be wise to ignore the results of evaluations by high status bodies whose results apply generally or very particularly to questions of global citizenship. But there are very many tensions and challenges about evaluation and below we explore just some of those that are particularly pertinent to our characterization of global citizenship education.

Some of the debates are rather technical. Statisticians will argue about the merits of different methods. An example of this may be easily seen (e.g. Adams 2003). There will be questions about what to evaluate, who to evaluate and whether the work should be conducted cross-sectionally or longitudinally. And once that work has been done, there will be questions about whether that research is of value and, if so, for what. It is possible that professionals and others will not know where to look to find the results of these evaluations. Perhaps many professionals will simply feel overwhelmed by the data. Distinctions will need to be made between data and indicators (whereas the former is information; the latter is evidence being used in relation to an argument). All of this requires technical knowledge and expertise to know how to judge the worth of the data and not everybody will have these things.

But more important in the context of the central purpose of this book are issues about the purpose and nature of the evaluation regarding types of global citizenship. Adams (2003) has argued that:

> The purpose of studies such as PISA and TIMSS is to stimulate debate about the relative merits of policy choices that are made in education systems. International studies provide a natural complement to in-depth system level analyses by systematically examining educational outcomes, practices and relationships across educational settings. (Adams 2003, p. 377)

For some this intention to stimulate debate is, at least, misleading. Some evaluators seem to adopt an almost Olympian approach in which they position themselves as objective and free from all interests. Even if certain purposes of evaluation are not explicitly acknowledged there is the possibility that – disingenuously or unintentionally – certain choices are being embraced. Wiseman (2010) refers to the three purposes of evaluation as 'to gauge quality, create equality, and establish control over schooling' (p. 18) and this, of course, indicates much more than just objective insight or the stimulation of debate. Kushner (2009) in an excellent piece of work refers to the work of Karlsson (2003) who suggests there are two distinct political ideologies operating in Europe about evaluation:

> New public management, designed to rationalize governmental budget cuts and reduce the public sector; and Democratic evaluation, designed to increase the role of stakeholders in public negotiation and decision making (p. 45).

Questions about purpose must be addressed directly if we are to consider what sort of global citizenship we want. Kushner outlines those questions that need to be asked in relation to these different possible purposes:

Why should evaluation be done? To improve programs? To influence decision making? To protect the public? To solve social problems? To promote social diversity?

- What are the proper social roles for the evaluator as a professional? Researcher? Teacher? Advocate? Facilitator? Judge?
- What should we consider acceptable evidence for making evaluative decisions? Causal claims? Moral conclusions? Expert opinion? Aesthetic judgments? Stakeholder consensus?
- How do we arrive at the most valid understandings of quality? Controlled experiments? Moral deliberation? Phenomenological renderings?
- How can stakeholders best be involved in evaluation studies? As served clients? As participants? As collaborators? As empowered citizens?
- What is the most effective way to ensure the quality of evaluation practice? Advanced training? Accreditation and licensing? Consensual professional standards? Mandatory meta-evaluation? (p. 48)

The above then needs to be considered in detail about particular studies (Kushner 2009, p. 49):

- power relationships, patterns of information flow, and access to resources that follow familial or tribal lines; for example, in an African context (Chapman 1992)?
- group interests that are prioritized over individual rights; for example, in a South Korean context (Smith & Jang 2002)?
- greater respect being accorded elders and those with senior authority; for example, in a South Korean context (Smith & Jang 2002)?
- the quality of social interaction being viewed as important, or more so, than task completion; for example, in a Cameroonian (Smith 1991), Caribbean (Cuthbert 1985), or Maltese (Chircop 1987) context?
- written communication that is associated with authority and so used sparingly, with oral communication dominating; for example, in an Egyptian context (Seefeldt 1985)?

- ancestry and locating current projects in ancestral place and time being considered important; for example, in a Polynesian context (Kawakami et al. 2008)?

The drive to democratic evaluation is, obviously in light of the above, not so straightforward as identifying what works or aiming to stimulate debate. The evaluator has choices about what is done. This is highly complex and not a matter of simply choosing whether we wish to be democrats or not. We do not have simple choices between acting exclusively as a colonialist or as a post colonialist. Indeed the very idea of much of the democratic evaluation that is practised today emerged from a Western context and to impose it on all peoples risks a newer, albeit more anguished, colonialism. The idea of establishing a global conversation around evaluation is incredibly challenging. If the channels for global dialogue are not enjoyed by all then it is somewhat patronising to insist that the perspective and rights of people in all contexts are being considered.

In short there may be three fundamental difficulties. Firstly, as Hood (2014) explains, globalization is not in the interests of some groups. And democratic evaluation may have emerged from – and be part of – globalization. If localization is required then it will be hard to speak a global language in relation to evaluation. Secondly, there are technical and cultural differences about what can be achieved. Any consideration of the Millennium Development Goals, for example, is difficult: what does enrolment mean (is it an indication of quality of process, outcomes for learners or simply years served?); should boys and girls be seen in the same or in different ways in the context of debates about equality and equity and because of the need to recognize group as well as individual identities are repeated years to be counted as single years of schooling; and so on. Thirdly, what sort of relationship should exist between the evaluators and the policy makers? At one level the evaluators are perhaps only fuelling the intense competition over status that is essential to national politicians who wish to be respected on the international stage. But more fundamentally is it possible given global diversity to identify simply and technically what works?

The above three difficulties are hugely challenging. In a sense they replicate debates about the nature of global citizenship itself. Is global citizenship attainable in an appropriately democratically inclusive manner or will it be forever entangled with the struggle between particular groups? Is the fight for universal democracy not a universalist struggle? We take an optimistic view in this book. We wish, of course, to recognize difference but we are not willing to carry the logic of relativism to its ultimate goal. We do not wish to stand back unable to identify what is valuable for all people. We do want to identify those things that are locally relevant in cultural or other terms. Our view is that these foundational challenges to global citizenship education and its evaluation may be met, at least in part, by exploring and explicitly specifying the preferred balance between democracy and rights. The value of technical expertise needs to be culturally interpreted. It is not always the right thing to do to insist that the same is good for all. But neither is it acceptable for powerful groups to insist that those with less power must follow a particular route. Sensitively established international and global evaluation is not easy to achieve.

Annotated bibliography

Kushner, S. (2009). Own goals: democracy, evaluation, and rights in millennium projects. In K. E. Ryan & J. Bradley Cousins (Eds). *The SAGE international handbook of educational evaluation.* (pp. 413–29). London: Sage.

This is an excellent book chapter which is extremely valuable for anyone wishing to understand the nature of evaluation in the context of global citizenship education. A lot of writing on evaluation tends to see that work as simply a job that needs to be done as well as possible. Evaluation by those people is seen as a branch of science. The technical experts must do their job properly. The strength of Kushner's chapter is that he acknowledges the need for technical expertise but also provides excellent explanations of the nature of social science that must be informed by social and political and cultural perspectives.

International Civic and Citizenship Education Study 2009. The International Civic and Citizenship Education Study (ICCS) 2009 was the third IEA study (after projects conducted in 1971 and 1999) on civic and citizenship education.

This is not an evaluation of one specific initiative but rather it is a richly detailed overview of what is happening around the world in relation to civics and citizenship. It is not obviously global; there are countries missing from its international reach but it does provide fascinating insights into the nature of what has been done in policy and professional practice and what young people know and feel they are capable of doing. http://www.iea.nl/iccs_2009.html.

Shaw, I., Greene, J. C. & Mark, M. M. (2006). *The Sage Handbook of Evaluation.* London, Sage.

This is a very valuable publication in which there are detailed descriptions and analyses of the meaning of evaluation and how it is conducted in various contexts. It is a little dated. Its breadth – it goes far beyond education – may be seen as a strength or a limitation depending on one's perspective. The early chapters on democratic evaluation are especially interesting and useful.

Activities

Design an evaluation project (please note, not an assessment project) that seeks to explore the value of recent work on global citizenship education in four schools. One school is based in New York City; another in a rural part of England; one in central Shanghai; and one in rural Nigeria. The initiative that you are evaluating aims to 'help young people understand key issues about global citizenship; to help them to make connections with young people beyond their own country; and to help them to develop an action project in their own area'.

You need to decide:

1. What is your precise evaluation question?
2. What style of evaluation will you follow?
   a) To what extent is your evaluation aligned with the cultural and other differences between the three sites?
   b) To what extent is your project designed to illuminate generally applicable insights?
   c) Is your project designed to allow a measure of control from your respondents? If so, how much control and in what ways is that control to be exercised?
3. Who will you gather data from?
4. What sort of data will you gather?
   a) Will the data be about perceptions of the initiative (i.e. what do respondents and others feel about things?)
   b) Will the data be about outcomes that have emerged from the initiative? (e.g. differences between amounts and types of knowledge before and after the initiative)
   c) How will you collect the data?
      - Interview? Questionnaire? Observation? Documentary analyses? Test scores? Other?
      - Will you gather the data in face to face settings following your travel? Will you ask people based locally to help with the initiative? Will you gather data through virtual communication (e.g. by Skype)?
   d) How will you analyse your data? (Will you rely on software packages such Nvivo to analyse interviews, for example, or will you seek to establish a less explicitly scientific approach?)
5. What are the key aspects of your ethical procedures?
6. To whom will you report? (You are obliged to report formally in a seminar to the funder of the initiative. There are no other restrictions placed on reporting).
   a) Will you see the development of recommendations as a key part of your report or is that possible future work for others?

Bibliography

Abdi, A. A. (2008). De-subjecting subject populations. In A. Abdi & L. Shultz (Eds). *Educating for human rights and global citizenship* (pp. 65–80). Albany, NY: SUNY Press.

Abdi, A. A. (2013). Decolonizing educational and social development platforms in Africa. *African and Asian Studies*, 12, 64–82.

Abdi, A. A., Shultz, L., & Pillay, T. (2015). *Decolonizing Global Citizenship Education*. Rotterdam: Sense Publishers

Adams, R. J. (2003). Response to 'Cautions on OECD's Recent Educational Survey (PISA). *Oxford Review of Education,* 29(3), 377–89.

Adwan, S., Bar-On, D., & Naveh, E. J. (Eds). (2012). *Side by Side: Parallel Histories of Israel-Palestine*. New York: New Press.

Agenda 21: An action plan for the twenty-first century (1992). https://sustainabledevelopment.un.org/content/documents/Agenda21.pdf

Ahmed, F. (2012). Tarbiyah for shakhsiyah (educating for identity): seeking out culturally coherent pedagogy for Muslim children in Britain, *Compare*, 42(5), 725–49.

Ainley, J., Schulz, W., & Friedman, T. (Eds). (2013). *ICCS 2009 Encyclopedia: Approaches to Civic and Citizenship Education Around the World*. Amsterdam: IEA.

Althusser, L. (1972). Ideology and ideological state apparatuses. In B. Cosin (Ed.) *Education, structure and society* (pp. 242–80). Harmondsworth: Penguin.

Amin, S. (2011). *Global History: A View from the South*. Dakar: CODESRIA/Pambazuka Press.

Anderson, B. (1983/2006). *Imagined Communities: Reflections on the Origin and Spread of Nationalism*. London: Verso.

Andreotti, V. (2006). Soft vs critical global citizenship. *Policy & Practice: A Development Education Review*, 3, 40–51.

Andreotti, V. (2011). *Actionable Postcolonial Theory in Education*. Basingstoke: Palgrave Macmillan.

Andreotti, V. (2014). Actionable curriculum theory: AAACS 2013 closing keynote. *Journal of the American Association for the Advancement of Curriculum Studies*, 10(1–10). Retrieved from http://www.uwstout.edu/soe/jaaacs/upload/v10-Andreotti.pdf.

Andreotti, V., & de Souza, L. M. (2013). *Postcolonial Perspectives on Global Citizenship Education*. London: Routledge.

Andreotti, V., & de Souza, L. M. T. M. (2008). *Learning to Read the World: Through Other Eyes*. Derby: Global Education.

Andreotti, V., Stein, S., Ahenakew, C., & Hunt, D. (2015). Mapping interpretations of decolonization in the context of higher education. *Decolonization: Indigeneity, Education & Society*, 4(1), 21–40.

Amnesty International UK. (2014). *Amnesty International Resources*. Retrieved from https://www.amnesty.org.uk/resources/1635/1553/all/1580/0/1#.V9wLboWcEcS.

Appadurai, A. (1996). *Modernity at Large*. Minneapolis, MN: University of Minnesota Press.

Aragon, M. J., Bittencourt, T., & Johnson, K. A. (2011). *The Curriculum Companion for Immigration: The Ultimate Teen Guide by Tatyana Kleyn*. New York: Teachers College, Columbia University. Retrieved from https://immigrationcurriculum.files.wordpress.com/2011/03/immigration-curriculum-final-draft.pdf.

Arthur, J. (2003). *Education with Character: the Moral Economy of Schooling*. London: RoutledgeFalmer.

Arthur, J. (2015). Extremism and neo-liberal education policy: a contextual critique of the trojan horse affair in Birmingham schools. *British Journal of Educational Studies*, 63(3), 311–28. http://doi.org/10.1080/00071005.2015.1069258.

Arthur, J., Davies, I., Kerr, D., & Wrenn, A. (2003). *Citizenship through Secondary History*. London: Routledge.

Assié-Lumumba, N. T. (2017). The Ubuntu paradigm in comparative and international education: epistemological challenges and opportunities in our field. *Comparative Education Review*, 61 (1), 1–21.

Association for Citizenship Teaching. (n.d.). *Political literacy*. Retrieved from http://www.teachingcitizenship.org.uk/democracy-government-politics-economy/political-literacy.

Australian Government. (n.d.). *Global education*. Retrieved from https://www.globaleducation.edu.au.

Bamber, P., & Hankin, L. (2011). Transformative learning through service-learning: no passport required. *Education + Training*, 53(2/3), 190–206.

Barca, I., Castro, J., & Amaral, C. (2010). Looking for conceptual frameworks in history: the accounts of Portuguese 12–13 year-old pupils. *Education 3–13*, 38(3), 275–88.

Barton, K. (2005). History and identity in pluralist democracies: reflections on research in the U.S. and Northern Ireland, *Canadian Social Studies*, 39(2), n2.

Battiste, M. (Ed) (2000). *Reclaiming Indigenous Voice and Vision*. Vancouver: University of British Columbia Press.

Benedito Vidagany, B., Morales Hernández, A. J., Parra Monserrat, D., & Santana Martin, D. (2016). *El concepto de ciudadanía global y su representación social en la educación primaria: proyectos escolares innovadores y educación para la ciudadanía planetaria*. In C. R. García Ruiz, A. Arroyo Doreste & B. Andreu Mediero (Coord.). *Deconstruir la alteridad desde la didáctica de las ciencias sociales: educar para una ciudadanía global* (pp. 615–24). Las Palmas de Gran Canaria (Spain): Universidad de la Palma y AUPDCS.

Berna, K. A. Y. A., & Aytaç, K. A. Y. A. (2012). Teacher candidates' perceptions of global citizenship in the age of technology. *Sakarya University Journal of Education*, 2(3), 81–95.

Biesta, G. (2009). Good education in an age of measurement: on the need to reconnect with the question of purpose in education. *Educational Assessment, Evaluation and Accountability*, 21(1), 33–46.

Biesta G. (2016). Say you want a revolution... Suggestions for the impossible future of critical pedagogy. In A. Darder, P. Mayo & J. Paraskeva (Eds). *International Critical Pedagogy Reader* (pp. 317–26). New York: Routledge.

Biesta, G., & Lawy, R. (2006). From teaching citizenship to learning democracy: overcoming individualism in research, policy and practice. *Cambridge Journal of Education*, 36(1), 63–79.

Bourn, D. (2014). What is meant by development education? *Diálogos educativos para a transformação social*, 1, 7–23.

Bourn, D. & Hunt, F. (2011). *Global Dimension In Secondary Schools*. London: Development Education Research Centre.

Bradbery, D. (2012). *Using Children's Literature to Build Concepts of Teaching about Global Citizenship*. Australian Association for Research in Education (NJ1).

Breit, R., Obijiofor, L., & Fitzgerald, R. (2013). Internationalization as de-westernization of the curriculum: the case of journalism at an Australian University. *Journal of Studies in International Education*, 17(2), 119–35.

British Council. (2015). *Why Partner with a School?* Retrieved from https://schoolsonline.britishcouncil.org/partner-school/why-partner.

British Council (2016). *Emerging Infectious Diseases: How Do We Stop New Diseases Spreading?* Retrieved from https://schoolsonline.britishcouncil.org/classroom-resources/list/emerging-infectious-diseases-how-do-we-stop-new-diseases-spreading.

Brookes, M., & Becket, N. (2010). Developing global perspectives through international management degrees. *Journal of Studies in International Education*, 15(4), 374–94.

Brooks, D. (2015, January 8). I Am Not Charlie Hebdo. *The New York Times*. Retrieved from http://www.nytimes.com.

Brown, G. (2006). Speech to the Fabian society, January 2006. Retrived from http://news.bbc.co.uk/1/hi/uk_politics/4611682.stm (accessed 14 August 2014).

Brown, T., & England, J. (2005). Identity, narrative and practitioner research: a Lacanian perspective. *Discourse: Studies in the Cultural Politics of education*, 26(4), 443–58.

Bryan, A. (2013). 'The impulse to help':(Post) humanitarianism in an era of the 'new' development advocacy. *International Journal of Development Education and Global Learning*, 5(2), 5–29.

Buckner, E., & Russell, S. G. (2013). Portraying the global: cross-national trends in textbooks' portrayal of globalization and global citizenship. *International Studies Quarterly*, 57(4), 738–50.

Butler, J. (1997). *The Psychic Life of Power: Theories in Subjection*. Berkeley: Stanford University Press.

Camicia, S. P., & Franklin, B. M. (2011). What type of global community and citizenship? Tangled discourses of neoliberalism and critical democracy in curriculum and its reform. *Globalisation, Societies and Education*, 9(3–4), 311–22.

Caruana, V. (2014). Re-thinking global citizenship in higher education: from cosmopolitanism and resilience and resilient. *Higher Education Quarterly*, 68(1), 85–104. doi:10.1111/hequ.12030.

Castro, C. J. (2004). Sustainable development: mainstream and critical perspectives. *Organization & Environment*, 17(2), 195–225.

Cho, Y. H., & Chi, E. (2015). A comparison of attitudes related to global citizenship between Korean-and US-educated Korean university students. *Asia Pacific Journal of Education*, 35(2), 213–25.

Chong, E. K. (2015). Global citizenship education and Hong Kong's secondary school curriculum guidelines: from learning about rights and understanding responsibility to challenging inequality. *Asian Education and Development Studies*, 4(2), 221–47.

Chui, W. H., & Leung, E. W. (2014). Youth in a global world: attitudes towards globalization and global citizenship among university students in Hong Kong. *Asia Pacific Journal of Education*, 34(1), 107–24.

Clifford, V., & Montgomery, C. (2014). Challenging conceptions of western higher education and promoting graduates as global citizens. *Higher Education Quarterly*, 68(1), 28–45. doi:10.1111/hequ.12029.

Colley, L. (1992). *Britons: Forging the Nation 1707–1837*. London: Pimlico.

Coloma, R. S. (2013). Empire: an analytical category for educational research. *Educational Theory*, 63(6), 639–658.

Colomer Rubio, J. C., Campo Pais, B., & Santana Martin, D. (2016). Aportaciones al conocimiento de la ciudadanía global del alumnado del grado de magisterio en la universidad de valencia. In C. R. García Ruiz, A. Arroyo Doreste & B. Andreu Mediero (Coord). *Deconstruir la alteridad desde la didáctica de las ciencias sociales: educar para una ciudadanía global* (pp. 594–694). Las Palmas de Gran Canaria (Spain): Universidad de la Palma y AUPDCS.

Connell, R. (2007). The northern theory of globalization. *Sociological Theory*, 25(4), 368–85.

Connolly, W. (1991). *Identity/Difference*. Ithaca: Cornell University Press.

Cooper, D. (2004). *Challenging Diversity: Rethinking Equality and the Value of ifference*. Cambridge University Press.

Coryell, J. E., Spencer, B. J., & Sehin, O. (2013). Cosmopolitan adult education and global citizenship: perceptions from a european itinerant graduate professional study abroad program. *Adult Education Quarterly*, 64(2), 145–64.

Cox, C., & Scruton, R. (1984). *Peace Studies: A Critical Survey*. New York: Hyperion Press.

Credit Suisse. (October, 2015). *Global Wealth Report 2015*. Retrieved from https://publications.credit-suisse.com/tasks/render/file/?fileID=F2425415-DCA7-80B8-EAD989AF9341D47E.

Crick, B. (1962). *In Defence of Politics*. Harmondsworth: Penguin.

Crick, B. (2000). *Essays on Citizenship*. London: Continuum.

Crick, B., & Porter, A. (eEds.) (1978). *Political Education and Political Literacy*. London: Longman.

Crutzen, P., & Schwagerl, C. (2011). Living in the anthropocene: toward a new global ethic. *Environment 360*. Retrieved from http://e360.yale.edu/feature/living_in_the_anthropocene_toward_a_new_global_ethos/2363/ Accessed July, 10, 2016.

Daquila, T. C. (2013). Internationalizing higher education in singapore: government policies and the NUS experience. *Journal of Studies in International Education*, 17(5), 629–47.

Davies, I., & Fülöp, M. (2010). 'Citizenship': what does it mean to trainee teachers in England and Hungary? *Napredak*, 8–32.

Davies, I., Evans, M., & Reid, A. (2005). Globalising citizenship education? A critique of 'global education' and 'citizenship education'. *British Journal of Educational Studies*, 53(1), 66–89.

Davies, I., Gorard, S., & McGuinn, N. (2005). Citizenship education and character education: similarities and contrasts. *British Journal of Educational Studies*, 53(3), 341–58.

Davis, W. (2009). *The Wayfinders: Why Ancient Wisdom Matters in the Modern World*. Toronto: Anansi Press.
Dawkins, R. (1976). *The Selfish Gene*. Oxford: Oxford University Press.
Dean, H. (2014). A post-Marshallian conception of global social citizenship. In E. Isin & P. Nyers (Eds) *Routledge handbook of global citizenship studies* (PP. 128–38). London: Routledge.
De Mol, Y. (2007). Radios Africaines Pour la Paix. Retrieved from https://www.sfcg.org/programmes/rfpa/pdf/RAPP_1-11.pdf
Department for Education. (2015). Character education: apply for 2015 grant funding. Retrieved from https://www.gov.uk/government/news/character-education-apply-for-2015-grant-funding (accessed 4 July 2016).
Department for International Development. (DfID). (2005). *Developing the global dimension in the school curriculum*. Retrieved from http://www.globaldimension.org.uk/docs/dev_global_dim.pdf
de Sousa Santos, B. (2014). *Epistemologies of the South: Justice Against Epistemicide*. London: Routledge.
DFE/QCA. (1998). *Education for Citizenship and the Teaching of Democracy in Schools*. London: QCA.
Dolby, N. (2007). Reflections on nation: American undergraduates and education abroad. *Journal of Studies in International Education*, 11(2), 141–56.
Dooly, M. (2015). Note of the editor. *Bellaterra Journal of Teaching & Learning Language & Literature*, 8(2), 1–12.
Dorling, D. (2014). *Inequality and the 1%*. London/New York: Verso Books.
Draxler, A. (2014). International investment in education for development: public good or economic tool? *International Development Policy/Revue internationale de politique de development* (Online), 5. Retrieved from http://poldev.revues.org/1772 (accessed 21 February 2017).
Duczek, S. (1980). *The Peace Studies Project: A Case Study*. York, University of York: unpublished MA thesis.
Duczek, S. (1984). Peace Education. Unpublished MA dissertation, University of York.
Dussel, E. (2013a). Agenda for a South-South philosophical dialogue. *Human Architecture: Journal of the Sociology of Self-Knowledge*, XI(1), 3018.
Dussel, E. (2013b). *Ethics of Liberation in the Age of Globalization and Exclusion*. Durham/London: Duke University Press.
Education Scotland. (n.d.). *Global citizenship*. Retrieved from http://www.educationscotland.gov.uk/learningandteaching/learningacrossthecurriculum/themesacrosslearning/globalcitizenship/
Ekman, J., & Amnå, E. (2012). Political participation and civic engagement: towards a new typology. *Human Affairs*, 22(3), 283–300.
Environmental Literacy and Inquiry Working Group at Lehigh University. (2015). *Environmental literacy and inquiry*. Retrieved from http://www.ei.lehigh.edu/eli/index.html
Equality and Human Rights Commission, (n.d.). *Lesson plan ideas*. Retrieved from https://www.equalityhumanrights.com/en/lesson-plan-ideas
Ermine, W. (2007). The ethical space of engagement. *Indigenous Law Journal*, 6(1), 193–203.
Escobar, A. (1995). *Encountering Development: The Making and Unmaking of the Third World*. Princeton: Princeton University Press.
Evans, M. (2015). Why South Korea is rewriting its history books. Retrieved from http://www.bbc.co.uk/news/world-asia-34960878 (accessed 30 June 2016).

Fonesca de Andrade, D. (2011). Challenging the focus of ESD a southern perspective of ESD guidelines. *Journal of Education for Sustainable Development*, 5(1),141–6.doi:10.1177/097340821000500116.
Foucault, M. (1982). The subject and power. *Critical Inquiry*, 8(4), 777–95.
Foucault, M. (2002). *The Order of Things: An Archaeology of the Human Sciences*. London: Routledge.
Frazer, N. (2009). *Scales of Justice: Reimagining Political Space in a Globalizing World*. New York: Columbia University Press.
Freire, P. (1970). *Pedagogy of the Oppressed*. New York: Continuum, 72.
Furco, A. (1994). A conceptual framework for the institutionalization for youth service programs in primary and secondary education. *Journal of Adolescence*, 17(4), 395–409.
Gaudelli, W. (2017). Geography and global citizenship. In I. Davies, L. C. Ho, D. Kiwan, A. Peterson, C. Peck, E. Sant, & Y. Waghid (Eds). *The Palgrave handbook of global citizenship and education*. Basingstoke: Palgrave Macmillan.
Gay, R. (2015). If je ne suis pas Charlie, am I a bad person? Nuance gets lost in groupthink. *The Guardian*. Retrieved from http://www.theguardian.com.
Geelan, D. (2017). Science and global citizenship. In I. Davies, L. C. Ho, D. Kiwan, A. Peterson, C. Peck, F. Sant & Y. Waghid (Eds). *The Palgrave handbook of global citizenship and education*. Basingstoke: Palgrave Macmillan.
Gomaa, E. H. (2014). Video production as a tool to reinforce media literacy and citizenship in Egypt. In S. H. Culver & P. Kerr (Eds). *Global citizenship in a digital world* (pp. 33–43). Sweden: Nordicom.
González, N. (coord.). *Educación para la ciudadanía global desde el currículo*. Barcelona: Fundació Solidaritat UB, 2012. Retrieved from http://hdl.handle.net/2445/34623.
Gove, M. (2011). *National curriculum review launched*. London, Department for Education. Retrieved from https://www.gov.uk/government/news/national-curriculum-review-launched (accessed 14 December 2016).
Grosfoguel, R. (2013). The structure of knowledge in westernized universities. *Human Architecture: Journal of the Sociology of Self-Knowledge*, XI (1), 73–90.
GTP. (n.d.). *Global teenager project*. Retrieved from http://www.ict-edu.nl/gtp/wat-is-gtp/.
Guth, S., & Helm, F. (2010). *Telecollaboration 2.0: Language, Literacies and Intercultural Learning in the 21st Century (Vol. 1)*. London: Peter Lang.
Haigh, M. J. (2002). Internationalisation of the curriculum: designing inclusive education for a small world. *Journal of Geography in Higher Education*, 26(1), 49–66.
Hall, S. (2000). Who needs 'identity'? In P. Du Gay, J. Evans & P. Redman (Eds) *Identity: a reader* (pp. 15–30). London: Sage.
Haraway, D. (2016). *Staying with the Trouble: Making Kin in the Chthulucene*. Durham: Duke University Press.
Hargreaves, D. (1996). *The Mosaic of Learning*. London: Demos.
Harris, I. M. (1999). Types of peace education. In A. Raviv, L. Oppenheimer & D. Bar-Tal (Eds) *Children understand war and peace: a call for international peace education* (pp. 299–317). San Francisco: Jossey Bass.
Harshman, J. R., & Augustine, T. A. (2013). Fostering global citizenship education for teachers through online research. *The Educational Forum*, 77(4), 450–63.

Harvey, D. (2005). *A Brief History of Neoliberalism*. New York, NY: Oxford University Press.
Harvey, D. (2008). The right to the city. *New Left Review*, 53, 23–40.
Hayward, B. (2012). *Children, Citizenship and Environment: Nurturing a Democratic Imagination in a Changing World*. Cornwall, UK: Routledge.
Heater, D. (1997). The reality of multiple citizenship. In I. Davies & A. Sobisch (Eds). *Developing European citizens* (pp. 21–48). Sheffield: Sheffield Hallam University Press.
Heater, D. (1999). *What Is Citizenship?* Cambridge: Polity Press.
Held, D. (1995). *Democracy and the global order: from the modern state to cosmopolitan governance*. Cambridge: Polity Press.
Held, D. (2003). Cosmopolitanism: taming globalization. In D. Held & A. McGrew (Eds). *The global transformations reader* (pp. 514–29). Cambridge: Polity Press.
Held, D., & McGrew, A. (Eds) (2005). *The Global Transformations Reader*. Cambridge: Polity Press.
Hicks, D. (Ed.) (1988). *Education for Peace: Issues, Principles and Practice in the Classroom*. London: Routledge.
Hobsbawn, E., & Ranger, T. (ed.) (1983). *The Invention of Tradition*. Cambridge: Cambridge University Press.
Holden, C., & Hicks, D. (2007). Making global connections: the knowledge, understanding and motivation of trainee teachers. *Teaching and Teacher Education*, 23(1), 13–23.
Holt, J. (1964/1977). *How Children Fail*. Harmondsworth: Penguin Books.
Honneth, A. (1995). *The Struggle for Recognition: The Moral Grammar of Social Conflicts*. Cambridge: Polity Press.
Hood, S. (2014). Evaluation for and by Navajos: a narrative case of the irrelevance of globalization. In E. Isin & P. Nyers (Eds) *Routledge handbook of global citizenship studies* (pp. 447–65). London: Routledge.
Hopkins, C. (2012). Reflections on 20+ years of ESD. *Journal of Education for Sustainable Development*, 6(1), 21–35.
Horn, A. S., & Fry, G. W. (2012). Promoting global citizenship through study abroad: the influence of program destination, type, and duration on the propensity for development volunteerism. *VOLUNTAS: International Journal of Voluntary and Nonprofit Organizations*, 24(4), 1159–79.
Huckle, J., & Wals, A. E. (2015). The UN decade of education for sustainable development: business as usual in the end. *Environmental Education Research*, 21(3), 491–505.
Huddleston, T. (2004). *Citizens and Society*. London: Hodder and Stoughton.
Ikeno, N. (2011). *Citizenship Education in Japan*. London: Continuum.
Isin, E., & Nyers, P. (2014). *Routledge Handbook of Global Citizenship Studies*. Abingdon: Routledge.
Jefferess, D. (2008). Global citizenship and the cultural politics of benevolence. *Critical Literacies*, 2(1), 27–36.
Jones, E., & Killick, D. (2013). Graduate attributes and the internationalized curriculum: embedding a global outlook in disciplinary learning outcomes. *Journal of Studies in International Education*, 17(2), 165–82. doi:10.1177/1028315312473655.
Joppke, C. (2007). Beyond national models: civic integration policies for immigrants in Western Europe. *West European Politics*, 30(1), 1–22.

Journell, W. (2010). Standardizing citizenship: the potential influence of state curriculum standards on the civic development of adolescents. *PS: Political Science and Politics*, 43, 351–8.

Kapoor, I. (2008). *The Postcolonial Politics of Development*. London: Routledge.

Kennedy, K. J. (2012). Global trends in civic and citizenship education: what are the lessons for nation states? *Education Sciences*, 2(3), 121–35.

Kahn, R. (2010). *Critical Pedagogy, Ecoliteracy, & Planetary Crisis: The Ecopedagogy Movement*. New York: Peter Lang.

King, M. L. (1992). I have a dream. In C. Ricks & W. L. Vance (Eds). *The faber book of America* (pp. 206–9). London: Faber and Faber.

Kirkwood-Tucker, T. F. (2004). Empowering teachers to create a more peaceful world through global education: simulating the United Nations. *Theory & Research in Social Education*, 32(1), 56–74.

Kiwan, D. (2008). *Education for Inclusive Citizenship*. London: Routledge.

Kohlberg, L. (1973). The claim to moral adequacy of a highest stage of moral judgment. *The Journal of Philosophy*, 70(18), 630–46.

Kohn, A. (1997). How not to teach values. a critical look at character education. *Phi Delta Kappan*, 78(6), 429–439.

Kushner, S. (2009). Own goals: democracy, evaluation, and rights in millennium projects. In K. E. Ryan & J. B. Cousins (Eds). *The SAGE international handbook of educational evaluation* (pp. 413–29). London: Sage.

Kwan-choi Tse, T. (2007). Whose citizenship education? Hong Kong from a spatial and cultural politics perspective. *Discourse: Studies in the Cultural Politics of Education*, 28(2), 159–77.

Kymlicka, W. (1998). *Finding Our Way: Rethinking Ethnocultural Relations in Canada*. Don Mills, ON: Oxford University Press.

Kymlicka, W. (2011). Multicultural citizenship within multination states. *Ethnicities*, 11(3), 281–302.

Kymlicka, W., & Norman, W. (1994). Return of the citizen: a survey of recent work on citizenship theory. *Ethics*, 104(2), 352–81.

Laclau, E. (2005). *On Populist Reason*. London: Verso.

Larsen, M., & Faden, L. (2008). Supporting the growth of global citizenship educators. *Brock education*, 17, 71–86.

Latour, B. (2004). *Politics of Nature: How to Bring the Sciences into Democracy*. Cambridge, MA: Harvard University Press.

Lee, W. & Leung, S. (2006). Global citizenship education in Hong Kong and Shanghai secondary schools: ideals, realities and expectations. *Citizenship Teaching and Learning*, 2(2), 68–84.

Levstik, L. (2014). What can history and the social sciences contribute to civic education? In J. Pagès & A. Santisteban (Eds). *Una mirada al pasado y un proyecto de futuro: investigación e innovación en didáctica de las ciencias sociales* (pp. 43–52). Bellaterra: Servei de Publicacions de la UAB. Retrieved from http://didactica-ciencias-sociales.org/wp-content/uploads/2013/11/XXVSIMPO1_v2.pdf.

Lickona, T. (1994). Foreword. In H. A. Huffman. *Developing a character education program: one school district's experience* (pp. v–viii). Alexandria, VA: Association for Supervision and Curriculum Development and the Character Education Partnership.

Lim, C. P. (2008). Global citizenship education, school curriculum and games: learning Mathematics, English and Science as a global citizen. *Computers & Education*, 51(3), 1073–93.

Lunn, J. (2008). Global perspectives in higher education: taking the agenda forward in the United Kingdom. *Journal of Studies in International Education*, 12(3), 231–54.

MacIntyre, A. (1988). *Whose justice? Whose Rationality*. Notre Dame, Indiana: University of Notre Dame P.

Mance, H. (2016). Britain has had enough of experts, says Gove. *Politics and Policy*. Retrieved from http://www.ft.com/cms/s/0/3be49734-29cb-11e6-83e4-abc22d5d108c.html#axzz4DiUyedGJ (accessed 7 July 2016).

Manos Unidas. (n.d.). *Un juego peligroso*. Retrieved from http://www.unjuegopeligroso.org/.

Marshall, H. (2011). Instrumentalism, ideals and imaginaries: theorising the contested space of global citizenship education in schools. *Globalisation, Societies and Education*, 9(3–4), 411–26.

Marshall, T. H. (1963). *Sociology at the Crossroads*. London: Heinemann.

Mahon, R. (2010). After neo-liberalism?: The OECD, the World Bank and the child. *Global Social Policy*, 10(2), 172–92. doi:10.1177/1468018110366615.

Mannion, G., Biesta, G., Priestley, M., & Ross, H. (2011). The global dimension in education and education for global citizenship: genealogy and critique. *Globalisation, Societies and Education*, 9(3–4), 443–56.

Marcuse, H. (1992). Ecology and the critique of modern society. *Capitalism, Nature, Socialism*, 3(3), 38–40.

Marshall, H. (2009). Educating the European citizen in the global age: engaging with the post-national and identifying a research agenda. *Journal of Curriculum Studies*, 41(2), 247–67.

Matthews, J., & Sidhu, R. (2005). Desperately seeking the global subject: international education, citizenship and cosmopolitanism. *Globalisation, Societies and Education*, 3(1), 49–66.

Mbiti, J. S. (1969). *African Religions and Philosophy*. London: Heinemann.

McCormack, O., & O'Flaherty, J. (2010). An examination of pre-service teachers' attitudes towards the inclusion of development education into Irish post-primary schools. *Teaching and Teacher Education*, 26(6), 1332–39.

McCowan, T. (2015). Theories of development. In T. McCowan & E. Unterhalter (Eds), *Education and international development: an introduction* (pp. 31–48). London: Bloomsbury.

McLaughlin, T., & Halstead, M. (1999). Education in character and virtue. In T. McLaughlin & M. Halstead (Eds). *Education in morality* (pp. 131–62). London: Routledge.

Mignolo, W. (2000). *Local Histories/Global Designs: Coloniality, Subaltern Knowledges, and Border Thinking*. Princeton, NJ: Princeton University Press.

Mignolo, W. (2011). *Darker Side of Western Modernity: Global Future, Decolonial Options*. Durham, NC/London: Duke University Press.

Mill, J.S. (1861/2008). *Representative Government*. Norderstadt: Grin Verlag.

Miller, D. (2010). Against global democracy. In K. Breen & S. O'Neill (Eds). After the nation: critical reflections on post-nationalism (pp. 141–60). Basingstoke: Palgrave Macmillan.

Miller, G. (2013). Education for citizenship: community engagement between the global South and the global North. *Journal of Geography in Higher Education*, 37(1), 44–58.

Ministry of Education (2012). *Character and citizenship education syllabus primary*. (Ministry of Education, Singapore). Retrieved from https://www.moe.gov.sg/education/syllabuses/character-citizenship-education.

Mochizuki, Y., & Bryan, A. (2015). Climate change education in the context of education for sustainable development: rationale and principles. *Journal of Education for Sustainable Development*, 9(1), 4–26.

Mokuku, T. (2012). Lehae La Rona: epistemological interrogation to broaden our conception of environment and sustainability. *Canadian Journal of Environmental Education (CJEE)*, 17, 159–72. Retrieved from https://cjee.lakeheadu.ca/article/viewFile/1048/663.

Montgomery, C., & McDowell, L. (2009). Social networks and the international student experience an international community of practice? *Journal of Studies in International Education*, 13(4), 455–66.

Moore, J. (2013). *Capitalism in the Web of Life*. New York: Verso Books.

Mudimbe, V. Y. (1988). *Liberty in African and Western Thought*. Washington, DC: Institute for Independent Education.

Myers, J., & Zaman, H. (2009). Negotiating the global and national: immigrant and dominant-culture adolescents' vocabularies of citizenship in a transnational world. *The Teachers College Record*, 111(11), 2589–625.

Myers, J. P. (2010). 'To benefit the world by whatever means possible': adolescents' constructed meanings for global citizenship. *British Educational Research Journal*, 36(3), 483–502.

Mylius, B. (2013). Towards the unthinkable: Earth jurisprudence and an ecocentric episteme. *Australian Journal of Legal Philosophy*, 38, 102–38.

Naciones Unidas. (n.d.). *Simulaciones naciones unidas*. Retrieved from http://nacionesunidas.org.co/modelos/.

Nambiar, P., & Sarabhai, K. V. (2015). Challenges that lie ahead for ESD. *Journal of Education for Sustainable Development*, 9(1), 1–3.

Nancy, J. L. (2007). *The Creation of the World or Globalization*. New York: State University of New York Press.

Naqvi, R., Thorne, K., Pfitscher, C., Nordstokke, D., & McKeough, A. (2012). Reading dual language books: improving early literacy skills in linguistically diverse classrooms. *Journal of Early Childhood Research*, 11(1), 3–15. doi: 0.1177/1476718X12449453.

National Youth White Paper on Global Citizenship (2015). *National Youth White Paper on Global Citizenship*. Retrieved from http://unesco.ca/~/media/unesco/jeunesse/national_youth_white_paper_gc_2015%20-mtm.pdf.

Neill, A. S. (1966). *Summerhill. A Radical Approach to Education* (5th impression). London: Victor Gollancz.

Nelson, J., & Kerr, D. (2006). *Active citizenship in INCA countries: definitions, policies, practices and outcomes*. National Foundation for Educational. Retrieved from http://nzcurriculum.tki.org.nz/index.php/content/download/654/4291/file/Active_Citizenship_Report.pdf.

Nick, L., & Smith, N. L. (2009). Fundamental evaluation issues in a global society. In K. E. Ryan & J. B. Cousins. *The SAGE international handbook of educational evaluation* (pp. 37–52). London: Sage.

Ní Mhurchú, A. (2014). Citizenship beyond state sovereignty. In E. Isin & Nyers, P. (Eds) *Routledge handbook of global citizenship studies* (pp. 119–27). London: Routledge.

Norris, P. (2005). Global governance and cosmopolitan citizens. In D. Held & A. McGrew (Eds). *The global transformations reader* (pp. 287–98). Cambridge: Polity Press.

Nussbaum, M. (2002). Education for citizenship in an era of global connection. *Studies in Philosophy and Education*, 21, 289–303.

O'Donoghue, R., & Russo, V. (2004). Emerging patterns of abstraction in environmental education: a review of materials, methods and professional development perspectives. *Environmental Education Research*, 10(3), 331–51.

Odora Hoppers, C. (2009). From bandit colonialism to the modern triage society: towards a moral and cognitive reconstruction of knowledge and citizenship. *International Journal of African Renaissance Studies*,4 (2), 168–80.

OECD (2016). *Global competency for an inclusive world*. Retrieved from http://www.oecd.org/pisa/aboutpisa/Global-competency-for-an-inclusive-world.pdf.

Olssen, M. (2004). From the Crick Report to the Parekh Report: multiculturalism, cultural difference, and democracy – the re-visioning of citizenship education. *British Journal of Sociology of Education*, 25(2), 179–92.

Ortloff, D. H. (2011). Moving the borders: multiculturalism and global citizenship in the German social studies classroom. *Educational Research*, 53(2), 137–49.

Osler, A. (2011). Teacher interpretations of citizenship education: national identity, cosmopolitan ideals, and political realities. *Journal of curriculum studies*, 43(1), 1–24.

Oxfam Australia. (n.d.). *Term two featured resource: fair trade*. Retrieved from https://www.oxfam.org.au/get-involved/how-schools-can-get-involved/resources-for-teachers/term-two-features-resource-fairtrade/.

Oxfam Hong Kong. (2016). *Global citizenship education*. Retrieved from http://www.oxfam.org.hk/en/globalcitizenshipeducation.aspx.

Oxfam UK. (n.d.). *The world cup: a fair game?* Retrieved from http://www.oxfam.org.uk/education/resources/the-world-cup-a-fair-game.

Oxley, L., & Morris, P. (2013). Global citizenship: a typology for distinguishing its multiple conceptions. *British Journal of Educational Studies*, 61, 3, 301–25.

Parker, W. C. (2011). 'International education' in US public schools. *Globalisation, Societies and Education*, 9(3–4), 487–501.

Parmenter, L. (2011). Power and place in the discourse of global citizenship education. *Globalisation, Societies and Education*, 9(3–4), 367–80.

Patterson, L. M., Carrillo, P. B., & Salinas, R. S. (2011). Lessons from a global learning virtual classroom. *Journal of Studies in International Education*, 16(2), 182–97.

Peacock, N., & Harrison, N. (2009). "It's so much easier to go with what's easy" "mindfulness" and the discourse between United Kingdom. *Domestic Student Attitudes : A Brief*, 487–508.

Perkin, D., & Pearson, A. (2016). Presenting the world: country poster presentations. *The Language Teacher,* 40(4), Retrieved from http://jalt-publications.org/node/23/articles/5248-presenting-world-country-poster-presentations.

Philippou, S., Keating, A., & Ortloff, D. H. (2009). Citizenship education curricula: comparing the multiple meanings of supra-national citizenship in Europe and beyond. *Journal of Curriculum Studies*, 41(2), 291–9.

Phillips, D., & Schweisfurth, M. (2014). *Comparative and international education: an introduction to theory, method, and practice.* London: Bloomsbury.

Pike, G. (2008). Global education. In J. Arthur, I. Davies & C. Hahn (Eds). *The Sage handbook of education for citizenship and democracy* (pp. 468–80). Los Angeles: Sage Publications.

Pike, G. & Selby, D. (1986). Scrutinising Scruton: an analysis of Roger Scruton's attack on World Studies. *Westminster Studies in Education*, 9(1), 3–8.

Piketty, T. (2015). *The Economics of Inequality.* Translated by Arthur Goldhammer. Cambridge, MA/London: Belknap Press of Harvard University Press.

Porto, M. (2017). Language and global citizenship. In I. Davies, L.C. Ho, D. Kiwan, A. Peterson, C. Peck, E. Sant & Y. Waghid, (2017). *The Palgrave handbook of global citizenship and education.* Palgrave Macmillan.

Practical action (n.d.). *STEM challenges and awards.* Retrieved from http://practicalaction.org/stem.

Prahalad, C. K., & Hammond, A. (2002). Serving the World's poor profitably, *Harvard Business Review*, September 2002, 48–57.

Proposed Universal Declaration of the Rights of Mother Earth. (2010). https:// pwccc.wordpress.com/2010/04/24/proposal-universal-declaration-of-the-rightsof-mother-earth/.

Rainbow village. (2015). *The "Rainbow village" project.* Retrieved from http://therainbowvillageproject.blogspot.co.uk/.

Rapoport, A. (2010). We cannot teach what we don't know: Indiana teachers talk about global citizenship education. *Education, Citizenship and Social Justice*, 5(3), 179–90.

Rathzel, N. & Uzzell, D. (2009). Transformative environmental education: a collective rehearsal for reality. *Environmental Education Research*, 15(3), 263–77.

Ravitch, D. (2006). Should we teach Patriotism? *Phi Delta Kappan*, 87(8), 579–81.

Rawls, J. (1985). Justice as fairness: political not metaphysical. *Philosophy and Public Affairs*, 14(3), 223–51.

Reid, A., Teamey, K., & Dillon, J. (2002). Traditional ecological knowledge for learning with sustainability in mind. *The trumpeter*, 18(1), 113–36.

Reilly, J., & Niens, U. (2014). Global citizenship as education for peacebuilding in a divided society: structural and contextual constraints on the development of critical dialogic discourse in schools. *Compare: A Journal of Comparative and International Education*, 44(1), 53–76.

Rico, M., Ferreira, P., Dominguez, E.M., & Coppens, J. (2012). Get networked and spy your languages. EuroCALL 2012 Proceedings, Gothenburg. Retrieved from https://research-publishing.net/publication/978-1-908416-07-0.pdf.

Robbins, M., Francis, L., & Elliott, E. (2003). Attitudes toward education for global citizenship among trainee teachers. *Research in Education*, 69, 93–8.

Robertson, R. (1995). Glocalization: time-space and homogeneity-heterogeneity. In M. Featherstone, S. Lash & R. Robertson (Eds). *Global modernities* (pp. 25–44). London: Sage.

Rodney, W. (1972). *How Europe Underdeveloped Africa.* London: Bogle-L'Ouverture Publications.

Rodney, W. (1981). *How Europe Underdeveloped Africa.* Washington, DC: Howard University Press.

Root, E., & Ngampornchai, A. (2012). 'I came back as a new human being': student descriptions of intercultural competence acquired through education abroad experiences. *Journal of Studies in International Education*, 17(5), 513–32.

Ross, A. (2015). *Understanding the Construction of Identities by Young New Europeans: Kaleidoscopic Identities.* Abingdon: Routledge.

Ross, E. W., & Vinson, K. D. (2012). La educación para una ciudadanía peligrosa. *Enseñanza de las ciencias sociales*, 11, 73–86. Available in English at https://www.academia.edu/8137088/Dangerous_Citizenship.

Ruitenberg, C. (2009). Educating political adversaries: Chantal Mouffe and radical democratic citizenship education. *Studies in Philosophy and Education*, 28(3), 269–81.

Rutkowski, D. J. (2007). Converging us softly: how intergovernmental organizations promote neoliberal educational policy. *Critical Studies in Education*, 48(2), 229–47.

Sant, E. (2015). 'That would give us power …' Proposals for teaching radical participation from a society in transition. *Critical Education*, 6(6). Retrieved from http://ojs.library.ubc.ca/index.php/criticaled/article/view/184842.

Sant, E., & Gonzalez, G. (2017). Latin America and global citizenship. In I. Davies, L. C. Ho, D. Kiwan, A. Peterson, C. Peck, E. Sant & Y. Waghid. (2017). *The Palgrave handbook of global citizenship and education*. Basingstoke: Palgrave Macmillan.

Sant, E., & Pérez, S. (2011). La participación en democracia. In J. Pagès & A. Santisteban. (Coords.). *Educación para la ciudadanía y los derechos humanos. Educación. Guías para la enseñanza secundaria obligatoria*. España: Wolters Kluwer. Retrieved from http://www.guiasensenanzasmedias.es/materiaESO.asp?materia=ciuda.

Sant, E., Davies, I., & Santisteban, A. (2016). Citizenship and identity: the self-image of secondary school students in England and Catalonia. *British Journal of Educational Studies*. Retrieved from http://www.tandfonline.com/doi/abs/10.1080/00071005.2015.1070789.

Sant, E., Gonzales-Monfort, N., Santisteban Fernandez, A., Pages Blanch, A., & Oller Freixa, M. (2015). How do Catalan students narrate the history of Catalonia when they finish Primary Education?. *McGill Journal of Education*, 50(3), pp.341–62.

Santisteban, A., Pages, J., & Bravo, L. (2017). History and global citizenship. In I. Davies, L. C. Ho, D. Kiwan, A. Peterson, C. Peck, E. Sant & Y. Waghid, (2017). *The Palgrave handbook of global citizenship and education*. Basingstoke: Palgrave Macmillan.

Santos, B. de Sousa. (2014). *Epistemologies of the South: Justice Against Epistemicide*. London: Routledge.

Sarangapani, P. M. (2003). Indigenising curriculum: questions posed by Baiga vidya. *Comparative Education*, 39(2), 199–209.

Sawir, E. (2011). Academic staff response to international students and internationalising the curriculum: the impact of disciplinary differences. *International Journal for Academic Development*, 16(1), 45–57.

Schulz, W., Ainley, J., Fraillon, J., Kerr, D., & Losito, B. (2010). ICCS 2009 international report: civic knowledge, attitudes, and engagement among lower-secondary school students in 38 countries. Retrieved from http://eric.ed.gov/?id=ED520018.

Schumacher, E. F. (1973). *Small is Beautiful. A Study of Economics as If People Really Mattered.* London: Harper Collins.
Schwägerl, C. (2014). *The Anthropocene: The Human Era and How It Shapes Our Planet.* London: Synergetic Press.
Schweisfurth, M. (2006). Education for global citizenship: teacher agency and curricular structure in Ontario schools. *Educational Review,* 58(1), 41–50.
SCIC (2016). *Global Citizenship Education (GCE) in Saskatchewan.* Retrieved from http://earthbeat.sk.ca/wp-content/blogs.dir/10/files/2015/06/GCE-in-SK-Schools-Ph-1-Results-Mar-2016-FINAL.pdf.
Sears, A., Davies, I., & Reid, A. (2011). From Britishness to Nothingness and Back Again. In A. Mycock & C. McGlynn (Eds), *Britishness, Identity and Citizenship: The View From Abroad.* (pp. 291–312). Bern: Peter Lang.
Secretariat of the Convention on Biological Diversity (2010). Global Biodiversity Outlook 3. Montréal
Segall, A. (2003). Maps as stories about the world. *Social Studies and the Young Learner,* 16(1), 21-21.
Seixas, P. (2014). History and Heritage: What's the Difference. *Canadian Issues Thèmes Canadiens,* (Fall), 12–16.
Sen, A. (1989). Development as Capability Expansion, *Journal of Development Planning* 19, pp.41–58. http://morgana.unimore.it/Picchio_Antonella/Sviluppo%20umano/svilupp%20umano/Sen%20development.pdf (accessed 14 December 2016).
Shelat, M. (2017). Social Media and Global Citizenship. In I. Davies, L.C. Ho, D. Kiwan, A. Peterson, C. Peck, E. Sant & Y. Waghid, (2017). *The Palgrave Handbook of Global Citizenship and Education.* Palgrave Macmillan
Shields, R. (2013). *Globalization and International Education.* London: Bloomsbury.
Shultz, L. (2007). Educating for global citizenship: conflicting agendas and understandings. *Alberta Journal of Educational Research,* 53(3), 248–58.
Shultz, L., Pashby, K. & Godwaldt, T. (2016) .Youth voices on global citizenship: deliberating across Canada in an on-line invited space. *International Journal of Development Education and Global Learning.* IOE University of London. 8(2), 5–17.
Simpson, L. (2008). *Lighting the eighth fire: The liberation, resurgence, and protection of indigenous nations.* Winnipeg, CAN: Arbeiter Ring Publisher.
Singer, P. (2002). *One World: the Ethics of Globalization.* New Haven: Yale University Press.
Smith, A. D. (1991). *National identity.* Reno: University of Nevada Press.
Smith, A. D. (1996). Culture, community and territory: the politics of ethnicity and nationalism. *International Affairs* (Royal Institute of International Affairs 1944–), 72(3), Ethnicity and International Relations, 445–58 http://www.portmir.org.uk/assets/pdfs/culture–community-and-territory–the-politics-of-ethnicity-and-nationalism.pdf (accessed 12 December 2016).
Spiro, J. (2014). Learning interconnectedness: internationalisation through engagement with one another. *Higher Education Quarterly,* 68(1), 65–84.
Standish, P. (2003). The nature and purposes of education. In R. R. Curren (Ed.). *A companion to the philosophy of education* (pp. 221–31). London: Blackwell.
Steffen, W., Crutzen, P. J., & McNeill, J. R. (2007). The anthropocene: are humans now overwhelming the great forces of nature? *Ambio,* 36(8), 614–21.

Stein, S., & de Andreotti, V. O. (2015). Cash, competition, or charity: international students and the global imaginary. *Higher Education*, 72(2), 225–39. doi:10.1007/s10734-015-9949-8.

Stockholm Resilience Centre. http://www.stockholmresilience.org/ (accessed 30 August 2016).

Stoecker, R., & Tryon, E. (2009). *The Unheard Voices: Community Organizations and Service-Learning*. Philadelphia: Temple University Press.

Tarrant, M., Rubin, D., & Stoner, L. (2014). The added value of study abroad fostering a global citizenry. *Journal of Studies in International Education*, 18(2), 141–61.

Tarrant, M. A. (2010). A conceptual framework for exploring the role of studies abroad in nurturing global citizenship. *Journal of Studies in International Education*, 14(5), 433–51.

Taylor, Y. (2012). *Educational diversity: the subject of difference and different subjects*. Basingstoke: Palgrave Macmillan.

Think Global (n.d.). The global dimension: the world in your classroom. Retrieved from https://globaldimension.org.uk/resources/browse/.

Thiong'o, N. (2011). *Re-membering Africa*. Nairobi/Kampala: East African Publishers Ltd.

Tint, B. S., & Koteswara Prasad, G. (2007). Peace education in India: academics, politics, and peace. *The Canadian Journal of Peace and Conflict Studies*, 39(1–2), 23–37.

Tlostanova, M. V., & Mignolo, W. (2014). *Learning to Unlearn: Decolonial Reflections from Eurasia and the Americas*. Columbus: Ohio State University Press.

Torres, C. A. (2015). Global citizenship and global universities. *The Age of Global Interdependence and Cosmopolitanism*, 50(3), 262–79.

Trahar, S. (2010). Changing landscapes, shifting identities in higher education: narratives of academics in the UK. *Research in Education*, 86, 46–60.

Tuck, E., McKenzie, M., & McCoy, K. (2014). Land education: indigenous, post-colonial, and decolonizing perspectives on place and environmental education research. *Environmental Educational Research*, http://dx.doi.org/10.1080/13504622.2013.877708.

Tully, J. (2014). *On Global Citizenship. Green Teacher*. London: Bloomsbury.

UNESCO. (2005). The UN decade of education for sustainable development at a glance. Paris: UNESCO. Retrieved from http://unesdoc.unesco.org/images/0014/001416/141629e.pdf (accessed 23 February 2017).

UNESCO. (2015). *Global citizenship education. Topics and Learning objectives*. Paris: UNESCO. Retrieved from http://unesdoc.unesco.org/images/0023/002329/232993e.pdf.

UNICEF United States Fund (2015). *Global citizenship*. Retrieved from http://www.teachunicef.org/teaching-materials/topic/global-citizenship.

UNICEF. (n.d.). Fact sheet: a summary of the rights under the convention on the rights of the C.HILD http://www.unicef.org/crc/files/Rights_overview.pdf.

United Nations. (2007). Declaration on the rights of indigenous people. http://www.un.org/esa/socdev/unpfii/documents/DRIPS_en.pdf.

United Nations. (2016). General dialogue on harmony with nature. http://www.un.org/en/ga/search/view_doc.asp?symbol=A/RES/70/208 (accessed 16 November 2016).

Urry, J. (1995). *Consuming Places*. London: Routledge.
Vare, P., & Scott, W. (2007). Learning for a change: exploring the relationship between education and sustainable development. *Journal of Education for Sustainable Development*, 1(2), 191–8.
Veugelers, W. (2011). The moral and the political in global citizenship: appreciating differences in education. *Globalisation, Societies and Education*, 9(3–4), 473–85.
Wade, R. C. (2008). Service-learning. In L. S. Levstik & C. A. Tyson (2008). *Handbook of research in social studies education* (pp. 109–23). New York: London: Routledge.
Wagler, R. (2012). The sixth great mass extinction. *Science Scope*. National Science Teachers Association. March 1, 48–55.
Watson, A. L. (2015). How 'global' are global history teachers? Secondary social studies teachers' understandings of global awareness and global education" (2015). *Dissertations* – ALL. Paper.
Weidman, J. C. (2016). Framing international development education in the post-2015 era: suggestions for scholars and policymakers. *Asia Pacific Education Review*, 17(3), 403–12.
Wermke, W., Pettersson, D., & Forsberg, E. (2015). Approaching the space issue in Nordic curriculum theory: national reflections of globalisation in social studies/citizenship textbook pictures in Sweden. *Nordic Journal of Studies in Educational Policy*, 57, 57–69.
Westheimer, J., & Kahne, J. (2004). What kind of citizen? The politics of educating for democracy. *American Educational Research Journal*, 41(2), 237–69.
Whitaker, P. (1988). Curriculum considerations. In D. Hicks (Ed.) *Education for peace: issues, principles and practice in the classroom* (pp. 20–35). London: Routledge.
Whiteley, P. (2014). Does citizenship education work? Evidence from a decade of citizenship education in secondary schools in England. *Parliamentary Affairs*, 67(3), 513–35.
Wiseman, A.W. (2010). The uses of evidence for educational policymaking: global contexts and international trends. *Review of Research in Education*, 34(1), 1–24.
Woolley, R. (2008). Spirituality and education for global citizenship: developing student teachers' perceptions and practice. *International Journal of Children's Spirituality*, 13(2), 145–56.
Yamashita, H. (2006). Global citizenship education and war: the needs of teachers and learners. *Educational Review*, 58(1), 27–39.
Young, I. M. (2011). *Justice and the Politics of Difference*. Princeton: Princeton University Press.

Index

Abdi, A. A. 19, 44
activism 190
Adams, R. J. 210
African ethos 41
Ahmed, F. 33, 146
Althusser, Louis 46–7
Amnesty International 32, 139
   Campaigns 195
Anderson, Benedict 63
Andreotti, Vanessa 25, 27, 51, 107, 112, 201
anthropocene 72
anti-globalization social movements 14–15
anti-racist education 68
Apartheid South Africa 145
Apery, Roger 181
Arab Spring 190
'Asian style' of teaching maths 56
assessment 184–5. *See also* evaluation
Assie-Lumumba, N. T. 41
Association for Citizenship Teaching 203
Austen, Jane 119
Austrian identity 48
Avenell, S. 139, 141
Aztec civilization 55

Baiga community 58–9
Bamber, P. 172
Banks, James A. 145, 149
Barton, K., 2005 64
Bauman, Z. 51–2
behavioural capacities 23
'being educated' 24
Benwell, B. 47, 52
'Beyond 2015' campaign 113
Bhabha, Homi K. 60
Biesta, G. 22–3, 25, 86
Blunkett, David 83
Bourn, D. 111

Breit, R. 172
BRICS countries 102
British Values 146
Brown, Gordon 65
Brundtland Report 154–5
Buckner, E. 168
Burdon, Peter 73
Butler, Judith 46

Canada 84
capabilities theory 107
Capitalocene, The 72
Cardinal Principles 32
Caruana, V. 171
Castro, Fidel 91
character
   meaning in England 116
   Six Pillars of (US Character Counts) 116
character education 115
   defined 119
   differences between global citizenship education and 118
   nature of 116
   priority for morality 118
   in Singapore 117
   in US 117
Charter of Fundamental Rights of the EU 31–2
Chilean Native Americans 55
China
   context of nation state 66–7
   fundamental rights and duties of citizens in 32
Chong, E. K. M. 68
citizenship
   collective nature of 5
   defined 5
   education 3
   in terms of human rights 35
citizenship education 68, 81–5

civic engagement 189–90
civics 83
civil participation 189–90
civil society 140
Clauswitz 135
cognitive skills 22
Colley, L. 64
colonial/colonized mind 40
colonial dependency 106
colonial education systems 40
commodified identity 52
community actions 187
   on citizenship and citizenship education 188–91
   education and 191–4
community-based work 108
conflict mediation and resolution 136
Conflict Resolution Programs 136
Connell, R. 52
Connolly, William 91
corporate global citizenship 15–16
cosmopolitan identity 49
cosmopolitanism 167
Cox, C. 140
Creation of the World or Globalization, The 13
Crick 2000 118
Crick Report 82–3, 86, 187
critical consciousness 109
critical education school 26
critical global citizenship education 27
critical patriotism 65
critical thinking 22
Crutzen, P. 72
curriculum 177–9
   controversies related to 179–81
   global citizenship in 181–2
   national 182–3
   stakeholders 183–4

Dahl, Robert 147
Davies, I. 68, 132, 204
Davies, Lynn 28, 141
Davy, I. 185
de Andrade, Fonesca 157
decolonization 75–6
Delgado, L. E. 60
DemocraciaRealYa (RealDemocracyNow) 187
Deng Xiaoping 32

dependency theory 104–5
De Sousa, Mario 201
development
   economics 103
   education 136
   education for 110–12
   international 101–9
   meaning 101
Development Assistance Committee's Evaluation Network, OECD 208
Dewey, J. 85
dialogue 108
differential exclusion 145
differentiated citizenship 147
Dillon, J. 160
Disney, Henry 135
distributive justice 94–5
diversity education 143–9
   debate on diversity and citizenship 144–8
   forms of diversity 144
   global community and 148–9
   in Japan and France, comparison 150
   liberal assimilationist approach 145–6
   multiculturalist approach 146–7
   Muslim communities and 149–50
   pluralist approach 147–8
   'segregationist' approach 145
dominant knowledge systems 106
Duncan, Arne 91
Dussel, Enrique 40

e pluribus unum 67
Earth Charter 156, 162
Earth jurisprudence 73
Earth Jurisprudence 71
ecological footprint 158
economic globalization 93
ecopedagogy 75–6
Edmunds, June 149
education
   discourses on 125–9
   global influences 129–31
education, defined 6
education for sustainable development (ESD) 25, 153–4, 156–8
   citizenship education and 161–2
   environmental education and 158–9
   indigenous perspectives 159–60

electoral activities 188–9
emerging economies 102
empathy 23
English as a first language 24
Enlightenment principles 106
Environmental Education Research 160, 162
Epstein, T. 68
equal distribution 93
Ermine, Willie 39–40, 42
Ethical Internationalism in Higher Education Research Project 174
ethical space 42–3
ethnic groups, rights and duties of 33
evaluation
   2009 ICCS study 209, 213
   of civics and citizenship 208–13
   methods 208
   purposes of 207
Evans, M. 67
Experts Advisory Group (EAG) on Global Citizenship Education (GCED) 27

Fanon 129
Feixa, C. 52
Fielder, M. 60
'first-class' and 'second-class' global citizens 24
First World 102
foreign language education 202
formal political participation 188–9
Foucault, Michel 46, 73
Fraser, Nancy 96–8
Freire, Paulo 108
Freud, Sigmund 48
Furco, A. 192

Gandhi, Indira 91
Gandhi, Mahatma 108
Gaudelli, William 205
Gay, Roxane 143
Geelan, David 202
GENE Global Education Network Europe 132
Gill, J. 68
'global', concept of 57
   interpretations 57–8
global citizen award 23

global citizenry 24
global citizens 14
   defined 17
global citizenship
   in anthropocene/capitalocene/chthulucene 74–5
   anticolonial response to 18
   in Ecuador 168
   education, challenges 2
   in Hong Kong 168
   local–global dynamics 59–60
   in Philippines 168
   purposes of education activity 22
   rights and duties 31–4
   in Singapore 168
   tensions between nation-states and 67–8
   in United States 168
global citizenship education (GCE) 21–2, 60, 117–18
   commitment to human rights 24
   human capital theory 23
   integrated into 'mainstream' subjects 199–203
   link with 'appropriate knowledge and skills' 26
   as qualification 22–4
   as socialization 24–5
   as a subject 203
   as subjectification 25–6
global community 39, 41
global competences 93
   of a global citizen 22–3
global corporate citizenship. *See also* corporate global citizenship
global corporations 15
global designs 61
global education 3, 125
   discourses on 125–9
Global Education for Sustainability Citizenship
   ethics dimension 161
   political dimension 161
   relational dimension 161
   scale dimension 161
global identity 45, 51
   as enlightened self 47–8
   as narrative self 49
   as political self 50

as postmodern self 49
as psychoanalytic self 48–9
as romantic self 48
as social self 49
as Western self 50
global knowledge commons 42
global markets 15
global mention 23
global mobility 39
global modern culture 17
Global North 102, 106, 110–12, 157
Global Peace Foundation 139
global rights and duties 31
Global South 102, 106, 111–13, 157
Global Wealth Report, 2015 16
globalization 126
    anticolonial response to 18
    current form 4
    defined 3
    McDonald's menu, case of 59
    processes of homogenization and differentiation in 59
globalized citizenship 3, 7–8
Goffman, E. 47
Gove, Michael 180, 183
Greene, J. C. 213
Grimley, N. 69
Guatemalan identity 45–6

Hahn, Carole 174
Haigh, M. J. 170–1
Hall, Stuart 46
Hammond, A. 15
Hanking, L. 172
Haraway, Donna 72–3, 75
Hargreaves, D. 118
Hartman, E. 195
Harvard University 98
Harvey, David 14
Hayward, B. 158–9, 162
Heater, D. 34
Hicks, D. 135–6
higher education policies and practices 28
Ho, L.-C. 204
Hobsbawn, E. 64
homogenization 58–9
Hong Kong 67
    citizenship education 61

Honneth, Alex 95
Hopkins, C. 154, 156, 158
horizontal processes 109
Huckle, J. 157, 161
human capital discourse on global citizenship 128
human capital theory 103
human rights education 24
humanist approaches to global citizenship 128
humanist education projects 18
humanist perspectives of globalized system 17–18
hybrid identities 52
hyper-globalizers 126

'I', southern African view 41
identities
    constitution of 46
    flexibility of 50
    global 45, 47–50
    hybrid 52
    individual and social 47
    national 47
    postmodern 49
imaginary register 48
Inca civilization 55
intergovernmental organizations (IGOs) 129–30
International Civic and Citizenship Education Study (ICCS) 2009 203, 209, 213
International Civic and Citizenship Study (ICCS) 167
International Covenant on Civil and Political Rights 31
international development 101–9
International Organization for Cooperation in Evaluation 208
Islamic countries, fundamental rights and duties of citizens in 32

Jefferess, D. 19
Jefferson Center for Character Education 119–20
Joppke, C. 35–6
Jubilee Centre, University of Birmingham 120

Juhász-Mininberg, Emeshe 61
jus sanguinis 33
jus solis 33
justice orientated citizenship 194

Kahn, Richard 74–5
Kahne, J. 84
Keating, A. 167
Kiely, R. 195
Kiwan, D. 35, 204
Kohlberg, L. 118
Koteswara Prasad, G. 141
Kristjánsson, Kristján 116, 121
Kushner, S. 210, 213
Kwan-choi Tse, Thomas 61, 168
Kymlicka, W. 144, 145

La Via Campesina 162
Lacan, Jacques 48
Laclau, Ernesto 50–1, 66
Latour, Bruno 73
Lawy, D. 86
Lawy, R. 23
learning
  moral outrage and 112
  values-based approach to 112
liberal capitalist paradigm
  background 103
  critiques 104
  main concepts 103–4
liberal discourse on education 128–9
liberal egalitarianism
  background 107
  critiques 108
  key concepts 107–8
liberal school of education 26
Lickona, Thomas 117, 121
Loader, B. V. 195
'local', concept of 55–7
  links between global and 58–9
local histories 61
locality, concept of 55–6
localness 56

MacIntyre, Alastair 92
Mao Zedong 32
Mark, M. M. 213
Marshall, T. H. 34, 85
Marx, Karl 104

Marxist paradigm
  background 104
  critiques and context 105
  main concepts 104–5
Maya civilization 55
Mbiti, J. S. 41
McCowan, T. 108–9
McDowell, L. 171
Mignolo, Walter 42, 43, 59–61, 73, 75–6, 107, 129
Mill, John Stuart 64
Millennium Development Goals (MDGs) 110, 153, 212
Miller, G. 171
Misiaszek, G. 76
modernity 107
modernization theory 103
Mokuku, T. 159–60
mondialization 13–14
monoculture 40
Montgomery, C. 171
Moore, Jason 72
moral universalism 107
Moreira dos Santos Schmidt, M. A. 68
Morgan, Nicky 120
Mouffe, Chantal 50–1, 147
multicultural education 68
multiculturalism 146–7
Myers, J. 169
Mylius, Ben 73, 76

Nancy, Jean-Luc 13–14
nation
  and global citizenship 64
  defined 64
nation state 64
national identities 47
Neill, A. S. 135
Nelson, Brendan 65
neo-conservatism 126
neoliberal discourse to education 126
neoliberalism, ideas of 14–17, 103–4
  of global economic system 15
  as a hegemonic discourse 14
  impact of 15
Network of Networks Impact Evaluation (NONIE) 208
Ngugi Wa Thiong'o 40
Nigeria 21

Nilan, P. 52
non-cognitive skills 22–3
nonviolence
  education 136
Norris, P. 48, 51
North, Connie E. 98
Nussbuam, Martha 128

Occupy protests 187
Odora Hoppers, C. 19
openness 23
Organization for Economic Cooperation and Development (OECD) 101, 110, 131, 207–8
Ortloff, D. H. 167
Oxfam UK 202

Parker, W. C. 148, 169
Parmenter, L. 172
participatory citizenship 188–91, 194
participatory justice 96–7
patriotism 126
peace education 24–5
  aims of 136–7
  approaches to 136
  characterizations of peace in 136
  critiques of 138–40
  defined 135
  examples of 139
  in Germany 139
  in Japan 139
  view of the learner 137–8
Peck, C. L. 68, 204
personal peace 136
personally responsible citizenship 194
Peterson, A. 68, 204
Philippou, S. 167
Pike, G. 141
planetary citizenship 71–4
planetary collapses 72
pluralism 147–8
pluriverse, idea of 42
policy transfer, concept of 56
politics of recognition 95
postcolonialism
  background 106
  critiques and responses 106–7
  main concepts 106
postcolonialist discourse on education 129

post-development theories 106
postmodern self 49
post-national citizenship 35
Prahalad, C. K. 15
problem-solving 22
Program for International Student Assessment (PISA) 110, 131, 208
  evaluation for maths 56
Progress in International Reading Literacy Study (PIRLS) 208
progressive education school 26

qualification purpose of education 22–4
  dimension of global citizenship education 192
queer movement 46

radical discourse on education 129
radical humanism in education
  background 108
  critiques and elaborations 109
  example 108
  key concepts 108–9
Ranger, T. 64
Ravitch, Daina 126
Rawls, John 93, 147
real register 48
recognition justice 95
Reid, A. 68, 132, 160
Reiss, Michael 181
relativism 32
representativeness, in political injustice 96
research on global citizenship education
  on higher education 170–3
  policy and curriculum 167–8
  on primary and secondary education 168–70
rights and duties, global 31–4
rights-based approach to education 108
Roberston, Roland 59
Romero, R. J. 60
Ross, A. 68
Roy, Arandati 75
Russell, S. G. 168
Rutkowski, D. J. 130

Said, Edward 129
Sant, E. 204

Sarangapani, P. M. 58
Schooling the World 43
Schumacher, E. F. 135
Schwagerl, C. 72
Scopes, John 180
Scott, W. 158
Scruton, R. 140
Sears, A. 68
Secretariat of the Convention on Biological Diversity 72
Seixas, Peter 65
Selby, D. 141
semi-peripheral states 105
Sen, A. 135
Sharia Law 32
Shaw, I. 213
Shia community 144
Shultz, Lynette 19, 98
Simpson, Leanne Betasamosake 44
Smith, A. D. 64
Smith, Anthony 48
Smith, M. K. 178, 185
Smyth, A. D. 53
social engagement 23
social identity theory 49
social involvement 189
social justice 91–2
  orientated education 92–7
socialization purpose of education 22, 24–5
  dimension of global citizenship education 192–3
soft global citizenship education 27
Sonu, D. 68
South Korea 67
Soysal, Y. 35, 150
spatial identity 52
Spivak, Gayatri 129
Spring, Joel 132
Standish, Alex 132–3
Stein, S. 51, 112
Stokoe, E. 47, 52
structural adjustment policies (SAPs) 103
subjectification purpose of education 22, 25–6
  dimension of global citizenship education 193
Suša, R. 112
sustainable development and education 75, 153

history and debates 154–8
Sustainable Development Goals (SDG) 110, 112–13, 153
symbolic register 48

teaching and learning practices
  cross-curricular theme 197–9
  global citizenship as a cross-curricular theme 197–9
  global citizenship education as a subject 203
  global citizenship integrated into other subjects 199–203
  languages education 201–2
  science, technology, engineering and mathematics (STEM) subjects 202
  social sciences and humanities 200–1
Teamey, K. 160
Terence 2
Think Global 205
Third World 102
Tint, B. S. 141
Tlostanova, M. V. 43
Torres, Carlos Alberto 28, 126
traditional ecological knowledge (TEK) 160
transnationalism 140
Trends in International Mathematics and Science Study (TIMSS) 208

Ubuntu 41
UN Decade of Education for Sustainable Development (UNDESD) 154
unequal exchange, idea of 105
UNESCO 27, 60, 96, 98, 130
  Cultural Diversity 150
UNICEF 36
UK Rights Respecting School 36
United Nation's Evaluation Group 208
United Nations (UN)
  Declaration of the Rights of Indigenous People (UNDRIP) 5, 74, 98
  relation to nature 74
  teaching and learning resource 36
Universal Declaration of Human Rights 31–2, 50

'universal' knowledge 57–8
universalism 32, 40–1
    Western ideas of 18
Unterhalter, E. 112

valuable, notion of 95
Vans, M. 132
Vare, P. 158
Violence Prevention Programs 136
virtual identity 52
Vromen, A. 195

Wade, R. C. 191
Waghid, Y. 204
Wallterstein, Immanuel 105
Wals, A. E. 157, 161
Warren, K. 76
Wermke, Pettersson and Forsberg (2015) 168

Western modernity 72
Western philosophy and thinking 40, 46
    global identities 50
    mobility of 40
Westheimer, J. 84
Whitaker, P. 137
Wong, S. 150
Woolley, R. 171
World order 136
World Systems theory 105

Xenos, M. A. 195

Young, Marion Iris 95, 147
Youth Global Forums 97

Zaman, H. 169

www.ingramcontent.com/pod-product-compliance
Lightning Source LLC
Chambersburg PA
CBHW070310230426
43663CB00011B/2075